"With intellectual precision and autobiographical candor, this book unpacks the causes and consequences of ideological division. Buchanan skillfully weaves together philosophical analysis, empirical evidence, and personal insight to reveal how tribalism erodes our shared humanity and democracy itself. Both compelling and insightful, it is an invaluable resource for anyone committed to safeguarding democracy's future."

Michael Hannon, *Associate Professor of Philosophy,*
University of Nottingham, UK

I0091742

POLITICAL TRIBALISM

Combining hard data with the author's personal story of a life in the U.S. South and then as a university professor, this book sheds a new light on tribalistic ideologies. Such ideologies are a deeply troubling feature of civic life in America and in many Western democracies as they erode trust among citizens, sow divisions, and pervert a larger pursuit of truth and understanding. Philosopher Allen Buchanan weaves together his own autobiography with the latest research in psychology, politics, anthropology, and philosophy to better understand the nature and causes of ideological tribalism, its pernicious effects on the individual and society, and the best possible solutions for curbing its spread.

The story begins with Buchanan as a middle-class, White boy in 1950s Arkansas, absorbing and espousing the racist ideas of his parents, church, and community. This beginning intentionally inculpates the author in subsequent criticisms of tribalism and—because Buchanan left this world and came to reject its values—makes convincing his arguments at the book's conclusion on how to escape tribalism's tight grasp. Before offering such final prescriptions, Buchanan examines the evolutionary origins of tribalistic thinking and shows how unyielding group ideologies short-circuit truth-seeking, attack the meaning and purpose of a liberal education, undermine a shared national identity, and—thanks to social media—prop up a shallow and false self-identity.

With a sharp eye toward tribalistic ideologies on the Right and the Left, *Political Tribalism: How it Hijacks Our Minds and Diminishes Our Humanity* is a compelling call for a healthier and deeper intellectual life of a democracy's polity and for its individual citizens.

Allen Buchanan is Professor of Philosophy at the University of Arizona. His recent books include *The Heart of Human Rights* (2013) and *Ideology and Revolution* (2025).

POLITICAL TRIBALISM

How it Hijacks Our Minds and Diminishes Our Humanity

Allen Buchanan

Routledge
Taylor & Francis Group

NEW YORK AND LONDON

Designed cover image: Getty Images / Paul Taylor

First published 2025
by Routledge
605 Third Avenue, New York, NY 10158

and by Routledge
4 Park Square, Milton Park, Abingdon, Oxon, OX14 4RN

Routledge is an imprint of the Taylor & Francis Group, an informa business

© 2025 Allen Buchanan

ISBN: 978-1-041-00961-0 (hbk)
ISBN: 978-1-041-00960-3 (pbk)
ISBN: 978-1-003-61246-9 (ebk)

DOI: 10.4324/9781003612469

Typeset in Sabon
by codeMantra

CONTENTS

ACKNOWLEDGMENTS

The thinking that went into this book is the result of decades of conversations on a broad range of topics with many smart and cooperative people from a wide range of disciplines. A number of them generously commented either on drafts of chapters of this book or on other work of mine that I utilized in developing the ideas of this book. Among the most valuable inputs were those of Jonathan Bendor (a political economist); Robert O. Keohane (an international relations specialist and institutionalist political scientist); Rachell Powell (a philosopher, biologist, and lawyer); Ritwik Agrawal (a philosopher, journalist, and cognitive scientist); Alexandra Bacall, Elizabeth Levinson, Alexander Motchulski, Travis Quigley, Sukhvinder Kaur-sshahi, Alec Cohen, and Sam Mattingly (all philosophers); and Richard Mamelok (a physician, medical researcher, pharmaceutical company entrepreneur, and poet). Alexandra Bacall and Sam Mattingly provided valuable research assistance. Finally, I want to express my gratitude for being able to work with the keen and congenial graduate students in Political Philosophy at the University of Arizona in Tucson. My interactions with them contributed to my thinking in this book. I learn more from them than from anyone.

INTRODUCTION

The Motivation for This Book

Yet another book on tribalism? Do we need it? There are many recent books on tribalism, but that's appropriate, because tribalism is so regressive, destructive, and pervasive that it warrants a lot of attention. First, let me explain why I decided to clarify my own thinking about tribalism by writing a book on it and why I determined that the best way to think about tribalism is to see it as a particular type of ideology. Then I'll be in a better position to explain why I think the book I ended up writing is needed.

What I mean by tribalism will become clearer as the chapters unfold. For now, I'll just say that the label "tribalism" as I use it indicates not just an in-group/out-group distinction, but also the idea that the out-group is dangerous, hostile, untrustworthy, not amenable to reason, and responsible for the major ills of our society, while our group is virtuous, reasonable, and responsible for all that is valuable. There may be cases where such a negative characterization of another group is largely accurate and justified—the case of Third Reich Nazis comes to mind. But the problem is that the tribalistic mentality characterizes the Other in just that way when doing so is not justified. Tribalistic ideologies turn the Other into the enemy.

I find tribalism so repulsive that I've tried to ignore it. But that's proved impossible. You can't escape tribalistic behavior, not just on social media and in the rhetoric of politicians, but also in the most mundane daily activities. Here are three examples. I'll analyze two of them in detail in a later chapter. The first happened just outside my home. One day as I approached

DOI: 10.4324/9781003612469-1

my car, mask in hand (I was going to a doctor's office where masks were required during the COVID-19 pandemic), a neighbor said: "Oh, I see you voted Democrat." He then launched into a tirade about how corrupt and inept the Democratic party is.

The second incident occurred when I was joining a sports club. The membership chairman introduced himself and then said: "If Biden is elected President, this will become a communist country." I was tempted to reply in the factual, rational mode, explaining why there was no reason to believe such a prediction. But then I concluded that that would be futile, because it seemed to me that the guy's utterance wasn't an invitation to a discussion about the facts; it was a signal sent to probe who I was and to convey who he was. If I indicated agreement with his statement, he would know I was a member of his tribe; if instead I said what I believed, namely, that what he said was patently false, he would have relegated me to the Other, in his case, no doubt, those stupid, awful Democrats or Liberals.

The third example shows that there's tribalism on the Left, not just on the Right. In a conversation with a Liberal acquaintance who knew enough about me to assume I was a Liberal, too, I criticized Anthony Fauci, the Director of the Infectious Disease division of the Centers for Disease Control and Prevention, for some of his actions during the COVID-19 pandemic. I said that the policy of closing schools wasn't justified, because there wasn't good evidence that it would be effective, while there was good evidence that it would harm children, especially those from disadvantaged backgrounds. The person I was talking with replied: "So, do you think drinking bleach would be better? Are you anti-vax as well?" The reference to drinking bleach was a reminder of some of President Trump's rather imaginative speculations about how to cure COVID-19. My criticism of Fauci was interpreted as a sign that I agreed with Trump and with others who had some rather less plausible criticisms of Fauci. My acquaintance assumed that if I disagreed with someone whom most Liberals at that time were wholly uncritical of and whom people on the Right had criticized, then I couldn't really be a Liberal. To him, being a Liberal meant criticizing those people most Liberals criticized (like Trump) and not criticizing those that Conservatives criticized (like Fauci). His conception of Liberals was thoroughly tribalistic: being a Liberal meant complete conformity to the values that are predominant among Liberals. Any divergence, any departure from complete conformity, was taken as disloyalty to the tribe.

Key Features of Tribalistic Ideologies

The first example illustrates an important point about tribalistic thinking: it makes all sorts of things political, including whether you wear a mask during a pandemic, what kind of vehicle you drive, whether you display a flag on July fourth, whether you drive a ton-and-a-half truck or a compact hybrid, etc. My neighbor was ideologically primed to interpret almost anything I did or said, including my wearing a mask, as a political identity statement. His world was thoroughly politicized, in Us versus Them terms.

All three vignettes illustrate another, equally important feature: tribalism is all about signaling group identity and using the responses to those signals to sort people into the Us or Them categories. The third vignette exhibits a related feature of tribalism: if you disagree with any part of your tribe's dominant beliefs or agree with any part of the opposing tribe's beliefs, you run the risk of being regarded as a traitor, as not one of Us, but one of Them. Tribalistic ideologies put a premium on loyalty, unwavering, wholly uncritical loyalty.

My interest in tribalism didn't originate with these recent incidents. I've been interested in tribalism, or more precisely tribalistic ideologies, since about the age of 14. At that time, the terms "tribalism" and "ideology" weren't in my vocabulary, but that's when I began to see that your beliefs about your society can be systematically distorted by the nature of the social environment in which you develop your view of the world, your conception of right and wrong, and your very identity, your sense of who you are.

At that age, I came to the realization that a great deal of what I had been taught, by precept and example, by my parents, my other relatives, my pastor, my teachers, and in the textbooks I read in school, was not just wrong, but also wrong in morally dangerous ways. I grew up in a thoroughly racist society, as a middleclass White kid in Little Rock, Arkansas.[1]

I was born in 1948. The Arkansas of my youth was literally an Apartheid society, a world of institutionalized racism. It was illegal for Blacks and Whites to marry each other; drinking fountains, toilets, and other public facilities were rigidly segregated; Black people had to sit at the back of city buses; they couldn't dine at restaurants where White people ate; they were excluded from the professions and skilled crafts; and they were "educated" in grossly inferior schools and barred from secondary education. I took all of this for granted; I had no experience of any other way of living. And everyone I looked up to took it for granted and approved of it.

The really sinister thing about a racist (or sexist) ideology—or any type of tribalistic ideology—is that it creates a social experience that seems to confirm its constitutive beliefs. I was taught that Black people are of inferior intelligence and lack self-discipline and are therefore only suited for manual labor directed by White people. In a society where that ideology was embodied in the law and social practices that seemed to be true: the only Black people I ever saw were engaged in manual labor, working for White people and being directed by them. My ideologically distorted social experience contained nothing to indicate that they were capable of anything else. A society shaped by the belief that Black people are inferior creates experiences that seem to confirm the truth of that belief and prevents experiences that would disconfirm it. The same is true of all other tribalistic ideologies: they shape the world in their own image.

What It Is Like to Be a Racist

I was lucky; I didn't commit a hate crime or any act of violence against a Black person, although, given the right combination of factors, I might well have. That doesn't mean I'm innocent. Like other White people, every single day I inflicted indignities on Black people. For example, I followed the practice of addressing all Black people, including adults and the elderly, by their first names—something I would never do in addressing Whites. I also scrupulously avoided physical contact with them. I would never shake hands with a Black person or eat with them (though I was happy to have them prepare and serve my meals). That kind of behavior doesn't go unnoticed by the people on the receiving end: they know they are being regarded as inferior and even as unclean. Their existence is permeated with insults, assaults on their dignity. We White people affirmed our identity by assigning an inferior status to Black people. To a large extent, being White meant not being Black, signaling that you weren't Black and that you recognized the inferiority of Black people.

Only many years later, reflecting on childhood experiences from a perspective not so distorted by racist ideology, did I realize the full extent of the burdens that the racist practices I participated in imposed on Black people. Here's one example among many. There was a Black man everyone called Walter (no one knew or cared to find out his last name) who periodically appeared on our street asking if he could mow people's lawns (for a price far lower than he could expect were he White).

This was a time in America when the men went to work, and the women stayed home. Walter knew this and knew that it could be fatal if any White person thought he was bent on assaulting a White woman. Given that assumption, the way he behaved made perfect sense: to avoid startling a White woman who had been ideologically primed to fear of sexual assaults by Black men, he would loudly whistle a cheerful song just as he approached a house seeking employment. He knew how vital it was not to surprise anyone, so he used the cheerful whistle strategy. He was a cat who belled himself.

That was just one instance of the need to be constantly engaging in self-defensive behavior. Racist ideology created a mine field that Black people had to negotiate everyday of their lives. Or to use another metaphor, for them life was a high wire-balancing act. For example, people like Walter had to show just enough initiative to get a job, but not so much as to be regarded as "uppity."

Current tribalistic ideologies are analogous to the racial ideology that Walter had to cope with in this respect: they encourage self-protective behavior, including self-censorship. I've noted that every day, Walter had to negotiate a mine field. I have heard many of my university colleagues and students use the mine field metaphor: they feel that the most innocent remark may result in their being stigmatized or even "cancelled," and that fear causes them to engage in self-protective behavior in the form of self-censorship. Out of fear, they silence themselves.

In private conversations with colleagues who are good friends, I have heard them say words to this effect: "Of course, I'm in favor of a moderate affirmative action policy, but I think that the overwhelming weight put on the need to hire minorities is undermining the commitment to merit. I can't say that in public, of course." Or, "Yes, I think that diversity is very important. I'm just not sure that being a women or a person of color is the best indicator of the kind of diversity that's valuable. But don't quote me on that." Similarly, some of my students report that they feel they must refrain from voicing certain ideas on pain of being labeled racist or sexist.

I'm not suggesting that the predicament of students and faculty is nearly as dire as Walter's. I'm simply pointing out a similarity between racist ideologies and, ironically, contemporary ideologies that are anti-racist. In drawing parallels between the racism I experienced and participated in Little Rock and current tribalistic ideologies. I'm aware that the effects of the former were far more serious.

Self-censorship occurs on the Right as well as the Left. For example, in certain social settings, a person who aptly self-describes as Conservative will be reluctant to voice skepticism about whether Trump's border-wall-building policy has been effective—out of fear that this would call his loyalty into question. In a later chapter, when I explore the ways in which tribalistic ideologies undermine truth-seeking communication, I'll argue that such self-censorship impairs the processes that produce knowledge and arbitrarily excludes some people from contributing to that process.

Sometimes, when I am overwhelmed with sadness or anger in remembering the racist society I grew up in world and how complicit I was in its severe injustices, how often I treated Black people in demeaning ways, I try to divert myself with self-deprecating humor. For example, when people learn I'm from Arkansas, I say "People where I grew up thought *Deliverance* was a love story."[2] Or, "What do you call a blond from Arkansas with all her teeth?" "A golden retriever." The first joke alludes to the supposed sexual deviance of Arkansans, and the second (quite cruelly) to the pervasive poverty in that state. Both focus on matters other than the racist elephant in the living room. They acknowledge that Arkansas or Arkansans are deficient, but they steer you away from the most serious deficiency, the fact that until recently Arkansas was an Apartheid society—and that the negative effects of Jim Crow on Black people persist after its demise.

What Arkansas was like back then is no laughing matter. I eventually learned there are better ways to deal with the negative feelings thinking about my upbringing evokes. Understanding the nature of tribalistic ideologies and staying alert to signs of tribalism in my own case proved more productive. Writing this book helped me do that; it was also therapeutic.

My Moral Luck

I was lucky, and not just because I committed no acts of violence against Black people. I was lucky first and foremost because my brother Steve, who was four years older, was astonishingly precocious and a thorough-going rebel. For reasons I have never been fully able to fathom, he didn't drink the racist Cool-Aid the rest of us were mindlessly guzzling. He also didn't accept Christianity or any religion. He was skeptical about authority in general.

I was influenced more by him than by anyone else, once I matured enough to understand just how extraordinary and how intelligent he was. When my father died suddenly, my brother's influence increased. He didn't just replace my father; in my eyes he was a superior replacement, a better role model.

Why could he see through the seamless veil of racism that the rest of us weren't even aware of even though it shaped our reality? I don't really know, but I think two factors were important. First, until puberty, he was the fat, nerdy bookworm who was ostracized and made fun of. That meant he had to be more independent and had to create an identity for himself that didn't require the approval of others around him. He chose to be an intellectual and a skeptic. Second, he read voraciously, including a great deal of science fiction, and that helped him to imagine a world different from the one he and I inhabited.

My mother also played a role. She wasn't skeptical like my brother; she wasn't as widely read, and far from being ostracized; she was accepted everywhere because of her charm and film-star beauty. Yet, she was different from my father, from everyone else in her family of origin and her peer group: she empathized with Black people (and poor people, too, both White and Black).

She and my father had a small real-estate business. One day I overheard her say, in a phone conversation, "I'm sorry, we don't rent to Coloreds." When that ended the conversation and she put down the phone, she burst into tears. She participated in racist practices, including housing discrimination, but she knew something was amiss or at least that the behavior of White people like her was hurtful to Black people.

One feature of tribalistic ideologies, including the racist ideology that permeated my childhood environment, is that they limit empathy, make you unable to extend it to out-group members. My mother's ideological indoctrination must not have been wholly successful, because her empathy extended beyond the color line.

The combination of my brother's anti-authoritarian influence and my mother's empathy, along with reading books my brother told me I had to read (including Nietzsche's *Genealogy of Morals*), led eventually to a kind of epiphany: I realized that my world was ugly and filled with dangerous illusions and that I couldn't trust any of the authority figures in it. I began to understand what racism is. And I realized that I was a racist. I began to understand tribalistic ideologies, though I didn't yet use that label.

The Struggle against Tribalistic Ideology

I've spent the last 60 years trying to not be a racist. When I think about how thorough my racist socialization was, I describe myself as a recovering racist. That's to acknowledge that there are still probably latent racist attitudes and reactions waiting to be triggered. I believe that if they were to be triggered, I wouldn't act on them. That's progress.

Due to the process of disillusionment that began during my adolescence, when I encountered the concept of ideology as an adult, it resonated with me. During the years when I formed my identity as a philosopher in the Western, analytic tradition, almost nobody in my intellectual world was talking about ideology. It's still not a core topic in the type of Moral and Political Philosophy that is predominant in the United States. Believe it or not, there's no entry on "Ideology" in the generally excellent and widely cited *Stanford Encyclopedia of Philosophy*. That's surprising, given how much philosophers and philosophy students rely on this work. In fact, you might even say that it defines the subject matter of the discipline. Here's a suggestion I offer free of charge for any Philosophy grad student in search of a dissertation topic: execute an ideological critique of contemporary analytic Philosophy based on what *isn't* in *The Stanford Encyclopedia*.

I belatedly acquired the concept of ideology when, in the 1980s, I participated in the short-lived "Analytic Marxism" philosophical movement, which I'd describe as an attempt to use the methodology of analytic

Philosophy to develop the most plausible interpretation of Marx's views and to figure out what Marx got right and what he got wrong. To participate in the Analytic Marxism endeavor, you didn't need to be a Marxist. I wasn't.

A decade before that, I had become an ardent fan of John Rawls's book, *A Theory of Justice*, which I and many others still regard as the best statement of liberal-democratic Political Philosophy.[3] I liken the appearance of Rawls's book in 1971 to the opening frames of the film, *Two Thousand One: A Space Odyssey*. In an unforgettable scene, a monolith deposited on earth by advanced aliens emits energy that transforms a group of dim-witted, mouth-breathing, knuckle-walking primates into the beginnings of humanity. Rawls's book had a similarly dramatic impact on the low-status, largely unproductive, and unimaginative analytic Political Philosophy community: they came to life, recognized that there was more to their field than digging up bones in the graveyard of its history, and actually began to think. Instead of continuing to be ventriloquists who mainly presented their own views only indirectly, by advancing them under the cover of figures like Aristotle and John Locke, they began to speak in their own voices. It dawned on them that the history of Political Philosophy wasn't over.

Reading Rawls's book caused me to change my course of study, from Philosophy of Language to Moral and Political Philosophy. Yet I worried that I was being swept away by the general enthusiasm for that magisterial work. I also worried that I might be afflicted by liberal bias. I thought I should see whether my enthusiasm for Rawls was based on sound judgment or bias and that the best way to do that would be to stage a confrontation between Marx and Rawls.

I decided to write a book, which turned out to have the title *Marx and Justice: The Radical Critique of Liberalism*, that would force me to be critical of Rawls's book and my own views. I read almost all of Marx's works in German, including his discussions of ideology.[4] His claim that ideologies support oppressive orders triggered memories of Little Rock and reinforced my conviction that I needed to worry about ideological biases in my own case.

So, I had a professional reason to pay attention to ideologies, once I got the concept. I saw it as a matter of being faithful to my identity as a philosopher. Philosophers, of all people, are supposed to be not just critical but also self-critical. They're supposed to question just about everything that other people take for granted and to scrutinize their own most basic beliefs and assumptions. Unfortunately, they've often fallen short on that. They typically acknowledge that all the major figures in the history of philosophy have been in the thrall of racist, sexist, classist, or Eurocentric ideologies, or all of these. Yet, the majority of them don't include in their articles or books a consideration of whether they, too, may be afflicted with ideological distortions. Political philosophers are not an exception; yet they should be especially sensitive to the possibility of ideological bias, given the nature of their subject matter.

To sum up, there are three reasons why I got to the point of writing this book: my first-hand experience of how pernicious ideologies can be; my conviction that philosophers have a special obligation to ask hard questions about their own vulnerability to ideological thinking; and, of course, the fact that I see tribalistic ideologies doing damage all around me, not just in social media or so-called news media, but also in my everyday, offline life.

What Makes This Book Different

That explains why I'm interested in tribalistic ideology and in ideologies more generally. It doesn't fully answer the question "Why another book on tribalism?" My answer is that this book is different in several ways that were shaped by my motivations for writing it. Here are the most distinctive features of my approach.

You've no doubt already noticed one of them: this book draws heavily on my own personal experience to illustrate points I'm trying to make. Sometimes I mine my memory for experiences that occurred when I was growing up in a racist society, the Apartheid Arkansas of the 1950s and 1960s. Sometimes I relate contemporary experiences, including personal encounters with tribalism on the Left as well as the Right.

You might think that examples of blatant racism in Apartheid Arkansas don't have much to do with the sort of tribalism we're currently afflicted with, but I'm going to convince you that that's not the case. Institutionalized racism in Little Rock and our current tribalism have much in common, in terms of attitudes toward the Other, mechanisms for sustaining beliefs in the face of disconfirming evidence, and the focus on identities defined in terms of opposition to other identities. The kind of racist ideology I grew up with and current tribalistic ideologies have something else in common: as I'll explain shortly, they include stereotypes of the Other that prevent you from seeing individuals as individuals. So, my examples of experiences in Apartheid Arkansas will be relevant to achieving an understanding of our current predicament.

You might be wondering how it is that I, or anyone for that matter, can manage to have personal relationships that are so diverse as to provide examples of tribalism from both ends of the political spectrum, as I have already done in my vignettes about masks, communist take-overs, and anti-vaxxing. Given how divisive tribalistic ideologies are, how can I have relationships with people on both sides of the great divide? The answer is that although I'm an academic and most of the people I relate to in my professional life are Liberals, that's not the only kind of person I interact with. My wife and one of my best friends are both Conservatives, and two of my hobbies, engaging in several target-shooting disciplines and restoring antique firearms, bring me into contact with groups that are largely Conservative. That's why my knowledge of Conservative thinking and attitudes is grounded not just in reading about Conservatism, and regarding Conservatives abstractly as if they were exotic beings on some distant planet, but also in actually knowing a number of them.

Those personal connections, which are extremely rare for an academic, help me understand Conservative versions of tribalistic ideologies. They've also impressed me with the diversity of Conservative views. Similarly, because I know lots of Liberals, having worked for 50 years in universities, where they are the majority among the faculty, I'm in good position to understand Liberal varieties of tribalistic ideologies. And I have enough contact with Liberals to see just how simplistic, homogenizing, and overdrawn many Conservatives' conceptions of them are. I've observed the same phenomenon in Liberals: they tend to operate with cartoonish conceptions of what it is to be a Conservative. In Chapter 1, I'll emphasize that inaccurate, homogenizing stereotypes of the Other are an essential feature of tribalistic ideologies, on the Right and the Left.

In brief, I live in two different worlds. I'm fairly comfortable in both, though not fully at home in either. I think my ambivalent stance, with one foot in the Liberal world and another in the Conservative world, is an advantage when it comes to writing a book like this. And by the way, I'm constantly at risk of being expelled from one group or the other should my sympathy for and interactions with members of the opposing group be known. It's not easy, but I manage to maintain something akin to dual citizenship without too much in the way of acting like I'm a resident of only one territory or the other. This requires not talking much about my hobbies when I'm around Liberals and not saying just how much I dislike Trump when my Conservative friends praise him. To justify this somewhat disingenuous conduct, from time to time I make it a point to ask members of both tribes what I hope are disturbing questions about their assumptions. So far, I've been able to avoid being excommunicated from either tribe. That may change, if the people I interact with read this book. That's a risk worth taking. I don't want to engage in self-censorship to avoid being stigmatized by people afflicted by tribalistic ideologies.

As this book unfolds, we'll encounter an important fact about tribalistic ideologies—one that makes my living in two worlds easier: tribalistic ideologies impair the exercise of important cognitive skills and redirect moral motivation toward immoral behavior, but this cognitive and moral damage is usually limited and compartmentalized. That's why I still manage to like, have friendships with, and even admire people whose political views I find to be thoroughly tribalistic and even abhorrent. I may be repelled by what they say and do when they are in the tribalistic mode, but our interaction may be such that I don't witness much of that. And if they and I both sense that there are deep political disagreements that we'd best not air, we'll avoid certain topics. That further reduces the proportion of our time together in which I am likely to see their tribalistic self.

Later, I'll explain in detail the compartmentalization feature of tribalistic. As a preview, the nub of the explanation is this: tribalistic ideologies don't impair our cognitive abilities and distort out moral responses across the board; instead, they normally cause cognitive and moral dysfunction only when we feel threats to our identity. In other contexts, individuals in the thrall of tribalistic ideologies may think quite well and scrupulously comply with moral norms. The problem, as I'll show in Chapters 2 and 3, is that tribalistic ideologies are imperialistic: they tend to invade larger and larger portions of the territory of our lives, making ever more things political and all things political deeply personal. That will make it ever more difficult for one to be friends or partners or spouses of people of opposing tribes.

Another unique feature of this book, in addition to its personal, autobiographical aspect, is its claim that in producing cognitive disabilities, tribalistic ideologies turn back the evolutionary clock, undermining the exercise of distinctively human capacities—both cognitive and moral—that took tens of thousands of years to develop through the interaction of natural and cultural selection. That means that tribalistic ideologies "de-humanize," not just in the way they characterize the Other (as subhuman or less than fully human), but also because they undermine the exercise of some of the cognitive capacities that are distinctive of our species. That's why the subtitle of this book includes "diminishes our humanity" as part of what tribalistic ideologies do to us—or rather what we do to ourselves when we are in their thrall.

A word of caution: I am not saying that people in the grip of tribalistic ideologies are less than human in the way that tribalistic rhetoric characterizes the Other as less than human. I am saying that tribalistic ideologies undermine the *exercise* of certain distinctively human cognitive and moral capacities that took eons to develop. Whether one is "human" in the sense of being the kind of entity that has a high basic equal moral status depends on what capacities one has, not on whether one is presently exercising those capacities. When tribalistic ideologies characterize the Other as less than human, the implication is that they lack that high basic equal moral status because they fail to have certain distinctively human capacities, including the ability to reason—and that, as a consequence, they lack fundamental rights and that it is therefore permissible to harm them in ways that would be impermissible if they had that status. I'm not saying that when I say that tribalistic moralities diminish our humanity.

I also include in this book an analysis of how tribalistic ideologies change the meaning of key political terms, including "legitimacy," "statesmanship," and "patriot." I haven't seen that in other works on tribalism either.

Further, as far as I can tell, this book is novel in arguing that the concept of ideology is valuable both for understanding the failures of U.S. COVID-19 policies and the responses to those policies. I show that U.S. policy was significantly shaped by a flawed public health ideology that divided the population into the incompetent masses who can't handle the truth and can't be trusted to do what's best for themselves, on the one hand, and the enlightened, truly scientific, purely altruistic public health professionals, on the other. I'm not sure that this public health ideology strictly fits the definition of tribalistic ideologies, but I am confident that it has several key features in common with them, as I'll explain later. I *am* sure that reactions to the pandemic, and especially to the behavior of top public health officials, were often thoroughly tribalistic. Whether you praised or damned Anthony Fauci and whether you took seriously President Trump's suggestion that the virus originated in a Chinese laboratory became litmus tests for determining your tribal affiliation. Affirming your tribal allegiance was more important than impartially evaluating policy choices. Calm, fact-based assessment of COVID-19 policy was displaced by frenzied identity-group signaling.

One especially damaging feature of the public health ideology is that it encouraged the top public health officials to mislead the public by pretending that "the science" spoke with one voice (theirs) and to use personal attacks to discredit their critics rather than answering them on the merits. That kind of sleazy behavior was apparently thought by those ordinarily decent folks to be justified, because they were convinced that it was necessary in the pursuit of a higher moral good: dealing effectively with what they considered to be a national public health emergency. The radical distinction between Us (the public health professionals in this case) and Them (the public), combined with the belief that They are irrational or at least far less rational than We are, is a key feature of tribalistic ideologies. So is the tendency of the public health leadership to brand those who didn't get on board with their policies as wicked or stupid and unscientific. That's typical of tribalistic ideologies, too: they demean and/or demonize those who reject the beliefs and policies they support, instead of responding to the substance of their views on the merits. In the pandemic case, this meant characterizing people who refused to be vaccinated as imprudent and selfishly putting others at risk. For example, people who didn't get vaccinated were branded as selfish because they were exposing not just themselves but also others to a harmful disease. That was inaccurate, because, as their producers now admit, there was no good evidence that being vaccinated prevented one from contracting or spreading COVID-19. That doesn't mean vaccination was worthless; it did apparently reduce the severity of symptoms in some individuals. But its value was shamelessly over-sold. And whether this limited value exceeded the costs in terms of adverse reactions is another question.

There's another difference between this book and others on the same topic. Most works on tribalism make suggestions about how to combat it, but to my knowledge none of them comes close to considering the full range of possible strategies for doing so that I discuss. There's another difference: they don't ask which measures for dismantling toxic ideological beliefs are ethically permissible, under which conditions. I devote a chapter to laying out a total of ten strategies for combatting tribalism and to determining which are ethically permissible. In doing so, I fill a gap not only in the literature on tribalism, but also in contemporary analytic Moral Philosophy. Because that branch of analytic Philosophy has largely ignored ideologies, it hasn't confronted the question of which ways of combatting tribalistic ideologies are ethically permissible and which are not.

Perhaps most importantly, this book identifies a key feature of tribalistic ideologies that other accounts overlook or don't emphasize sufficiently: tribalistic ideologies turn the mind and the moral self against themselves. Only a species that is exceptionally cognitively developed can use its cognitive abilities to undermine its cognitive performance. Understanding that tribalistic ideologies turn the mind itself implies that it's misleading to say that tribalistic types are stupid and leave it at that. They are smart enough—cognitively sophisticated enough—to use their minds to undercut their cognitive performance. The same is true of our capacities as moral agents: only a species with highly developed moral capacities can violate moral rules for the sake of morality. That means that the common complaint that tribalism makes people immoral is true but misleading: it wrongly suggests that tribalism makes us abandon morality, when in fact tribalistic ideologies only produce immoral behavior because people care about being moral. Tribalistic moralities redirect moral motivation so that it fuels immoral behavior.

The dominant tone of the book is therefore irony: I show how, time and time again, ideologies damage us because we are very sophisticated creatures, cognitively and morally. We are the only species on the planet capable of harming ourselves so profoundly, using our own extraordinary powers to turn back the evolutionary clock, regressing in effect to a prehuman condition of stupidity and moral error.

Here's another way to look at it that's also ironic. Evolution in humans has produced cognitive abilities that enable cooperation for truth-seeking and cognitive abilities that enable cooperation for collective action (by fostering solidarity in groups, through the creation of robust group-based identities). The problem is that these two sets of abilities or systems can be in tension.[5] Truth-seeking can undermine solidarity in some cases, as when it brings to light facts that contradict the myths that ground solidarity (for example, by debunking inaccurate histories of the nation that make it seem more different and better than it really is). And, in the case of tribalistic ideologies, the cognitive abilities that enable cooperation for collective action can be exercised in such a way as to undermine truth-seeking. At present, it appears that the cooperation/group solidarity system is winning at the expense of truth-seeking system. Cooperation for winning in a struggle against another group is driving out cooperation for seeking the truth. Here's the irony: we've become so good at one kind of cooperation—cooperating to compete with the Other—that we've become very deficient in another kind of cooperation—cooperation in seeking the truth. If cooperation in seeking the truth is confined to our own group and excludes members of the Other, then we will miss out on important information; the knowledge we produce will be inferior to what it would be if our cooperation in seeking the truth was more inclusive.

At various points in the chapters to follow, I'll point out how my thinking about tribalistic ideologies differs from or is similar to the work of others on that topic, while trying to make it clear that some of what I say has also been said by others, though often with different framings. Nevertheless, it may be helpful in this Introduction to summarize the most important points about the relationship between this book and work by some of the best work of others.

Let me begin that task by noting how my view differs from that of perhaps the most influential and widely read moral psychologist of our day, Jonathan Haidt. His most recent book, *The Anxious Generation: How the Great Rewiring of Childhood Is Causing an Epidemic of Mental Illness,* is only partly and indirectly relevant to my topic.[6] As the title suggests, its focus is not on tribalistic political ideologies, but rather on understanding why there has been an upsurge in mental health problems among American minors. Nonetheless, what he says about the role of social media use in the causation of the mental health problems he discusses is fully compatible with what I say about identity-anxiety and about how social media use both expresses and fuels that anxiety.

Haidt's widely acclaimed book, *The Righteous Mind: Why Good People Are Divided by Politics and Religion*, comes closer to engaging the topic of my book.[7] Haidt is a "sentimentalist" in his approach to morality and to disagreements that have a moral element. That means that he thinks that our moral judgments and responses are overwhelmingly driven by emotions, not by reason. He thinks that when reason does play a role of morality, it is almost exclusively to provide *post hoc* rationalizations for judgments and responses that were emotional, not grounded in reasoning at all.

Ideologies involve emotions, but they also have a cognitive aspect: they include a set of relatively coherent beliefs and cognitive processes for managing beliefs. The belief management processes, as I'll show in the next chapter, involve reasoning. Haidt's sentimentalism makes it hard, if not impossible, for him to take the concept of ideology seriously as a resource for understanding what divides us. In contrast, I believe that as the chapters of my book unfold, it will become clear that the concept of ideology is an important tool for understanding tribalism.

His sentimentalism is also at odds with his recommendation for how to combat tribalism. All he says about the latter is that if we understand the sources of our tribalistic divisions, we may be able to overcome or at least moderate them. But he leaves it wholly unclear as to how this understanding would change the emotions that on his view overwhelming determine our moral judgments and responses, including those involved in our tribalistic divisions. He thinks that if we understand how large the role of emotions is in morality, we will be more empathetic toward others; but he doesn't explain why this would occur. Unless Haidt is willing to give a larger role to the influence of reasoning on our moral emotions than his sentimentalism allows, it will remain a mystery as to how greater understanding of the sources of our divisions would help us to overcome or reduce them.

The concept of ideology plays no significant role in either book; their indexes do not even include the term "ideology." That's a major difference between Haidt's approach and mine.

There is one respect, however, in which Haidt's view in *The Righteous Mind* adds something of potential value to my attempt to understand those divisions: one aspect of his theory could be employed to help explain why different ideologies appeal to different people. This is his theory of moral foundations, the view that all human beings have the same set of fundamental moral response categories. Although his list of foundations has changed over time, it currently includes these: authority/subversion, loyalty/betrayal, care/harm, purity/degradation, and fairness/cheating. He thinks that what divides Liberals and Conservatives is that they have different priorities among these foundations, that they give different weights to them: Liberals are more concerned with care and fairness and regard harming and unfairness as the most serious wrongs. Conservatives put a premium on loyalty and authority and regard betrayal and subversion of authority as especially wrong. So, one might conclude that the reason some people adopt Conservative ideologies and others Liberal ideologies is that there are differences in the weights they give to the various moral foundations. So far, so good. But then the question arises: why are there differences in the weightings?

I find his answer to this question unsatisfying. He says that the differences in weightings result from differences in the cultural influences to which individuals are subjected and perhaps other variations in environment. This does little to explain how Americans of the same social class and educational level and siblings who grew up in the same family can be so politically divided as they are in many cases. So, although I think that Haidt's hypothesis about people assigning different weights to various members of a common set of "moral foundations" may be useful in explaining why people gravitate to some political identities and their supporting ideologies rather than others, his theory does little to explain why there is such variation in how people assign weights to them.

There's one feature of Haidt's thinking that I am very much in harmony with: he makes a convincing case that the problem of tribalism is not that many people have suddenly become immoral. Like me, he recognizes that the tribalism that divides us is grounded in the potent motivational force of morality. Tribalism doesn't repudiate morality; it harnesses it or, you might even say, perverts it.

There are a number of thinkers who, like myself, believe that anxiety over perceived threats to identity plays a central role in tribalism.[8] That view is supported by a sizeable literature on "identity-protective cognition" that describes how people's cognitive performance degrades when they feel that their identity or some aspect of it is threatened.[9] Often, however, there is little discussion of the connections between this phenomenon and ideologies, and the consequences for political deliberation and democracy are not systematically explored. This book fills both of these gaps.

A Word about Morality

In what follows, I'm going to put a lot of weight on the idea that political ideologies, including tribalistic ones, include moral beliefs, in particular, beliefs about how a society ought to be and about which groups are to blame when it isn't as it should be. I'll even say that political ideologies, in part, include moralities, or at least some elements of moralities. That means that when a person has an ideology, they have certain moral commitments.

When write in that way, I'll be using the terms "moral," "moralities," and "moral commitments" in the descriptive-sociological sense. When the terms are used in that way, they just refer to the code or system of beliefs and commitments regarding what's right and wrong, permissible and impermissible that some group or individual happens to have. For example, when we are using the term "morality" in the descriptive-sociological way, it makes perfectly good sense to say that there was a Nazi morality.

But often we use the term "morality" in a different way, call it the critical sense of "morality." We're using the critical sense of the term when we say that Nazi morality (in the descriptive-sociological sense) included principles that advocated immoral acts, like persecuting Jews. It makes perfectly good sense to say that some moralities (in the descriptive-sociological sense) are immoral (in the critical sense).

When we use the terms "morality" or "moral beliefs" or "moral commitments" in the critical sense, we are implicitly rejecting moral nihilism, the view that there is really no right or wrong, and ethical relativism, the view that there's no right or wrong as such, merely what is right or wrong for some particular morality (in the descriptive-sociological sense) or other. If you are a moral nihilist, you can't say that genocide is wrong or slavery is wrong—for you those terms have no referents, make no sense. If you are an ethical relativist, you can't say that it is wrong for a committed Nazi to persecute Jews; you can at most say that, given your morality, doing that is wrong.

I'm pretty confident that most, if not all, of you who read this book are neither moral nihilists nor ethical relativists. You think there really is a right or wrong about some matters, not just different beliefs about what's right or wrong, with no way of ever that some beliefs are more cogent than others when they disagree.

In other words, you think that at least for some matters, there is an objective right or wrong. That's compatible with recognizing that in all too many cases people think that the domain of what's right or wrong, objectively speaking, is a lot more extensive than it is. In other words, you can reject moral nihilism and ethical relativism and still acknowledge that too often we think that morality in the critical sense includes a lot more rights and wrongs than it does or that we have a perfect grasp of what's included in morality in the critical sense. Keeping that in mind can help us be less certain of our own moral rectitude and more tolerant of people who disagree with us on some moral issues—without lapsing into moral nihilism or ethical relativism.

Two Views about Ideologies

My focus in this book is not ideologies in general, but rather *tribalistic* ideologies. I don't assume that all ideologies are toxic. For most people, however, or at least for most Americans, "ideology" is a pejorative term. In our culture, if we say someone's beliefs are ideological, it's not a compliment. For one thing, the implication is that they hold certain beliefs dogmatically, that they stick to them in the face of disconfirming evidence, and that their beliefs are unduly rigid.

There's more to it than that, however. When we treat "ideology" as a pejorative term, we may be implicitly making two other assumptions: first that ideologies only function to support oppression; second that ideologies seriously misrepresent reality, that they foster "false consciousness." These two assumptions about ideology are what I call the Marxist hangover—elements of Karl Marx's thought that have made their way into the thinking of people who would be horrified to be known as his heirs. People afflicted by this hangover ignore the fact that, since Marx, a less restrictive conception of ideologies that rejects both assumptions has become prominent among psychologists, political scientists, and sociologists. That is, contemporary social scientists recognize that there are ideologies that challenge, rather than support, oppressive orders, and they don't take false consciousness, if that means a fundamental misrepresentation of social reality, to be essential characteristics of ideologies.

Given the pervasiveness of the two Marxist assumptions, it's completely understandable that no American politician in their right mind would publicly acknowledge having an ideology. But among many politically active people in the global South, the term isn't pejorative. They often openly declare, without apology, their endorsement of a particular ideology, for example, some variety of democratic socialism. That's because they understand that ideologies can be powerful resources for mobilizing people and coordinating their participation in collective political action, including political action that is emancipating, not oppressive. They also recognize that some ideologies reveal, rather than obscure, the nature of a social order and can reduce false consciousness rather than foster it. For example, an emancipatory, revolutionary ideology can help expose the illusion that the current regime is largely just or legitimate or that the inequalities it supports are natural and unavoidable.

So, the lesson we should draw from an account of the damage tribalistic ideologies cause is *not* that we should try to do without ideologies. Understanding the positive potential of ideology will turn out to have important implications for how we should try to combat tribalistic ideologies. More precisely, it may be that the best way to combat a bad ideology is with a good (or at least less bad) one.

It may turn out that we can't do without ideologies. That would be the case if complex, diverse, large-scale societies need hierarchies, structures of authority in which some have power over others that others don't have over them, and if ideologies are needed to make hierarchies work without relying excessively on sheer force. Maybe ideologies supply the social glue needed to make people voluntarily follow the rules that make a complex, large-scale society work rather than just cooperating because they fear punishment if they don't. Furthermore, ideologies can include moral commitments that help people avoid or overcome obstacles to successful social cooperation, including the temptation to free-ride on the efforts of others or to pursue one's own particular interests at the expense of the common good.[10]

Puzzles to Be Solved

I've explained how my book differs from others on tribalism and therefore why there's a need for it. Those distinctive features allow me to solve a number of frustrating puzzles. I'm guessing that you've found yourself asking some if not all of the following questions and being unsure about the answers.

- Why are politicians today so prone to lie, cheat, and engage in such nasty attacks on their opponents?
- Why do their supporters accept such behavior?
- Why do people make such outrageously, patently false statements about political matters?
- Why do people keep using social media to criticize the views of people on the other side of the ideological divide when they know doing so won't change anybody's mind?
- Why is there so little respect for the truth nowadays?
- Why can't people in different political tribes even agree on basic facts?
- Why is there not just "polarization," disagreement on policy, but also "affective polarization," which involves regarding those you disagree with as despicable, devious, dangerous, insincere?
- Why do people who are civil and well-mannered in real life become so nasty when they go online?
- What happened to the idea of the common good?

By the end of this book, I will have answered all of these questions, and the answers will be principled and systematically connected, not *ad hoc* and unrelated.

I'm not going to focus on how foreign agents are using social media to exacerbate divisiveness or influence elections. That's a serious problem.

Fortunately, U.S. security agencies have made some progress on reducing that threat. I'll concentrate instead on how ordinary Americans are expressing and intensifying their tribalistic ideologies. That phenomenon by itself is serious enough to warrant this book. Deliberate exploitation of tribalistic ideologies by bad actors is a derivative phenomenon, because they don't create tribalistic ideologies, they merely exploit them. I'm concentrating on what's more basic.

American Exceptionalism?

This book analyzes tribalistic ideologies and their consequences by focusing mainly on manifestations of tribalism in contemporary America. There is good reason to do so, in addition to the fact that this book draws on my personal experiences as an American living in America. The chief reason for the American focus is that tribalism appears to be especially extreme and pervasive in this country.[11] If that is so, the question naturally arises as to why America is exceptional in this way.

From what I have been able to ascertain, there are two compatible explanations that, taken together, offer the most plausible account currently available as to why tribalistic political ideologies are more extreme and pervasive here than in most other developed countries. The first explanation is institutional: the two-party system, combined with the "first past the post" feature of American electoral politics, gives politicians incentives to emphasize and even exaggerate differences between the values and policies of the two major parties and to convince their supporters that politics is a zero-sum contest, that either We win (completely) or They do, and these same institutional arrangements lack the incentives for compromise and moderation that are present in multi-party, proportional representation, parliamentary systems, where governance usually requires coalitions across party lines. As I'll explain in more detail in the last two chapters, politicians and media-based political influencers in the American system have incentives to foster identity-bundling, to encourage people to see their group as sharing a set of identities or aspects of identities that are defined in sharp opposition to the bundles of identities attributed to the Other. If people can be convinced that one party will acknowledge and support the whole bundle, then it will be easier to gain and sustain their allegiance. Believing that the opposition poses a threat to the whole bundle, to all aspects of your identity, is very motivating; it can result in a strong commitment to the party you think will protect you, the whole you.

The second explanation is cultural: at least one of the most important factors that drive political ideologies, namely, anxiety over identity, appears to be due in part to the erosion of traditional forms of community, a phenomenon that arguably is more pronounced in America. The idea is that the loss of identity-conferring and -supporting traditional communities creates identity-anxiety and for some people relief from that anxiety comes in the form of allegiance to a political tribe. Everything I say in the rest of this book is compatible with both the institutional and the cultural explanation. As my analysis unfolds, it will provide some support for both.

Of course, there are features of American tribalism that are found in some other countries, in particular populism with its distrust of an animosity toward "elites," and the rising popularity of nationalist and even racist political beliefs and attitudes in response to increases in immigration and to threats to some identities posed by globalization and rapid social and technological changes that lower the status and reduced the power of certain groups. Nonetheless, there are advantages to this book's focus on the American case, not the least of which is that the relatively extreme nature of political tribalistic ideologies in this country makes the basic features and tendencies of that kind of ideology and its personal and political consequences all the clearer.

The Ishmael Problem

At this point, I feel compelled to address a worry you may have—in fact, a worry it is perfectly appropriate for you to have. Anyone who writes about tribalistic ideologies—or for that matter ideologies of any type—runs the risk of being accused of being ideologically biased themselves. After all, if ideologies are so pervasive, how did I escape their grip? You may be wondering, that is, why I think I can give a non-ideological account of ideologies and the role they play in tribalistic behavior.

That's what I call the Ishmael problem. At the end of Melville's *Moby Dick* (which tells you a lot more about how to dismantle a whale than most of us care to know), the main character, Ishmael, says "…and I alone escaped to tell Thee." Well, I probably can't fully convince you that I escaped ideological bias in writing this book. Perhaps the best I can do is to emphasize that I won't be assuming that either of the two major political groups in America today has a monopoly on tribalism. At least that should help allay the worry that I'll be criticizing tribalism on the Left from the perspective of tribalism on the Right or *vice versa*.

To repeat: I'm aware that tribalistic ideologies exist on the Left as well as the Right. That's not surprising because ideologies thrive on competition with other ideologies. In fact, as I've argued in another recent book, ideologies co-evolve with one another.[12] That's because, they are, among other things, strategic weapons in an age-old struggle between those who seek to dominate others and those who resist domination (or wish to become dominators).

Examples of Rightist tribalistic ideologies are not hard to find. Here's one, sometimes labeled White Christian Nationalism, whose main tenets are as follows. (1) America is a Christian nation. (2) Christianity is under siege in America today. (3) Government should promote Christian values. (4) There is a conspiracy to replace White Christians with Black people, Muslims, and various other "non-white" types. (5) Trump is the new Cyrus (an ancient Persian leader who, though not Jewish, acted in ways that helped the Jews). (6) There is an invasion of immigrants who are "wrecking the country," "poisoning its life-blood" (to use two favorite phrases of Trump's).[13] (7) The Democratic party wants to destroy individual liberty and extend government control over our lives. (8) Global warming is a hoax concocted by Liberals to attack capitalism and extend government control. (9) School textbooks should not include language that is divisive, leads students to question traditional authorities or that casts a negative light on American history.

Here's an example of an equally extreme Leftist tribalistic ideology, a variety of what is sometimes called Wokism. It's constitutive claims are (1) that the world divides neatly and exhaustively into (predominantly) White oppressors and non-White oppressed, (2) that virtually all of the disadvantages of non-Western people are due to European colonialism, (3) that colonialism is a peculiarly European or Western invention, (4) that all major U.S. institutions are racist, (5) that the primary mission of universities should be to promote social justice, (6) that We (the awakened, enlightened people) know exactly what social justice is, and that our being mistaken is out of the question, (7) that racists and sexists (and other oppressors such as neo-colonialists) should not be allowed to speak on college campuses or in other public venues, and (8) that when oppressed peoples, in resisting their White oppressors, use violence against civilians (aka terrorism), they're not culpable for doing so; if anyone is to blame, it's their oppressors, for making them resort to such acts (There was evidence of this last belief in the unqualified support some American college students and others voiced for Hamas in the wake of the atrocities that group committed against Israelis on October 7, 2023.).

If, after my acknowledgment that there are tribalistic ideologies on the Left as well as on the Right, you're still concerned that my theory may be ideologically biased, I can think of one more thing to do to lessen your concern: I can acknowledge that, so far as I'm aware of having one, my ideology is one that explicitly renounces all forms of tribalistic ideologies, mainly because they all fail to acknowledge the fundamental equal moral status of persons, by characterizing the Other as morally and intellectually inferior. The fact that my ideology is fundamentally anti-tribalistic in that sense reduces the risk that I'm providing a tribalistic analysis of tribalism.

The Most Regressive Aspect of Tribalistic Ideologies

The failure to acknowledge fundamental equal moral status in all people is evident in the way tribalistic ideologies on the Left and the Right both systematically characterize the Other as not just dangerous and insincere or stupid, but also as lacking an essential feature of human beings as proper objects of equal respect, namely, rationality. Because rationality is often thought to be part of what makes us human, when tribalistic ideologies refuse to recognize the Other as beings with whom you can reason, they deny that they are fully human and as such are our equals.

There's a long tradition of thinking of our rationality is a feature of our human nature that grounds basic rights.[14] Nowadays we think of human rights as rights we all have simply by virtue of being human. But if you leave it at that, human rights are vulnerable to the charge of speciesism.[15] That's the charge that in ascribing these rights to ourselves we assume that just being a member of the species *Homo sapiens* is in itself of great moral value, without explaining why it is, and ignoring the possibility that other creatures may also have rights.

Avoiding the charge of bias in favor of our own species requires saying just what it is about humans that gives them all certain rights. Rationality is probably the most widely offered answer to that question. There's nothing speciesist about the idea that rationality grounds basic rights, because it's easy to imagine creatures (say, from another galaxy) that are rational but of a different biological species, products of a different evolutionary path, with a radically different genome (if they even have DNA).

Given this connection between rights and rationality, to deny someone's rationality is not just to deny that they are fully human, which is bad enough, but also to pave the way toward denying that they have the rights of humans. So, when your ideology causes you to regard the Other as irrational, it's a small step to regarding them as having an inferior moral status and thinking that they don't have the rights that We have. Tribalistic ideologies on the Left and the Right encourage that kind of thinking.

I've already noted that tribalistic ideologies are regressive: they return us to a less cognitively and morally developed condition, undoing the work of eons of the interaction of biological and cultural evolution. Now I want to sharpen that point by taking note of a major instance of regression.

In two other books, one co-authored with Rachel Powell, I've argued that one of the humanity's greatest achievements in moral progress has been what we call the First Great Expansion: the recognition, embodied in law and social practices, of the equal basic moral status of all persons.[16] It's an expansion of the circle of moral regard. Its most recent and developed expression is the modern idea of human rights, the belief that all persons, regardless of race, nationality, gender, ethnicity, or religion, have the same set of basic moral rights.

To the extent that tribalistic ideologies, at least in their more extreme forms, regard the Other as fundamentally irrational and even less than fully human; they erode this great accomplishment. Why? Because of the deep connection between the concept of rationality and rights—at least the kinds of rights that are most valuable for persons and which are thought to be uniquely possessed by persons.

You and I have a concept—the concept of a human being—that most human beings, since there first were human beings, lacked. In fact, even today, some tribal groups refer to themselves by terms that can be translated as "the human beings" or "the people," while the terms they have for other groups are often rather less than flattering, in some cases, likening the Other to animals or attributing some rather unpleasant trait to them. To the extent that our concept of a human being implies some kind of basic equality that's of fundamental importance for how we ought to treat other people, all other people, not just members of our group, it's a rather new concept. And attaining it is a great accomplishment.

Tribalism threatens to destroy that accomplishment, robbing us of one humanity's greatest achievements—the recognition of our common humanity. That's because the way tribalistic ideologies demeans the Other can be so extreme as to amount to denying that they are human, at least so far as the assumption is that humans are rational, that they are the kinds of beings you can reason with, who are responsive to reasons. As far as I can tell, other contemporary works on tribalism don't make this point, at least not clearly. And to that extent, they profoundly underestimate just how damaging tribalistic ideologies are. It's one thing to say that tribalistic ideologies make us stupid and nasty, and that they divide us and are damaging to democracy; it's quite another to say they threaten to wipe out what is perhaps the single greatest instance of moral progress that has occurred so far.

A recent book is a perfect manifestation of the de-humanizing feature of tribalistic ideologies: *Inhuman: The Secret History of Communist Revolutions (and How to Crush Them)*.[17] This book states that an attempted communist revolution is now underway in the United States, led by Liberals and Progressives, whom the book characterizes as not being human and as being implacable enemies of humanity. Trump's choice for his Vice President, J.D. Vance, as well as the enormously influential Conservative media star, Tucker Carlson, provided glowing endorsements on the book's jacket.

This book exhibits what is perhaps the most dangerous aspect of tribalistic ideologies in their more extreme forms: they present current political issues as a Manichean struggle for the highest stakes, between the virtuous Us and the demonic, subhuman Them.[18] In *Inhuman*, what Holocaust and genocide scholars call "eliminationist" discourse abounds: if all Liberals and Progressives, all of those on "the Left," are not only less than human but are also implacable enemies of humanity, bent on destroying all that is valuable in human life, then the proper response is extermination. If they are demonic "inhumans," then there is no prospect of reforming them; elimination is the only option. They either never had rights or have forfeited them through their horrible conduct.

Some tribalistic types may not consider the Other as literally less than human in the sense of lacking the capacity for rationality or some other essential feature of human beings; they may simply regard them as deeply and irredeemably irrational, as failing to exercise their capacity for rationality, without making any assumptions about a connection between rationality and human nature. But that can by itself lead in the direction of denying that they have rights. It is quite common, after all, to assume that minors who have not yet fully developed their capacity for rationality or people with certain severe mental disabilities that impede the exercise of the capacity for rationality do not have the rights that normal adults do. When your tribalistic ideology leads you to regard the Other as permanently, deeply irrational, you may in effect relegate them to a lower status, that of a being who doesn't possess all of the rights you have. At best, you'll regard them the way you do minors or people who are severely mentally impaired. You certainly won't regard them as your equals, mentally or morally.

My Ideology

Though I run some risk of misunderstanding in using this label, if pressed, I'd describe my ideology as a variety of Enlightenment ideology that has two main positive features: the belief that some moral progress has occurred and that more is possible, though far from inevitable, and the belief that all persons have an equal fundamental moral status that can be cashed out in a set of human rights. In my updated version of Enlightenment ideology, the first belief's expression of optimism about the possibility of moral progress is tempered by an appreciation of three facts about power. First, there are great disparities of power. Second, those with greater power have a tendency to use it in ways that produce injustices. And third, they often win in contests with the less powerful. That means that making moral progress is hard and that the achievement of it is highly contingent and fragile, not inevitable and durable (as some Enlightenment philosophers thought).

That's the best I can do for now in response to the Ishmael problem. Ultimately, the only way for you to tell whether my analysis is ideologically biased is to read this book to the end, with your ideological bias antennae fully extended. Keep this in mind, however: It's one thing to say that my analysis in this book is influenced to some extent by an ideology; it's another to say that this means that what I say isn't illuminating. Remember, ideologies can reveal, not just obscure, important features of the social world. Whether they reveal more than they obscure, or *vice versa*, depends on the ideology.

My examination of tribalistic ideologies won't be value-free. It couldn't be an evaluation, as opposed to purely a description, if it didn't rely on assumptions about values. I'll make negative judgments about tribalistic ideologies on the Left and the Right, and of course that means I'll be expressing my own values, which no doubt are influenced by my updated Enlightenment ideology. But I'm not going to be focusing so much on the specific substance of various tribalistic ideologies as on their common structure. I'll emphasize their shared features that impair our cognitive features and that operate across tribalistic ideologies that differ substantively from one another in dramatic ways.

More of my examples of tribalistic ideology come from the Right rather than the Left, because I think they come closer to being instances of the "ideal type" of tribal ideology I'm trying to explain. (An ideal type is a kind of model that exhibits the key features of tribalistic ideologies most clearly.) That's consistent with studies that purport to show that people with Conservative ideologies are "more ideological," on average than those with Liberal ideologies. What that means is that in surveys a higher percentage of self-identified Conservatives say they are very or extremely Conservative than the percentage of self-identified Liberals say they are very or extremely Liberal.[19]

Tribalistic Ideologies as Responses to Identity-Anxiety

A major theme of my analysis of tribalistic ideologies is that they are expressions of anxiety over identity—that these ideologies are empowered by the worry that society is moving in a direction that will make it impossible for you to live your identity or at least to do so without stigma. It may be that at present in America more and more Conservatives are coming to believe that society is increasingly rejecting the values that constitute Conservative identity and therefore that identity-anxiety is more prevalent and intense among Conservatives. If that's the case, then it shouldn't come as a surprise that Conservatives describe themselves as more ideological than Liberals do. That can change. If, in his second term as president, Trump does much of what he has said he'll do and the Supreme Court continues to make rulings that support Conservative values, then Liberals may come to experience increased identity-anxiety and come to describe themselves as being more ideological, as "very Liberal" rather than just as "Liberal."

Even though I've found more examples of Rightist tribalistic ideologies, I'll also give examples of how Leftist ideologies disable our most sophisticated cognitive abilities and damage us as moral agents in the process. And I'll show just why it is that we are all vulnerable to being taken in by tribalistic ideologies, regardless of our location on the Left-to-Right spectrum. In other words, my diagnosis of the source of tribalistic ideologies doesn't exhibit a bias against Conservatism. I don't assume that Conservatives are less intelligent or more gullible than Liberals, for example.

To anticipate: we're all vulnerable, because we're all shaped by the same evolutionary history, a journey of hundreds of millennia that produced a creature who has two traits that make us easy prey for tribalistic ideologies. First, we crave an identity that others will recognize and approve of and that gives us a sense of belonging, an assurance that we are not alone, and second, we tend to have inflated views about the virtues of our group and overly negative assessments of other groups. Those two traits were probably highly beneficial—important adaptations that helped humans survive and thrive in early environments. But now they are exploited by tribalistic ideologies in extremely harmful ways. In the next to the last chapters, when I consider how we can combat tribalistic ideologies, I will show that although our evolutionary history makes us vulnerable to tribalistic ideologies, that doesn't mean we are powerless to resist them. Our moral nature is not tribalistic, or at least not wholly so—not in the extreme sense of tribalism indicated by the term "tribalistic ideology." So, combatting tribalistic ideologies is not futile; it may well succeed. Given how pernicious they are, it's worth a try.

Notes

1 White according to the dominant way of classifying people, but in fact of Cherokee descent on my father's side. If you are part Native American, you are considered White; if you are part African-American, you are considered Black. The implication is that being part White can cancel out whatever sorts of inferiorities are associated with being Native American or that the latter aren't serious enough to matter, but that the inferiority of Black people is so severe that being part Black means you aren't White.

2 This film, based closely on a novel of the same title by James Dickey, graphically depicts a male raping another male.

3 "Liberal" here does not mean what it does in contemporary American popular discourse. It refers to a Political Philosophy that emphasizes individual freedom, typically by prescribing a set of rights that are to be entrenched in a constitution, and limited government.

4 I didn't find learning German to be easy. I had trouble with sentence structure, including the tendency in philosophical German to compose sentences with a large number of clauses and all of the verbs at the end. There's a joke about that: at academic conferences in German, you have two days of lectures, followed by a day for the verbs.

5 I thank Jonathan Bender for this insight.

6 Jonathan Haidt, *The Anxious Generation: How the Great Rewiring of Childhood Is Causing an Epidemic of Mental Ilness*. New York: Penguin Press, 2024.

7 Jonathan Haidt, *The Righteous Mind: Why Good People Are Divided by Politics and Religion*. New York: Vintage, 2012.

8 Christopher Bail, *Breaking the Social Media Prism: How to Make Our Platforms Less Polarizing*. Princeton, NJ: Princeton University Press, 2021; Roy F. Baumeister, "Tribal Hostility in Political Conflict." In *The Tribal Mind and the Psychology of Collectivism*, edited by Joseph P. Forgas, 1st ed., 271–85. New York: Routledge, 2024. Shanto Iyengar, Yphtach Lelkes, Matthew Levendusky, Neil Malhotra and Sean J. Westwood, "The Origins and Consequences of Affective Polarization in the United States." *SSRN Scholarly Paper*. Rochester, NY, May 1, 2019. Blake Roeber, *Political Humility: The Limits of Knowledge in Our Partisan Political Climate*. New York: Routledge, 2024; Henri Tajfel and John C. Turner, "The Social Identity Theory of Intergroup Behavior." In *Political Psychology*. New York: Psychology Press, 2004; Ori Weisel and Ro'i Zultan. "Social Motives in Intergroup Conflict: Group Identity and Perceived Target of Threat." *European Economic Review* 90 (November, 2016): 122–33.

9 Dan M. Kahan, *Misconceptions, Misinformation, and the Logic of Identity-Protective Cognition*. 2017. papers.ssrn.com; Dan M. Kahan, Donald Braman, John Gastil, Paul Slovic and C. K. Mertz, "*Culture and Identity-Protective Cognition: Explaining the White-Male Effect in Risk Perception*." *Journal of Empirical* 129, (2007): 1–30. Wiley Online Library; Geoffrey L. Cohen and David K. Sherman, "The Psychology of Self-Defense: Identity-Protective Cognition in the Wake of Collective Threat." *Psychology Bulletin* 140, no. 1, (2014): 1–37; Roy F. Baumeister, *Identity: The Most Underestimated Force in Political Psychology*. New York: Oxford, 1988.

10 Allen Buchanan, "The Explanatory Power of Ideology," in a forthcoming issue of *Social Philosophy & Policy*.

11 See, for example, Michael Dimock and Richard Wike, "America Is Exceptional in the Nature of Its Political Divide." Pew Research Center, November 13, 2020. https://www.pewresearch.org/short-reads/2020/11/13/america-is-exceptional-in-the-nature-of-its-political-divide/, which cites several empirical-survey-based studies indicating that the problem of affective polarization or tribalistic ideologies is especially severe in the United States.
Thomas Carothers and Andrew O'Donahue, "Why Americans Were Driven to Extremes," *Foreign Affairs* (September 25, 2019): 10–12; Ezra Klein, *Why We're Polarized*. First Avid Reader Press. Hardcover ed. New York: Avid Reader Press, an imprint of Simon & Schuster, Inc, 2020. Klein describes the "stacking" of identities on top of partisan identities.

12 Allen Buchanan, *Ideology and Revolution: How the Struggle Against Domination Drives the Evolution of Morality and Institutions*. Cambridge: Cambridge University Press, 2024.

13 Ginger Gibson, "Trump Says Immigrants Are 'Poisoning the Blood of Our Country.' Biden Campaign Likens Comments to Hitler." *NBC News*, December 17, 2023. https://www.nbcnews.com/politics/2024-election/trump-says-immigrants-are-poisoning-blood-country-biden-campaign-liken-rcna130141; Nathan Layne, Gram Slattery and Tim Reid, "Trump Calls Migrants 'Animals,'

Intensifying Focus on Illegal Immigration." *Reuters* (April 3, 2024), sec. United States. https://www.reuters.com/world/us/trump-expected-highlight-murder-michigan-woman-immigration-speech-2024-04-02/.

14 Kant develops this idea in more detail in his seminal *Groundwork for the Metaphysics of Morals*. Translated by Mary J. Gregor and Jens Timmermann, *Cambridge Texts in the History of Philosophy*. Revised ed., 1785. Reprint. Cambridge: Cambridge University Press, 2012.

15 "Speciesism" is the belief or practice of treating members of one species as morally more important than members of other species, solely on the basis of their species membership. The term was originally coined in 1970 by Richard Ryder, a British psychologist and animal-rights activist, see "Speciesism." In *Wikipedia*, August 17, 2024. https://en.wikipedia.org/w/index.php?title=Speciesism&oldid=1240794399.

The term was further popularized by Peter Singer, with his landmark book *Animal Liberation: A New Ethics for Our Treatment of Animals*. London: Cape, 1976.

16 The Second Great Expansion is the recognition that at least some nonhuman animals have moral standing, that they count morally in their own right and hence are not properly regarded as mere things, to be used as we see fit. The two books in which I discuss the Two Great Expansions are *The Evolution of Moral Progress: A Biocultural Theory*, co-authored with Rachel Powell, and *Our Moral Fate: Evolution and the Escape from Tribalism*.

17 McFaul. Michael J. Inhuman: The Secret History of Communist Revolutions (and How to Crush Them). New York: HarperCollins, 2022.

18 Among these books, many gross errors are lumping together in the category "communists" not just communists but also Socialists, Leftists, and Progressives.

19 Lydia Saad, "U.S. Political Ideology Steady; Conservatives, Moderates Tie." *Gallup* (January 17, 2022). https://news.gallup.com/poll/388988/political-ideology-steady-conservatives-moderates-tie.aspx. This source shows that 9% of people identify as "very conservative" while only 7% of people identify as "very liberal." However, it does not say that amongst those who self-identify as conservative, people are more likely to be "very conservative." This 2014 Pew study, Abigail Gieger, "Section 1: Growing Ideological Consistency." Pew Research Center, June 12, 2014. https://www.pewresearch.org/politics/2014/06/12/section-1-growing-ideological-consistency/ shows that "Fully 84% of those who are consistently conservative in their ideological positions call themselves conservative, as does a smaller majority (61%) of those who are 'mostly conservative' on the scale. But those who express consistently or mostly liberal values, are less likely to embrace the 'liberal' label. About six-in-ten (62%) consistent liberals say they are liberal, with 31% saying they are moderate, and a handful (6%) calling themselves conservative. And among those who are mostly liberal on the ideological consistency scale, more (44%) say they are moderate than say they are liberal (32%)."

1

ZOMBIES ARE REAL AND SOME OF THEM ARE US

Real-Life Zombies

Orb-weaving spiders are excellent craftsmen. The webs they weave consist of concentric orbits, hence the spider's name. But sometimes the spider stops spinning that way and constructs an entirely different kind of web. The spider's nervous system has been hijacked and reprogrammed by a parasitic wasp. The wasp deposits an egg in the spider's abdomen. The egg contains chemicals that alter the spider's nervous system. This changes the spider's web-weaving behavior. Instead of circular webs, the spider moves robotically back and forth, spinning a straight-line, thick, very strong web. The wasp attaches a cocoon with a wasp pupa inside to this new web, which is so tough that the cocoon doesn't get washed off in heavy rains or blown off by the wind. After hanging securely for a while in the new web, the developed pupa turns into a wasp—which then seeks another host spider. The parasitic invasion ultimately results in the spider's death and greater reproductive success for the wasp.[1]

This phenomenon is called "host manipulation": a parasite changes the behavior of its host organism in ways that harm the host but increase the reproductive fitness of the parasite, which means raising the probability that it will have offspring that survive long enough to reproduce.

Another example is zombie ants. A fungus invades the ant and reprograms its nervous system. This causes the ant to climb to a high location (where it is exposed to predators, something it generally avoids). The fungus consumes the ant from within and as the ant's body collapses and disintegrates, it disperses the fungus spores, producing more fungi.

DOI: 10.4324/9781003612469-2

The same phenomenon occurs in a species of fly. The parasite hijacks the fly's nervous system, causing it to climb to a high perch, spread its wings, and thrust its hind legs straight out. The parasite destroys the insides of the fly and, as it literally falls apart, the parasite's offspring are dispersed and dispersed more effectively because of the fly's abnormal posture and location.

When I first read about these gruesome examples of host manipulation, the chill that went up my spine was quickly followed by a sigh of relief. I thought to myself "Thank God, evolution didn't produce this kind of thing in humans!"

Ideological Zombification

I was wrong. Our brains do get hijacked and reprogrammed, not by some critter that invades us from without, but by our own ideological beliefs. The difference between us and the spiders, ants, and flies that parasites zombify is that we create what make us zombies.

I don't mean that tribalistic ideologies literally turn us into zombies (zombies, after all, are hardly conscious if at all). I'm drawing an analogy between host manipulation and the way tribalistic ideologies affect us. It's an analogy, not an identity. Tribalistic ideologies aren't parasites, but like the parasites that engage in host manipulation; they hijack and re-purpose normal functions, in the human case, functions that determine how we acquire and manage beliefs, that determine our understanding of what others are saying and doing, and that shape our behavior. And when we are hijacked by a tribalistic ideology, we don't become mindless robots; instead, our most impressive cognitive abilities are turned against themselves.

Of course, if you think you're ideology-free, you won't worry that you may be zombified. If that's the case, I suggest you ponder what Michael Freeden, an expert on ideologies, says: ideologies are like bad breath; you only notice them in *other* people.

Freeden is right. Many of us quite confidently call other people ideologues, but bristle with indignation at the suggestion that we have an ideology. That's not surprising, because it's in the nature of ideologies that those who have them are usually not aware of it. So, you shouldn't assume that a discussion of how ideologies can hijack the brain doesn't apply to you because you are ideology-proof.

The point is that none of us may be ideology-proof, at least not under all circumstances. Think of it this way: ideologies don't just produce delusions about the way the world is; they produce delusions about our ability to perceive how it is. They delude you into thinking that you're not deluded.

Nevertheless, if you prefer, much of what I have to say can be conveyed without using the term "ideology." For a moment, let's avoid the I-word and concentrate on beliefs, more specifically, political beliefs, and certain ways the brain manages these beliefs when they are ideological beliefs. My claim is that some types of beliefs, when accompanied by certain ways of managing beliefs, undermine normal brain functions and replace them with dysfunctions. In effect, our political beliefs cause cognitive disabilities. The kind of political beliefs and belief management processes that cause these disabilities are sometimes called *tribal*. Here's the irony: these beliefs do this damage by hooking up with normal cognitive functions. They hijack normal cognitive functions in ways that diminish our cognitive performance, make us unable to do what humans are normally capable of. In that sense, they make us less than fully human, turning back the evolutionary clock.

At this point it's hard to avoid using the term "ideology." It's an economical way of referring to a complex package of beliefs, attitudes, and thought processes for managing beliefs. So, I'll take the plunge. Here's my preliminary definition of "ideology."

What Are Ideologies?

An ideology is an evaluative, action-guiding map of the social world. It's evaluative in that it doesn't just describe, it includes positive and negative judgments about some of what it describes, and that makes it action-guiding or prescriptive: it provides guidance about what to believe and what to do. In the case of political ideologies, the evaluative aspect of the map includes beliefs about legitimate institutionalized power and how it ought to be exercised. That has implications for how we ought to respond to the institutional exercise of power.

Political ideologies also single out groups as important features of the landscape and typically draw a sharp distinction between Us and Them. Because it is evaluative and action-guiding, an ideology is more than just a description of the social world. A merely descriptive map, without the evaluative element, would be a theory. An ideology is more practical than a theory.

Tribalistic ideologies are a type of political ideology. What distinguishes them from other political ideologies is the extreme character of their division between Us and Them, which includes the idea that They are not just inferior, but dangerous, insincere, and hostile toward all We value. It's also a hallmark of tribalistic ideologies that they represent the world in Manichean terms, as a life-or-death, no-holds barred struggle for the highest stakes. Recall the recent book I noted in the Introduction: *Inhuman: The Secret History of Communist Revolutions (and How to Crush Them)*. It perfectly exemplifies the Manichean aspect of tribalistic ideologies.

Perhaps the most important feature of ideologies to keep in mind is that they don't just orient an individual in the social world: they orient many individuals in the same way. They tell us what We believe and stand for and what We should do. They also tell us that We are quite different from (and superior to) Them. They coordinate beliefs, attitudes, and actions by forming group identities that are not just descriptive but also prescriptive, that is, action-guiding. This coordination motivates and enables collective action.

With this preliminary understanding of what ideologies are, we can now restate the crucial point about the mind turning against itself. When tribalistic ideologies take hold, cognitive functions that evolved for certain purposes, including preeminently cooperation within a group, are re-purposed in such a fashion as to impair cognitive performance, and impair it in ways that make cooperation between groups very difficult if not impossible. Soon I'll explain exactly how all of this works, but for now I want to emphasize that ideologies aren't just sets of beliefs and attitudes. They also have mechanisms for managing beliefs—for excluding some beliefs and preserving others.

Ideological Belief Immune Systems

More specifically, all ideologies, political ideologies included, have ways of preserving the beliefs they contain in the face of contradictory experience or information. I call this feature "the belief immune system," because it's analogous to the way an organism's immune system resists invasion by parasites or infectious agents. The belief immune system utilizes cognitive dissonance resolution mechanisms that are flawed from the standpoint of getting at the truth and avoiding error. Here's an example from my own experience growing up in Apartheid Arkansas.

When I was a child, I was taught that Black people are of inferior intelligence. I noticed that our Black housekeeper, Louise, was very smart. So, I asked my mother how this could be, given that Louise was Black. My mother replied: "She must have some White Blood." My mother's racist ideology had a cognitive dissonance resolution mechanism that operated on the basis of the belief that some quantity of "White Blood" could ameliorate the defects of being Black. That allowed her to sustain her belief that Black people are mentally inferior in the face of Louise's obviously high intelligence. The "White Blood" theory eliminated the psychological dissonance that was produced by the juxtaposition of the belief that Black people are mentally inferior and the belief that Louise was highly intelligent.

In 1988, I spent two months in Apartheid South Africa.[2] From the moment I arrived there, the sense of *deja vue* was overwhelming: I felt like

I had traveled back in time to the Little Rock, Arkansas, of my youth. When I heard Afrikaners say that Nelson Mandela must have had a White father, I thought of my mother's comment about Louise. Saying that Mandela's father was White was their way of reconciling a begrudging acknowledgment of his exceptional character and accomplishments with their belief in the inferiority of Black people. That's cognitive dissonance resolution at the expense of truth, rationality, and the correction of false beliefs. The cognitive dissonance mechanisms of tribalistic ideologies tend to be "epistemically defective," as philosophers would put it. They aren't conducive to knowledge or justified belief.

Later, I'll explain how this feature of ideologies that I observed in Little Rock and South Africa—their uncanny knack for preserving beliefs that ought to be abandoned—plays a role in the hijacking not just of our cognitive abilities, but also our moral abilities. The latter include the ability to apply moral concepts, to judge behavior to be right or wrong, and to know how we ought to act toward other people. For now, I want to focus on one of the most sinister ways in which ideologies invade and transform cognitive abilities, causing something that looks a lot like a mental illness.

Theory of Mind

One important cognitive ability our evolved brain gives us is "theory of mind" (also called "mind-reading"). This includes the ability to make generally reliable inferences about a person's mental states—their intentions, their beliefs, whether they are hostile or friendly, etc.—on the basis of their behavior, including what they say. For example, if I see several members of the audience eyeing the clock on the wall or looking at their watches, I reasonably infer that they think it's past time for me to wrap up my lecture.

Sometimes, rightly or wrongly, we infer not just a particular intention or a belief, but also a personality trait from behavior. Here I'm reminded of one of the few jokes about philosophers. It's apt because it's a theory of mind joke. How do you tell an extraverted philosopher? He looks at *your* shoes when he's talking to you.[3] That's an inference about a personality type made on the basis of shoe-viewing behavior.

Theory of mind is an awfully important ability. It's essential for predicting what others will do and hence for trust, and trust is essential for cooperation. Theory of mind is also important for communication. Sometimes I can only know what you're saying if I've already inferred what your intentions are on the basis of your previous behavior. If I make a mistaken inference from your behavior to your mental states, wrongly thinking you intend one thing when in fact you intend something quite different, I may systematically misunderstand what you are saying. And that misunderstanding can cause me to act toward you in ways that I shouldn't.

The point is that when others speak, we don't just hear various sounds; we interpret. And theory of mind plays a crucial role in our interpreting. That's why failures of theory of mind can cause failures of communication. And those failures of communication can do more than just hinder cooperation; they can also spark conflict, including violent conflict.

How Tribalistic Ideologies Disable Theory of Mind

Tribalistic ideologies undermine this vital ability and replace it with a tendency to make unreliable inferences from behavior to mental states, substituting a defective theory of mind for the normal, reasonably well-functioning one. One way this works is through stereotyping. A tribalistic ideology not only makes a sharp distinction between Us and Them, but it also represents all of Them as being the same. In philosophical terms, it ascribes a shared essence or nature to all of Them, and this shared essence or nature is thought to determine their behavior. So, let's call this aspect of tribalistic ideology "essentialized, deterministic stereotyping," EDS for short.

Psychologist Laurence has studied the EDS phenomenon in great detail.[4] He shows that from a very early age, children implicitly ascribe a shared, deterministic essence to all individuals they categorize as being Other, as not belonging to the group the child normally associates and identifies with. Hirschfeld also says that, depending on the child's cultural environment, this psychological trait can become the basis for racism. Hence, the title of his book *Race in the Making*.

A natural way to describe Hirschfeld's findings about EDS is to say that the apparently innate tendency to ascribe a shared deterministic essence to members of out-groups can come to be expressed in the form of racism, if a racist ideology is pervasive in the cultural context in which the child is developing. In a different cultural context, under the influence of a different type of ideology, the child's EDS might be focused, not on a racial group, but rather upon the members of a religious or ethno-national group different from her own. In my childhood environment, the innate tendency Hirschfeld describes developed into racism, which included racial stereotypes of African Americans. If I had been a Serbian child in the early 1990s, then I would most likely have developed negative, essentialized, deterministic stereotypes of Croats and Bosniak Muslims.

I think Hirschfeld's extremely valuable work can be made even better by adding the idea that differences in ideologies explain how the innate tendency he describes plays out differently in different cultural contexts, thereby avoiding an exclusive emphasis on race. What follows are some examples of how this type of stereotyping, as an aspect of tribalistic ideologies, undermines our normal theory of mind.

Recall the experience I related in the Introduction: when a neighbor saw me wearing a mask, he said "Oh, I see you voted Democratic," and then went on to describe how the Democrats were bent on destroying individual liberty and extending government control.

If your Conservative tribal ideology tells you that all Liberals are alike, that what defines them as Liberals is that they all want to increase government's control over us, then you will interpret what they say and do accordingly. If you and your fellow Conservatives are resistant to mask-wearing, when you see someone wearing a mask during a pandemic, you will infer that they are a Liberal, someone who's onboard with the Liberal project of gradually increasing government control.

The mere sight of someone wearing a mask can trigger the stereotype: you'll assume that person is a Liberal. Once you do that, you'll interpret their behavior through the lens of your stereotype of what Liberals are like. That can lead you to make serious mistakes about what they believe, their intentions, and attitudes. If it weren't for the stereotype, you might simply conclude that I'm wearing a mask because I don't want to get COVID and think wearing a mask reduces the risk that I will. Or, as was in fact the case, that although I didn't think masks did much to stop the spread of infection, I didn't want to have a confrontation with the receptionist at my doctor's office.

Appreciating the EDS aspect of tribalistic ideologies helps explain another feature of them that has received a good deal of attention from social scientists: the fact that those in the grip of tribalistic ideologies tend to exaggerate the scope of disagreement on political issues. Social science research shows that there is more "affective polarization" than "substantive polarization," the latter being disagreement on various political issues. In addition, there's evidence that people tend to assume that there is much more disagreement on the latter than there really is.[5] If your ideological stereotype of the Other presents Them as wholly different from Us and diametrically opposed to Us, then you will naturally assume that they disagree with everything We believe. In the next to the last chapters, where I consider solutions to our tribalism problem, I'll suggest that we have to think hard about how to combat this tendency to exaggerate political disagreement. Doing so will no doubt prove very difficult, in part because, politicians and other promoters of tribalistic ideologies are keen to foist on us bundled identities that are defined in part by their contrast with the bundled identities attributed to the Other. If you define yourself as radically opposed to everything They stand for, you'll tend to think that you disagree with them on every matter of importance.

Here are two more examples of how the EDS of a tribalistic ideology works. The late Rush Limbaugh, the most influential Right-wing radio show host until his death several years ago, repeatedly said that Liberals don't really care about migrants; they just want more of them to come to the United States, because they think they'll vote Democratic. If you buy that, then whenever somebody you sort into the Liberal category advocates loosening border controls on the grounds that tight controls result in human rights violations, you won't hear what he or she is saying or at least you won't take it at face value. You won't be able to make reasonable inferences about what they believe and intend. And you'll feel no obligation to engage the Liberal on the facts—in this case the facts about the relationship between tight controls and human rights violations. You won't take what they say as an indication that they really believe in human rights; instead, your essentialized, deterministic stereotype of Liberals will lead you to infer quite a different mental state, namely, the intention to increase the Democratic vote. And you will do this without providing or feeling the need to provide any evidence whatsoever for the claim that all or even most Democrats have this intention.

In the Limbaugh example and similar instances, theory of mind has been derailed by ideology, due to rigid ideological stereotyping of the Other. The stereotype prevents you from making reliable inferences about the Other's mental states on the basis of their behavior. Your stereotype of the Other prevents you from discerning their intentions and beliefs. But it's worse than that: your ideology replaces a normal theory of mind with a very defective one, one that produces unreliable inferences from behavior to mental states (in this case, the Liberal's supposed beliefs about how to increase the Democratic vote). The result is that you will systematically misunderstand what the other person does and says, in ways that simply reinforce your stereotype of "those people."

Here's another example of how ideological stereotypes impair cognitive functioning, this time from the Left. Trump suggested and his Conservative followers sometimes confidently asserted that the COVID-19 virus originated in a Chinese lab. Many Liberals automatically dismissed this hypothesis just because of who was saying it. They viewed Trump as unreliable and saw his speech as a device for drawing attention to himself or stroking (and stoking) his base. When Conservatives agreed with Trump on the origin of COVID-19, Liberals interpreted this as just another sign of Conservatives' xenophobia and their tendency to be swayed by their demagogic leader. In other words, Liberals didn't regard remarks about the Chinese lab as a statement that should be evaluated as such, to try to determine whether it was true or false, justified or not. Instead, due to their stereotype about who was saying it, they didn't engage with the content at all. Their ideological beliefs about the nature of Trump and his followers prevented them from regarding what they said as statements, propositions that can be and ought to be evaluated as to their truth or justification. Because of their ideological assumptions about the character, motives, and intentions of the speaker, they saw no point in addressing the content of what was said.

Consequently, they didn't ask themselves whether there was evidence for his claim; they didn't evaluate it on the merits—they just dismissed it. I'm ashamed to admit it, but this is exactly what I did. It was a long time till I felt obligated to actually look at the facts that can be construed to support the Chinese-lab-origin hypothesis. I'm not 100% convinced that COVID-19 originated in the Wuhan lab, but I think there is considerable evidence that it did.

Even worse, I and a lot of Liberals were remarkably uncritical about U.S. pandemic policy precisely *because* people on the Right were so critical of it. When our political enemy attacked something, we felt we had to defend it. Our focus on *who* was criticizing policy, shaped by our theory of mind regarding Conservatives, not only prevented us from taking seriously anything they said, but it also led us to act as if any criticism of individuals that people on the Right were criticizing was disloyalty to our tribe. If you think anything a Conservative says is just stupid or disingenuous because of your ideological stereotype of what Conservatives are like, you aren't likely to try to determine whether their criticisms are valid. And if you even so much as suggest that their criticism might be plausible, you run the risk of being considered one of Them.

These last two examples illustrate how an ideological beliefs divert attention from the actual content of the Other's speech and focus it on the speaker, characterized in a negative way. This is what philosophers call the *ad hominem* fallacy: rejecting a statement or argument, not on the merits, but by discrediting the person who advances it. An ideologically distorted theory of mind does the discrediting.

The Importance of Theory of Mind for Democracy

The Limbaugh and Chinese lab examples illustrate something else that's central to tribalistic ideologies—and very dangerous: by replacing a normal theory of mind with a bogus one, they misinterpret behavior in a way that blocks sincere, mutually respectful discourse that focuses on facts and reasons. As we'll see shortly, that has dire consequences not just for civil-ity, and for the pursuit of truth, but also for democracy. If your stereotype of the Other characterizes them as stupid and/or insincere, there's no point in engaging respectfully with them in a discussion aimed at finding out the truth about some political issue. In a later chapter I'll elaborate on this point, showing how tribalistic thinking and discourse replaces truth-seeking communication while simulating it.

Political scientist Robert Jervis gives us a masterful analysis of how impairments of theory of mind affect international politics, though he doesn't use the phrase "theory of mind." He describes how time and time again leaders of one country erroneously interpret the behavior of leaders of another country, act according to that interpretation and then are misunderstood in turn by those other leaders. For example, country A may undertake what it views as a purely defensive action (e.g., the United States puts missiles in Turkey, near the Soviet border, to deter a first strike by the U.S.S.R.), but leaders of country B (the Soviet Union) see this not as a defensive action but rather as an aggressive one, a prelude to a first strike. Then country B responds to this interpretation of country A's behavior with an action (putting missiles in Cuba) that it sees as purely defensive, but which country A sees as aggression, and so on. This spiral of misunderstandings can produce increasingly risky behavior. It can even result in a war that nobody wanted.[6]

At each stage, the misinterpretation is due to rigid stereotypes of the Other, rooted in a political ideology. Jervis makes it clear that this spiral of misunderstandings occurs regardless of whether the participants' ideologies are Left-wing or Right-wing. Both varieties feature stereotypes of the Other that lead to systematically skewed inferences from behavior to mental states.

A sound theory of mind enables one to infer a more varied range of mental states to the Other by discerning nuances in their behavior and speech. An essentialized, deterministic stereotype automatically attributes only a more limited set of mental states, all of which are negatively characterized.

When tribalism is rife, there is tremendous pressure for conformity within the opposing groups. To that extent, ideological stereotypes of the Other may be accurate, but only as very broad generalizations. Tribalistic ideologies cause us to mistake probabilities for certainties, generalizations for universal truths. Worse than that, they are sometimes not even accurate as broad generalizations. I think that is the case with the belief that Democrats only care about loosening border controls because they think migrants will vote Democratic. I think it is very unlikely that most Democrats believe that.

For eight years, I served as a volunteer in Samaritans of Tucson, participating in over 150 "patrols," backpacking in water, medical aid, and food to migrants in the Tucson sector of the Southern border. I never heard any of my co-workers (virtually all of whom were Liberals) so much as hint at the view Limbaugh attributed to Liberals. Given their behavior and discourse among themselves, I think the simpler and more plausible hypothesis is that they, like myself, just wanted to save human lives. We weren't participating in some liberal conspiracy to increase the Democratic vote.

All of the preceding examples of ideology-induced cognitive disfunctions are eerily similar to the zombie spider, ant, and fly cases described earlier. The brain gets hijacked by an ideology. The cognitive capacities that normally tend to produce good results are replaced by defective counterparts.

You Have to Be Smart to Use Your Mind to Make Yourself Stupid

Only in a species that has the cognitive sophistication to have an ideology can the mind disable its own most valuable functions. In neurological terms, it's a matter of ideological beliefs causing the brain to rewire itself in ways that make it dysfunctional.

I've already noted that ideologically caused cognitive and moral dysfunctions aren't across the board, that they typically only occur when triggered by threats to our identity. Ideologies provide the cues that do the triggering. People can be decent, respectful of the truth, and critical about what they are asked to believe in other areas of life, but just the opposite in the political realm.

In the usual host manipulation cases, the hijacker is external; in the case of ideology, the enemy is within us. Of course, in most instances, the enemy didn't *originate* within you or me. Most of us don't invent our ideologies; we get them from elsewhere. But once they have taken hold, they affect us in the depths of our being, in our mind. As I noted before, ideologies don't do this by themselves. They exploit or re-purpose evolved cognitive abilities to undermine cognitive performance. The true "enemy within" (to use one of Trump's favorite phrases) is our tribalistic morality in alliance with the cognitive and moral abilities it hijacks.

How Tribalistic Ideologies Create Separate Worlds

Now I want to suggest that it will help us understand the nature of tribalistic ideologies if we appreciate the relevance of a fascinating biological concept, that of an *Umwelt*. The character of our minds, combined with the nature of our sense organs, and how our physical form shapes our interaction with the environment determine what biologists call our *Umwelt*, reality as we experience it. Different types of creatures have different *Umwelten*, because they have different sense organs, nervous systems, and physical capacities for encountering items in their environment, capacities that are shaped by their body designs. Because of these differences, they experience reality in different ways. From their standpoint, what is real is only what their constitution gives them access to. For example, a tick has a very limited *Umwelt*. It only senses heat, hair texture, and the smell of butyric acid emanating from skin.[7] Humans have a much richer *Umwelt*.

Your dog's *Umwelt* is much richer than a tick's, but it is largely olfactory, and rather limited compared to yours. A dog's sense of smell is at least 1,000 times more sensitive than ours. As your dog moves through the world, its consciousness is mainly an awareness of a kaleidoscope of smells, in an almost infinite, ever-changing variety of intensities and flavors.

It's quite different with us. Smells are typically an episodic and relatively minor feature of the human *Umwelt*. In the canine *Umwelt*, smells are all-pervasive and persistently dominant. Our human *Umwelt* is predominantly visual and auditory, but all our sensations are filtered, organized, and interpreted through our beliefs and attitudes. That makes our *Umwelt* largely mentalized. In fact, it's so mentalized that we can explore a thought-world with very little new sensory input, at least for a while.

The general contours of the human *Umwelt* are fixed by the evolution of our species. Yet for a number of reasons, your *Umwelt* and mine may differ within those contours, if only in which particular items among those that all humans have the capacity to be aware of we happen to notice and attach significance to.

Different ideologies can produce remarkable differences within the parameters of the evolved human *Umwelt*. If the differences in the *Umwelt* created by a group's tribalistic ideology become great enough, that group and its political *Umwelt* break away, secede from the common political *Umwelt*. When this occurs, there will no longer be a shared political *Umwelt*. As I'll show later, *Umwelt* secession can lead people to think seriously about real, territorial secession: in particular secession of the Red states from the Union.

Without a shared political *Umwelt*, there can be no democracy, because democracy requires common ground, which includes agreement on at least some of the relevant facts, as well as agreement, in broad outlines, on what government is for. If your political *Umwelt* and mine are wholly distinct, with no significant overlap when it comes to our understanding of politically relevant facts, we can't regard ourselves as working together, through democratic institutions, to pursue a common good. We won't be able to identify a common good. And the idea that we are one people will no longer apply. In Chapter 4, I elaborate the point that tribalistic ideologies make "We the people" a term without a single referent, and I explain the dire consequences this has for democracy.

If you and I have opposing ideologies, my evaluative map of the social world may magnify certain features of the landscape that are relatively insignificant in your map. And it may diminish or completely obscure other features that are very prominent in the map your ideology supplies. I may see mountains where you see mole hills and *vice versa*. For you, news of a surge of migrants across the Southern border may dominate your map. The bright light your ideology shines on the immigration issue may relegate almost everything else that's going on to darkness. If my ideology tells me that abortion rights are the key issue and I hear that the Supreme Court has struck down *Roe vs. Wade,* that news will tower above the landscape of my map, casting an obscuring shadow over other important events.

If our maps differ enough, we may not be able to locate a common landmark at which we can meet. Instead, the maps our ideologies supply will lead us farther and farther apart. If we have profoundly different, non-overlapping political *Umwelten,* then, politically speaking, we will inhabit different worlds and communication between the inhabitants of those separate worlds will be limited, if it is at all possible. It won't be a matter of our evaluating the same set of facts differently. We won't even be able to agree on the facts. This inability to agree on the facts that are relevant to political issues is damaging to democracy, because it makes genuine deliberation across partisan lines impossible.

From the human point of view, the tick has a very limited *Umwelt,* a profoundly impoverished experience of the world. But it would be wrong to say it suffers from a disability. That's just the way ticks are when their sensory organs and nervous systems are working normally. The inability to detect anything but heat, hair texture, and the smell of butyric acid isn't a disability (or a disease, if "disease" is defined as an adverse departure from normal functioning—in this case, normal functioning for a tick).

It's different with humans. If an ideology limits a person's ability to perceive some important features of reality that normal human beings have the ability to perceive, that's a disability and in some cases, perhaps even a disease or mental illness.

It took millions of years for evolution to produce a species (*Homo sapiens*) that has an unparalleled repertoire of capacities for interacting with its environment in ways that generate a myriad of perceptions and ways of knowing. And that resulted in an amazingly rich human *Umwelt.*

The same capacities that create our rich *Umwelt,* including especially our language-based knack for abstractions, also allow humans to do something no other species can do: we can enter, to some extent, into the *Umwelten* of other creatures. For example, knowing what we do about dogs and ticks, we can imagine, though imperfectly, what it is like to be them (more so with dogs than ticks, I think). The more scientific knowledge about other species we gain, the better we will be able to imagine what their *Umwelten* are like.

We now know that some animals that we treat very badly, like factory-farmed cows and pigs, have nervous systems so very much like ours that it is undeniable that they experience physical suffering pretty much the same way we do. We know that no matter how much the bovine or porcine *Umwelt* differs from the human one, it includes pain, and we know that pain, as such, is bad. We know, then, that the suffering we inflict on them is very similar to the suffering we'd experience were we treated that way. That knowledge has implications for how we should treat them.

Being able to imagine the *Umwelt* of another creature is important for being able to empathize with it, and empathy can be crucial for including that creature in the moral community, the class of beings that have moral standing, that matter morally in their own right, the beings toward whom we owe moral obligations, whom we shouldn't treat as if they were mere things, just means toward our ends. Moral progress in our treatment of non-human animals has depended, in part, on getting better facts about what it is like to be such creatures, using that knowledge to begin to comprehend their *Umwelten*, and using our understanding of their *Umwelten* to determine how we ought to treat them. Perhaps the biggest reason why we've been so bad at understanding the *Umwelten* of non-human animals is that our interaction with them has mainly been a matter of exploiting and killing them.

When we realize that cows and pigs feel pain much as we do, a powerful tool, moral consistency reasoning, may kick in. If pain in us is bad, then pain in other creatures is also bad and we shouldn't inflict it on them. Because they understand the power of moral consistency reasoning, animal rights activists have tried hard to convince people that factory farming inflicts terrible suffering on animals.

Here's another example. Recent research shows that octopi are highly intelligent, playful creatures, capable of interacting with humans and apparently enjoy doing so. You are not likely to notice those impressive characteristics if you "interact" only with dead octopi by eating them or if your "interaction" with live ones consists of "harvesting" them to sell them as food.

Learning about the impressive abilities of octopi has changed me. Grilled octopus used to be one of my favorite foods. Now I find the thought of eating an octopus repugnant. Why? Because I now believe that these creatures have some of the same qualities that persons have and that are among the qualities that give persons moral status, that make them not mere things. If I value certain traits in humans, I ought to value them in octopi. And if valuing them in humans requires treating them in certain ways, then valuing those traits in octopi requires similar treatment of them. Valuing them is not compatible with treating octopi as mere stuff to be killed and eaten when there are plenty of other things to eat that lack those valuable traits.

So, I came to find the thought of eating an octopus repugnant because of moral consistency reasoning: I value traits X, Y, and Z in humans and I think their having those traits has moral implications, that there are certain things it's wrong to do to persons because they have those traits. Octopi also have traits X, Y, and Z. It's the traits that make a moral difference, not whether the creature that has them is a member of my species. Therefore, I ought to recognize that there are certain things it's wrong to do to octopi and act accordingly.

Later, I'll stress that the ability to engage in moral consistency reasoning is one of our most powerful resources as moral agents. I'll also show how tribalistic ideologies can either prevent us from engaging in moral consistency reasoning when we should and subvert it when we do engage in it. That's one way in which tribalistic ideologies undermine us as moral beings.

The Ideological Disabling of Empathy

Now for the main point of my discussion of Umwelten: *Ironically, as science has increased our ability to enter the Umwelten of creatures remarkably unlike us, our tribalistic ideologies have diminished our ability to imagine what it is like to inhabit the Umwelten of some members of our own species.* I've heard Liberals say they can't understand Conservatives and Conservatives say they can't understand Liberals. They're both right! Their ideologies disable the cognitive and emotional capacities needed for understanding how the Other experiences the world. Due to the pervasiveness of tribalistic ideologies, some of us are better at empathizing with cows, pigs, and octopi than we are with some of our fellow human beings.

There's another way to look at the effect of tribalistic ideologies' EDS: it not only produces unreliable inferences from behavior to mental states, but it also impairs our ability to perceive individuals as such. It makes us unable to distinguish one individual from another because they are all seen through the ideological essentialized, deterministic stereotype. That, too, is a cognitive disability. It's also profoundly disrespectful.

If you are Liberal with a tribalistic political ideology and classify someone as a Conservative, you'll assume that they have certain views, certain commitments, and goals. You won't pay them the respect of finding out what they are really like, what they really think or value. You won't take seriously the possibility that even if most of Them have those goals and commitments, not all of them do. And your interactions with them will be shaped by the stereotype; they won't be responsive to their characteristics as individuals. Some Conservatives you encounter might well share some common ground with you, be someone you could cooperate with. But you'll miss that opportunity, because your ideology tells you they're a Conservative and that Conservatives are all alike in getting everything important completely wrong.

Here's an example. As I noted earlier, my wife is a Conservative. When people learn this fact about her, they make certain assumptions and some of them are quite wrong. Unlike many Conservatives, she thinks the death penalty should be abolished, she thinks the Second Gulf War was unjustified, and she believes that abortion should be a legal option. She gets pretty angry when people attribute the opposite views to her just because they classify her as a Conservative. What bothers her most about this is that, when people make those assumptions, they don't give her credit for being independent in her political beliefs. They treat her like a herd animal. In effect, they deny her separate identity as the person she is, because they've assigned the identity their stereotype of Conservatives prescribes.

If tribalistic ideologies have produced a high level of conformity among their adherents, interpreting people's behavior on the basis of stereotypes can actually become rational, from a purely epistemic point of view, that is, in terms of what you have evidence for believing. But sometimes what's "epistemically justified" (to use the philosophical jargon) and what's morally justified can diverge. Even if you know for sure that someone is, say, a Liberal, and even if it's true that most Liberals believe X, there may be moral reasons to disregard that fact and try to find out what *this* Liberal believes. Not acting on the basis of the high probability that this individual believes X may be required in order to show due respect for them as an individual, and it also may be the right thing to do from the standpoint of seeking agreement and compromise. Even if, due to the accuracy of the stereotype, it's unlikely that this particular Liberal will be somebody you can find some common ground with, finding common ground may be important enough, from a moral point of view, for you to buck the odds and disregard the stereotype. So, whether the ideological stereotype is accurate or not, letting it determine how you act toward others can have bad consequences.

It's not news that ideologies can have negative features, in particular, that they can include false beliefs that encourage bad behavior (think of antisemitic ideologies that attribute global conspiracies to the Jews). My point is that stopping there grossly underestimates the damage ideologies can do. They can cause serious malfunctions of our brains. They can make us blind to what other people are really like and deaf to what they are really saying.

It's common knowledge that one way ideologies produce dangerous beliefs and bad behavior is by supplying false premises in inferential reasoning. It can do this without undermining normal cognitive functions, in this case inferential (If..., then...) reasoning. Bad premises can result in arguments that are valid, but unsound. For example, "If Joe committed the murder, he ought to be punished. Joe committed the murder. Therefore, he ought to be punished." This little argument is valid—the "Therefore" is perfectly correct in the sense that given the premises, the conclusion does follow. But that's compatible with the conclusion ("Joe ought to be punished") being false for the simple reason that one premise ("Joe committed the murder") is false. Ideologies can produce bad beliefs and behavior simply by feeding false premises into inferential processes that are impeccable. When that happens, the ideology hasn't produced a genuine mental disability; it hasn't undermined the capacity to draw valid inferences (though it has damaged our ability to use it to get at the truth). The proper operation of cognitive functions—in this case, the ability to make valid inferences—remains intact.

My focus is on something more insidious than the fact that ideologies supply false premises for valid arguments. I'm homing in on something much more basic: how ideologies actually undermine normal cognitive processes rather than just supply faulty inputs for them.

How Ideologies Insulate Themselves from Criticism

Remember that I've emphasized that ideologies include ways of sustaining their core beliefs in the face of challenges to them. They also have ways of preventing challenges from even arising. Tribalistic ideologies, on the Left and the Right, provide explanations of what's gone wrong in our society that obscure their own role in making things go wrong and thereby insulate themselves from challenges. They impair our ability to understand why we're currently in such a lamentable state by diverting attention from their own contribution to it.

Here's a classic example. Suppose you're in the grip of a Conservative tribalistic ideology, here's what it tells you:

Yes, all American politicians are immoral, they all lie, cheat, and play dirty. But Our politicians didn't start that, Theirs did. Liberals will do anything to advance their big government, freedom-destroying agenda. Our politicians have to respond in kind—otherwise we lose. And given what's at stake, losing isn't an option! You can't expect Our politicians to play nice when their opponents are utterly unscrupulous. Unilateral disarmament isn't an option in a total war to the finish.

Liberal tribalistic ideologies tell the same story, with the role of aggressive immoralists and defensive immoralists reversed.

Both ideologies divert attention from the role *they* are playing in the current disgusting state of American politics. That's one way they preserve their constitutive beliefs, make them immune to challenges. If people saw what their ideologies were doing, they might think twice about their allegiance to them. They won't see what their ideologies are doing if their ideologies convince them that the real problem is the opposing ideology and what it causes people to do. That, too, is a cognitive impairment, and impairment of our ability to identify the true causes of certain states of affairs, to develop plausible causal explanations of why they are as they are. So, tribalistic ideologies not only do a great deal of damage, but they also make it harder to make things better by providing false explanations of why the damage has occurred.

More Ideological Cognitive Impairments

Impairing theory of mind, blinding us to differences among individuals, and providing bogus explanations of bad behavior that conceal their own role in producing it are not the only ways ideologies disrupt normal cognitive functions. So far, I've emphasized these two impairments because I think they're especially dangerous and as far as I can determine haven't received enough attention in the psychological literature.

That literature does have a good deal to say about several other ideology-induced cognitive disabilities. One is impairment of our ability to evaluate evidence and draw correct conclusions from it. For example, a person who is very good at reasoning on the basis of evidence when the cognitive task has nothing to do with politics suddenly is "dumbed down" if they now have to perform the same type of task, but the task is framed in political terms or as involving political issues.

A major contributor to that literature, psychologist Dan Kahan, has studied yet another way in which ideologies damage cognitive performance: he shows how biases, including those that ideologies cause, can rob us of the ability to make good judgments about who has expertise.[8] When questions about expertise connect with political issues, our judgments of who has expertise are distorted by our partisanship. People who are generally good at identifying true experts perform badly when the question is "Who has political expertise in general?" or "Who is the expert on this particular political issue?"

There's a subdiscipline of Philosophy called "social epistemology." Epistemology is the critical study of how we come to know and to believe. It also explores the questions: what is knowledge and when is belief justified? Social epistemology starts with the assumption that as knowers we are social beings, and that for the most part we are able to come to know things because there are social practices that enable us to benefit from information that others have and that guide us in the making of judgments about what is and what isn't the case.

Humans are extraordinary knowers compared to other creatures because they're able to capitalize on the knowledge of other humans, living and long dead. We have what anthropologists call cumulative culture[9] and that includes the accumulation of knowledge over time. The kind of culture humans have is cumulative in this sense: we create, preserve, and transmit an increasingly large stock of cultural items that can be modified, combined, and recombined in novel ways.

The point is that much of our information is second-hand. In fact, it's probably not an exaggeration to say that most of what we know about the world is borrowed, second-hand knowledge. Even when it isn't borrowed, it's often only available to us through cooperation in knowledge-producing activities with others.

That means that we are profoundly dependent on being able to identify reliable sources of knowledge. We have to be good at determining who is an expert if we are to be successful social knowers. Figuring out who is an expert can be hard, because we can't evaluate a supposed expert by seeing whether they have all the knowledge an expert of that sort is supposed to have. To do that, we'd have to be experts and if we were experts we wouldn't need to rely on somebody else's expertise.

Social epistemologists call the need to determine who is a genuine expert "the novice/expert problem." Tribalistic ideologies make the novice/expert problem all the more difficult.

They do this in two ways. First, and most obviously, in a deeply tribalistically divided world, some experts, perhaps many of them, will in fact be partisan and their partisanship will distort their judgments. So genuine, unbiased expertise may be harder to come by.[10] Second, tribalistic ideologies undermine the exercise of the cognitive abilities we need to solve the novice/expert problem.

Reliable judgments about who is an expert on a certain matter are supposed to be based on an accurate assessment of whether the person has the relevant knowledge and can be trusted to share it truthfully, but when ideology takes over, they aren't. Instead, irrelevant factors, including whether the person in question is identified as one of Us and holds the same political beliefs We do, influence our judgments about who has expertise.

What Triggers the Most Severe Ideology-Caused Cognitive Impairments

Kahan and other researchers have provided evidence for an intriguing—and scary—hypothesis: ideologies have the greatest "dumbing down effect," make us stupidest, when we believe that our identity is threatened. For example, suppose we believe we are in a political crisis: our group is threatened with losing out to the Other, the enemy. They are about to gain control of the whole political process and they will use it against us. If they do that, we won't be able to live in a way that expresses who we are so far as our ideology tells us who we are. That is an existential threat, a threat to who we are, to our identity, the identity our ideology affirms.

We all have multiple identities—you may be a mother, a professional, a Presbyterian, a Liberal (or a Conservative), a quilter, and a martial arts expert. And all of those "selves" may be important to you, though some are more important than others, and which are the most important can vary, depending on the circumstances.

Multiple Identities: Strange Bedfellows

Identities can blend—I once heard someone describe herself as "lesbyterian." They can also co-exist in improbable ways. I recall a social ritual I participated in my youth that involved the near simultaneous affirmation of two distinct and, one might say, inconsistent identities. At football games in Arkansas and I suspect throughout the South in that era, prior to the first kick-off, people in the stands stood up, put their hands over their hearts, and first sang the National Anthem, immediately followed the Confederate anthem, "Dixie." Combatants in the Civil War were so thoroughly convinced that you couldn't be an American and a Confederate that they were willing to slaughter one another in staggering numbers, yet we seemed to think our dual allegiance wasn't a problem. Or rather, the thought that it might be a problem never even occurred to us. Maybe that means that the Southern identity had changed, so that the idea of the Lost Cause and the rightness of secession have disappeared or receded into the background, while other elements of the regional identity remained or became more prominent. I don't think such a sanitized Southern identity was at work in this case, because the second flag we saluted was the Confederate battle flag.

One more anecdote will reinforce the fact that identities can come in improbable bundles. My maternal grandparents were children of immigrants from Germany. They and their children and grandchildren had a triple identity. They thought of themselves as Germans (and thereby superior to the other people in their town by virtue of being cleaner, more self-disciplined, and more industrious). They also thought of themselves as Southerners (and as such superior in a number of ways to Yankees). And they thought of themselves as American (and thereby as superior to all other nationalities). Their ability to sustain the combination of a German identity and an American identity was put to the test during two world wars in which Germany was the enemy. But they pulled it off.

During World War II, women from our Lutheran Church (where sermons were in German until World War I) periodically took socks, food, and toiletry articles to give to German soldiers in a POW (Prisoners of war) camp outside of Little Rock. Three of the POWs stayed in the United States after the war ended and married women in our congregation.

One of them, Otto, a Wehrmacht sergeant captured in Italy, was my Sunday school teacher—in a room in the church basement that had pictures of young men of the congregation who had been killed by people like Otto. This puzzled me, so I asked my mother about it. Her reply: "Otto's a *good* German, like us." She reconciled the apparent German/American identity incompatibility by distinguishing a subclass of Germans, the good ones, who weren't really enemies of America. Apparently, to be a good German, all Otto had to do was to fit into our Lutheran culture. He did that very well, becoming one of the most active and hard-working members of the congregation. As far as I know, no one ever asked him about what he did in the war.

The football game ritual and my mother's mental gymnastics in dealing with Otto illustrate an important point about ideology-grounded identities: they're highly flexible and their flexibility doesn't follow the rules of logic.

In Chapter 6, when I consider how to combat tribalistic ideologies, the fact that identities are flexible and that people can have multiple identities without one being dominant will turn out to be important. It will open up the possibility of dismantling the tight, political-identity-dominating bundles of ideologies that tribalistic ideologies foster, allowing people to feel that everything is not about politics, that is, about the contest for control over powerful institutions, social practices, and norms. If people can cultivate multiple identities across partisan lines, that may reduce the power of tribalistic ideologies. To some extent, that's what I've done in combining my identity as a member of the largely Liberal university community with my identity as someone who appreciates the history of firearm design and likes to discharge weapons at (inanimate) targets and associate with people who have those same interests.

Tribalistic ideologies bundle multiple identities together in a way that makes your political identity include most of the rest while being the most important. That's why if you know whether someone identifies as a Republican you can predict with some degree of accuracy the kind of vehicle he drives, his taste in music (more likely Country than Jazz), whether he owns an American flag, whether he owns a firearm, and how prominent red meat is in his diet. Similarly, if someone identifies as a Democrat, it's more likely that he drives a Prius than a big pickup truck, has a passport, has a rainbow sticker on his car, is a vegetarian, shops at Whole Foods, and is "un-churched" (to use a phrase churchgoers use to characterize the impoverished existence of those who aren't members of some religious congregation or other).

When any component of the bundled identity that your ideology creates is threatened—or when it's not but you think it is—your ideology supplies defense mechanisms. And these defense mechanisms make you stupid and in some cases immoral, because they undermine the exercise of your normal cognitive capacities, including those involved in making sound moral judgments.

For example, if you think that people like you will be suppressed, unable to live their shared identities, if the opposing group gains control of the Presidency and both the House and the Senate, you will react defensively to even the most innocuous, inconsequential policy proposals of the opposing political party. You'll see them as trying to execute a master plot. You'll take evidence of what in fact is perfectly innocent behavior to be conclusive proof of a conspiracy. And to avert the extinction of your identity that the successful execution of that plot would entail, you'll be willing to do anything. And you'll be willing to accept the most indecent, outrageous behavior of any politician you think is the best bet for averting the threat.

When Identity-Threats Activate, rather than Override Moral Commitments

It's not that the perceived threat to your identity suddenly makes you immoral or amoral (i.e., turns you into a sociopath). Rather, because your identity is framed by your ideology in moral terms (We are the good guys; They are evil), when your identity is threatened, you'll violate normal moral rules for the higher moral good of protecting Us and our wonderful values from an existential threat. Tribalistic ideologies motivate good people to do immoral things for the sake of their quite respectable basic moral values.

The research team of Jonas Kaplan, Sarah Gimbel, and Sam Harris provides further support for the hypothesis that perceived threats to identity are central in tribalistic ideologies. In an article in *Science Reports*,[11] they showed, using brain scans, that the same regions of the brain that are activated when you are under threat of physical harm light up when your ideological beliefs are challenged. They conclude that when ideologies are in play, disagreements with your political beliefs are taken as personal insults, as threats to your identity. They think this helps explain why ideological beliefs are so rigid, and why people cling desperately to them even when this means denying obvious facts. That makes sense if your brain is acting as if what is really just a political disagreement, perhaps a minor one, is a threat to your identity, a threat as serious if not more so than a threat of physical harm. If your identity includes certain beliefs, challenges to those beliefs are attacks on *you.*

Feminist used to promote the slogan "The personal is political." They meant that oppressive power relations don't just exist between governments and citizens, in the public space, but also within the private sphere of the family, in intimate personal relations. The apt slogan for this book reverses the feminist mantra: "The political has become the personal."[12] Tribalistic ideologies do their most serious damage, provoke the most indecent and extreme behavior and the most astonishing reductions in intelligence, because they make the political the personal. Political disagreements become struggles for whose identity will be recognized and approved and whose will be denied and denigrated. Challenges to your political beliefs are perceived as the worst, most threatening insults, as assaults on your most encompassing, most cherished identity. There's nothing more personal than that. And by the way, that explains why current political discourse is rife with personal attacks. If you feel personally, deeply personally, attacked by the opposition—even personally threatened by their very existence—then why shouldn't you respond in kind? Tribalistic ideologies have blurred or even erased the distinction between challenging someone's beliefs and assaulting their identity.

Once the political has become the personal and almost everything feels political and hence personal, people don't notice that they responded with a personal attack to some remark by the Other that really, objectively speaking, isn't personal at all. If I say "We ought to give equal marriage and inheritance rights to gay and transgender people," what you will hear, if you are in the grip of a particular tribalistic ideology, is "We disdain and want to destroy heterosexual marriage and we want to corrupt your children." If you respond accordingly by saying "You're a filthy pedophile who doesn't care about children but just wants to groom them," in your mind, then you're just responding in kind to a personal attack, not shifting an impersonal conversation into the personal mode. You've done nothing wrong.

The statement that tribalistic ideologies make so many things political sounds like it's inconsistent with social science studies that show that most Americans don't care much about politics and refrain from discussing it. It's not inconsistent, because when I say that "all sorts of things have become political," that's shorthand for "so many things nowadays are felt to implicate identity and the assumption is that whoever captures a preponderance of power will affirm some identities and denigrate others." Everything can be political for you in that sense even if you don't care much about politics as that's ordinarily understood and don't engage in what are ordinarily understood to be political activities.

The reference to power is important: many political scientists *define* politics as the struggle for power. People can treat everything that they link to their concern for identity as politics in that sense, whether or not they regard what they're doing as engaging in politics. That's why surveys that ask people whether they are interested in or engaged with politics don't provide any evidence whatsoever that it's wrong to say that tribalistic ideologies make everything political and make the political the personal.

There's another way to unpack the idea that tribalistic ideologies have made a remarkably broad range of things political and the political has become the personal: they convince us that the most mundane choices and the most minor disagreements are potential tipping points in a contest to determine whether the society you live in will approve of and help you live your identity or whether it will make you feel like an unwanted stranger, an alien intruder who doesn't belong here, who isn't one of Us. When you are in the tribal mode, there are no minor political issues.

Are Ideological Cognitive Impairments Mental Illnesses?

You might think the suggestion that tribalistic ideologies cause cognitive disabilities that perhaps could qualify as mental illness is hyperbolic, even a bit hysterical. Nothing in my analysis depends on that suggestion panning out. I'll get my points across if you just think of it as an *analogy* between tribalistic ideologies and mental illness, rather than a claim that the former are or cause the latter. Nevertheless, I want to make the idea that tribalistic ideologies and mental illnesses are more than analogous at least initially plausible by comparing the damage tribalistic ideologies inflict on the mind with what goes wrong in a condition that no one denies is a mental illness: paranoid schizophrenia.

A person suffering from paranoid schizophrenia automatically imposes a delusional mold on their experience. Benign behavior is interpreted as malicious; coincidences are seen as evidence of elaborate, well-organized plots. The mind's normal powers of inference play an important role here: given the paranoid schizophrenic's false assumptions, the conclusions he draws are perfectly valid. But his theory of mind has been corrupted by the delusion that there's a plot against him. That leads to systematic misinterpretations of other people's behavior. The mind is working against itself, creating a seamless web of false beliefs that are immune to correction.

The same is true with tribalistic ideologies. They can cause cognitive disabilities that are very similar to those caused by mental illnesses like paranoid schizophrenia. That's why I think it's not implausible to suggest that (some) ideologies cause—or are—mental illnesses. That makes sense if an illness (or disease) is defined as an adverse departure from normal species functioning. That is, if an ideology causes an adverse departure from a normal human cognitive function (like theory of mind inferences from behavior to mental states), then why not say it causes a mental illness?

A thought experiment will increase the credibility of my mental illness suggestion. Suppose that you and I are ideology-free and so is everyone in our social world, except for one person. That person, call him Jones, has thoroughly absorbed a tribalistic ideology that inflicts a wide range of cognitive disabilities on him. His political views are uniquely deranged—you and I and everybody else but Jones hold political views that are utterly inconsistent with his. Unlike the situation in which almost everybody has a tribalistic political ideology and many people have the same one Jones does, Jones sticks out like a sore thumb. It's obvious to us that his way of thinking and perceiving and judging is permeated with adverse departures from normal functioning for human beings, that he has a mental illness.

The point of this thought experiment is that the biggest obstacle to recognizing that tribalistic ideologies cause cognitive dysfunctions that count as mental illness is the pervasiveness of those dysfunctions, along with the fact that most people who suffer from them are unaware that they do. That lack of awareness is characteristic of many mental illnesses. As I've already noted, it's also an inherent feature of ideologies that people often don't know they have them and are unaware of the damage they cause. It's a testimony to the power of tribalistic ideologies that most people are unable to imagine that they cause mental illness—or even take seriously the possibility that they have an ideology.

Ideologies, Beliefs, and Brains

In drawing an analogy with host manipulation, I've said that ideologies can hijack your brain because I've assumed, quite reasonably, that the cognitive abilities that ideologies undermine are the result of activity in the brain. There are two radically different views about the relationship between ideology and the brain. The first view is that some particular brain states cause us to see the world in ideological terms and to experience cognitive deficits as a result; that is, ideologies are outputs of certain brain states. The other view is that ideological beliefs and thought processes change the brain, creating brain states that wouldn't exist were it not for the ideology. That is, certain brain states are outputs of ideological beliefs and thought processes. That's what's going on when brain imaging shows that the same parts of the brain are activated when someone's political beliefs are challenged as when they are physically threatened.

I think both views about the relationships between brains and ideologies are probably correct. The causal arrows go in both directions, from brains to ideologies and from ideologies to brains. Of course, we couldn't have ideologies unless our brains had certain characteristics. The same is true of some conditions we call mental illnesses. Paranoid schizophrenia is a clear example. The brain of a person with this malady acts differently from a normal brain. There is even some evidence that there are structural differences, that some regions of a schizophrenic person's brain are different in size from those of a neurotypical person and that the proportions of different types of brain tissues may vary as well.[13] It's also likely that only certain types of brains are more prone to schizophrenia, but equally likely that schizophrenia changes the brain. If you substitute "tribalistic ideology" for "schizophrenia" in that sentence, it remains just as plausible. Because of the particular way their brains have developed (as a result of a combination of genetic and environmental influences), some people's brains may make them more prone to be captured by an ideology. Differences among brains may also help explain why some people gravitate toward Conservative ideologies and others toward Liberal ones.

All of that is pretty speculative, however. Research on the interactions between ideologies and brains is in its infancy, so I'm cautious about saying much more about them than I already have. I'll concentrate on how tribalist ideologies use the capacities our brains support. In other words, I'll operate in more in the domain of cognitive psychology than in that of neuroscience.

Even the Smartest People Are Vulnerable to Tribalistic Ideologies

Some of you may be inclined to believe that the cognitive disabilities I've described so far may be a problem for other people, but not for you. You may be thinking:

> Yes, that's all well and good; maybe you're right. Maybe those who are in the grip of tribalistic political ideologies do suffer certain cognitive impairments and maybe in some extreme cases they qualify as mental illnesses. But some of us (myself included) are not likely to succumb to that sort of ideology. We know enough about how the mind works and about the dangers of ideologies to avoid them. We know about confirmation bias, the *ad hominem* fallacy, and about epistemically defective cognitive dissonance mechanisms. We're not so easily fooled.

My response is simple: don't be so smugly confident. Even the thinking of contemporary scientists exhibits ideological distortions, and they are supposed to be especially good thinkers, especially careful in forming beliefs. Here's one example. Until recently, the received view in ornithology (the scientific study of birds) was that only male birds have songs. That view persisted—until the ranks of ornithologists came (quite recently) to include significant numbers of women. Then, some women ornithologists began to study female birds and quickly discovered that they, too, have songs.[14] When the discipline was a males-only club, no one noticed that female birds sing. Until women joined their ranks, ornithologists were so much in the grip of a patriarchal, sexist ideology that they focused exclusively on the interesting and admirable traits of male animals that they were deaf to the songs of female birds.

I can't resist relating an even more dramatic case of science being led astray by ideology. In the early years of the emergence of genetics as a scientific discipline—roughly the 1880s–1900s—some genetic scientists hypothesized that "love of the sea" (thalassophilia) was an inherited trait, or as we would say, that there is a gene (they called it "germ plasm") for love of the sea. Further, they thought that this trait was only inherited in the male line. Why? Because (at that time) sea captains and sailors were all men.[15]

As with the bird song case, it's hard to understand how such absurd reasoning could occur within a group of people that in many ways were better thinkers than the general public, unless a patriarchal, male-focused ideology was at work. In the love of the sea case, that sort of ideology blinded scientists to the possibility that sexist social practices and laws were producing a biased sample, that their experience of behavior indicating a love of the sea was limited, due to the fact that the very ideology that produced this blindness was acted out in institutions and social practices in their society. As in the ornithology example, patriarchal ideology was undermining a cognitive ability that is crucial for science, the ability to gather and evaluate evidence for or against a hypothesis. In both cases, that ability was undermined because, due to their patriarchal ideology, the scientists did not consider the possibility that the evidence they had was not representative, that they were unwittingly relying on a biased sample, and that their data was faulty because they only had experience of life in a patriarchal society. They were making the same type of mistake as the lousy lover who was convinced that the female orgasm is a myth because he'd had sex with several women and none of them had one.

I've said that ideologies can be the enemy within. But of course, that's compatible with an invasion model of the sort that applies in host manipulation and addiction, because (at least in most cases) people get ideological beliefs from sources outside themselves—that's Truth Number One of social epistemology.

Meme theory takes the invasion metaphor literally: it claims that some bits of information (ideas, images, phrases, etc.) coming from sources outside the individual's own mind invade it like a virus.[16] And certain of these mind viruses become predominant because they have characteristics that give them superior reproductive fitness, that cause them to out reproduce rival memes. While meme theory may shed light on why some ideologies spread more widely than others, it tells us virtually nothing about why humans are attracted to ideologies or about how tribalistic ideologies undermine normal cognitive functions and moral performance.

The biggest problem with meme theory, however, is that it portrays us as hapless victims, purely passive in the face of invasion by brain parasites. That's odd, considering that in many other cases of parasitism, the host develops countermeasures, evolves an immune system to resist the parasite invasion. Given how sophisticated our brains are and our ability to understand the phenomenon of memes, it would be surprising if we were totally helpless against them.[17] In Chapter 6, when I consider how to combat tribalistic ideologies, I'll identify several different strategies of resistance.

In the chapters that follow, I'll describe the nature and destructive effects of several other serious impairments in addition to those I've noted in this chapter. And then I'll show that, taken together, these disabilities have dire consequences for civility, mutual respect, democracy, and national identity. In the next chapter, I explain how ideologies can systematically rob us of one of our most important and uniquely human skills: the ability to communicate with one another for the sake of discovering the truth.

Before proceeding further, however, I want to acknowledge that there's risk in my suggestion that certain ideologies may actually cause mental illness. The risk is that if someone exhibits an ideology you reject, you'll say their just crazy, mentally ill and treat them in an even less respectful way. In fact, I've heard Liberals say that about Conservatives and Conservatives about Liberals.

Medicalizing behavior you don't approve of has a long, sordid, tragic-comic history: the disease of masturbation (a disease that causes blindness and insanity), drapetomania (a disease that causes slaves to try to run away), nymphomania (a disease that makes women as interested in sex as men are and in severe cases even leads them to enjoy it), etc. And I'm aware that saying someone has a mental illness can be stigmatizing.

My reply is that the risks of acknowledging that ideologies can cause mental illness or at least conditions that are strongly analogous to mental illness can be minimized if people heed the rest of what I say about ideologies. More importantly, I believe it's a risk worth taking, because if some

ideologies do cause mental illnesses or conditions that are very similar to them, that may turn out to have important implications for knowing how to combat them effectively and in ethically permissible ways. Also, if people become convinced that tribalistic ideologies cause (or are) mental illnesses or are at least very much like them, maybe they take these ideologies more seriously. Nonetheless, nothing I say in this book depends on the assumption that tribalistic ideologies literally are or cause mental illnesses. I do think, however, that there is at the very least a strong analogy between mental illness and the damage to our cognitive and moral abilities that tribalistic ideologies inflict. And I think that this damage can be at least as serious as that caused by mental illness.

Notes

1 Sharon Moalem and Jonathan Prince, *Survival of the Sickest: The Surprising Connections between Disease and Longevity*. Harper Perennial ed. New York: Harper Perennial, 2007.
2 I gave talks at universities on medical ethics and on human rights. I also attended illegal African National Congress (ANC) meetings and illegally transported copies of letters from Nelson Mandela smuggled out of his prison cell on Robbin Island. I engaged in these illegal activities because I had decided that it was okay to violate the ANC-endorsed cultural boycott of travel to that country so long as I participated in some way in resistance to the regime. What I did wasn't much, but it qualified as resistance. I got caught transporting the Mandela letters, but I was released from custody with no more than a stern warning, because I was an American. Technically, I committed an act of terrorism under South African Apartheid law. But I don't include "anti-Apartheid terrorist" in my c.v., because, given how minimal and nonviolent what I did was, that would be misleading.
3 Why are there so few philosopher jokes compared to jokes about lawyers and doctors? Answer: because philosophers don't have enough power or status to make it worth the effort to use humor to bring them down a notch.
4 Lawrence A. Hirschfeld, *Race in the Making: Cognition, Culture, and the Child's Construction of Human Kinds*. Cambridge, MA and London, England: MIT Press, 1996.
5 Carnegie Endowment for International Peace. "Polarization, Democracy, and Political Violence in the United States: What the Research Says," n.d. https://carnegieendowment.org/research/2023/09/polarization-democracy-and-political-violence-in-the-united-states-what-the-research-says?lang=en.
6 Robert Jervis, *Perception and Misperception in International Politics*. New ed. Princeton, NJ: Princeton University Press, 2017.
7 Ed Yong, *An Immense World: How Animal Senses Reveal the Hidden Realms around Us*. 2023 Random House trade paperback ed. New York: Random House, 2023.
8 Dan Kahan, "The Supreme Court 2010 Term - Foreword: Neutral Principles, Motivated Cognition, and Some Problems for Constitutional Law." *SSRN Electronic Journal* 129 (2011): 1–30. https://doi.org/10.2139/ssrn.1910391.
9 Kevin Laland, *Darwi's Unfinished Symphony: How Culture Explains the Evolution of the Human Mind*. Princeton, NJ: Princeton University Press, 2017; Joseph Henrich, *The Secret of Our Success: How Culture Is Driving Human*

Evolution, Domesticating Our Species, and Making Us Smarter. Princeton, NJ: Princeton University Press, 2015.

10 Blake Roeber, *Political Humility: The Limits of Knowledge in Our Partisan Political World*. New York and London: Routledge, 2024.

11 Jonas Kaplan, Sarah Gimbel and Sam Harris, "Neural Correlates of Maintaining One's Political Beliefs in the Face of Counterevidence." *Scientific Reports* 6, no. 1 (December 23, 2016): 39589. https://doi.org/10.1038/srep39589.

12 Shanto Iyengar, Yphtach Lelkes, Matthew Levendusky, Neil Malhotra and Sean Westwood, "The Origins and Consequences of Affective Polarization in the United States." *SSRN Scholarly Paper*. Rochester, NY, May 1, 2019. https://doi.org/10.1146/annurev-polisci-051117-073034.

13 Nora Dunne, "Analyzing Brain Structure in Schizophrenia." Northwestern Medicine News Center, July 2, 2015. https://news.feinberg.northwestern.edu/2015/07/02/analyzing-brain-structure-in-schizophrenia/; Katherine H. Karlsgodt, Daqiang Sun and Tyrone D. Cannon, "Structural and Functional Brain Abnormalities in Schizophrenia." *Current Directions in Psychological Science* 19, no. 4 (August 2010): 226. https://doi.org/10.1177/0963721410377601.

14 "Why We Didn't Know That Female Birds Sing: Why Science and Science Communication Are Better When They're Inclusive," *Scientific American*, Opinion (November 26, 2021).

15 In 1919, Charles Davenport, a prominent geneticist, argued that thalassophilia was a recessive, sex-linked genetic trait. See, Garland Allen, "Eugenics and Modern Biology: Critiques of Eugenics, 1910–1945." *Annals of Human Genetics* 75, no. 3 (May 2011): 314–25. https://doi.org/10.1111/j.1469-1809.2011.00649.x.

16 Richard Dawkins, *The Selfish Gene*. Oxford: Oxford University Press, 1976.

17 There's another problem with meme theory: it implicitly rejects the plausible view that in some cases which memes spread most widely depends in large part upon how well our reliance on them furthers our interests. If that is so it is very misleading to view beliefs as invasive parasites afflicting a hapless host.

2

HOW IDEOLOGIES REPLACE TRUTH-SEEKING COMMUNICATION WITH SORTING, SIGNALING, AND SCORE-KEEPING

Tribalistic Ideologies Divide the World into Us versus Them

Tribalistic ideologies are all about an Us versus Them conflict. They depend on and exploit a primal feature of human psychology, what is sometimes called the friend/foe or in-group/out-group distinction (or dichotomy). In Chapter 6, I'll explain the evolutionary roots of that phenomenon.

As I noted earlier, sociological research shows that tribalistic political tribalism is more a matter of opposing partisan identities than of opposing policy positions.[1] That's why one of the most basic functions of these ideologies is to distinguish Us from Them. We need to know whether someone shares, approves of, and will defend our identity or whether they disparage it and threaten it.

Sorting, Signaling, and Score-Keeping: Not Truth-Seeking

The obsession with the Us versus Them distinction has a profoundly damaging effect on one of the most valuable cognitive abilities humans have: the ability to engage with one another in communication aimed at discovering the truth. Tribalistic political ideologies undermine the exercise of this ability and replace it with what I call sorting, signaling, and defensive score-keeping. Or, to put the same point differently, through a process of cultural selection, sorting, signaling, and defensive score-keeping drive out truth-seeking and become the dominant forms of communication in increasingly wider contexts of interaction.

What makes this really harmful is that, on the surface, sorting, signaling, and defensive score-keeping behavior looks like truth-seeking behavior even

DOI: 10.4324/9781003612469-3

while replacing it. That's why most people are oblivious to the fact that we are suffering from a catastrophic loss, the destruction of one of the most valuable distinctively human activities, engaging in truth-seeking communication.

Sorting and Signaling

Here's an elaboration of an example of sorting and signaling I sketched briefly in the Introduction. When I moved to another city, I went to join a gun club (so that I could shoot sporting clays and compete in 100-yard rimfire benchrest matches).[2] Please don't take my joining a gun club as a reliable signal that I should be sorted into the "gun nut" and arch-Conservative categories and that accordingly I'm against gun control legislation, believe the right to bear arms extends to Rocket-propelled grenades (RPGs), machine guns, and killer drones for remote hunting, etc. None of that is true of me.

When I approached the fellow in charge of membership, he said to me, just after introducing himself, "If Biden wins the election, this will become a communist country." If you don't understand how tribalistic ideologies work, you might think he was just accurately reporting his belief about the consequences of a Biden electoral victory and setting the stage for a discussion of the future of the country in which I could offer my view, just as he had offered his.

I don't know whether he really believed that we were headed for a communist takeover. He may have believed that. But there's an alternative: he was simply signaling his allegiance to a particular tribe and using that signal to prompt me to reveal my tribal affiliation by my response to it. He wasn't trying to initiate a dialogue aimed at establishing the facts about the outcome of a Biden electoral victory; he was simulating that in order to signal his tribal affiliation and prompt me to send a signal that would enable him to sort me into the proper tribal category. If that's what he was doing, he wasn't engaged in truth-seeking communication. Of course, the nature of his signal was influenced by his ideological beliefs about what the facts are. I suspect that he was doing what the authors of *Inhumans* do: expanding the definition of "communist" to include not just socialists but also all leftists and progressives. Or, he was assuming that socialist, leftist, or progressive policies inevitably lead us down a slippery slope to communism.[3]

If you're in the grip of a tribalistic political ideology, it will equip you with a repertoire of signals designed to reveal your allegiance and at the same time determine the allegiance of the person you aim those signals at. The signal may look like a straightforward report of the speaker's belief or a statement about the facts, but that's not what it's really about.

If I had responded to this guy's statement about a communist takeover by saying "Yes, that's very likely," he would have been confident that I was a member of his tribe and that I was trustworthy, on the right side in the momentous struggle between good and evil that he believed was playing out in American politics. Suppose that instead I replied as follows, kicking into the truth-seeking mode, rather than the sorting and signaling mode.

> No way. Biden isn't even a socialist, much less a communist; and besides, entrenched wealth and powerful institutions are big obstacles to a communist take-over in America. Also, there has never been a successful communist revolution in a wealthy, economically developed country.[4]

Hearing that, he would have sorted me into the Them box, as someone who clearly was a Biden supporter, applied the deterministic, essentialized stereotype that goes along with that, and then not taken anything I said after that at face value.

Having put me in the Liberal box, he wouldn't feel any need to respond to what I said on the merits. He wouldn't feel obligated to try to refute the factual claims I was making about the conditions under which a communist takeover can or cannot occur. According to his ideology, there is no point in arguing with Liberals because they are hopelessly misguided and insincere to boot. What makes them pursue the Liberal agenda isn't the reasons they give in support of it; instead, it's their contempt for individual liberty and their vastly over-optimistic belief in the efficacy and trustworthiness of government. And there is no way to disabuse them of those dangerous, patently false beliefs because they aren't rational; Liberals are dogmatic true-believers or too stupid to learn.

There are lots of different ways of signaling tribal allegiance and of emitting probes to determine the tribal allegiance of others. These days, a prominent way of signaling your allegiance to Conservative Nationalism is to display the American flag—as a lapel pin, as a decal on your pickup truck (and I do mean pickup truck), on a pole in your front yard, or on a tee-shirt. On the other side of the yawning tribal divide, there are different signaling devices, both intentional and unintentional: driving an electric car or at least a hybrid, not driving a pickup truck, having a rainbow bumper-sticker, shopping at Whole Foods, not being able to sing along at your high school reunion when everybody else knows by heart the words to Lee Greenwood's "I'm proud to be an American."

Defensive Score-Keeping

Smith says, "Biden is corrupt, he used his power as President to get lucrative business deals for his son." Jones replies, "Trump does that sort of thing for his daughter and son-in-law."

In some contexts, score-keeping discourse is appropriate and is aimed at discovering the truth: more specifically, the truth about which candidate we should support when our options are limited. If our only choice is between candidate A and candidate B, then "keeping score" as to which one has the most transgressions is valuable for deciding whom we ought to support.

But there's also a dark side to score-keeping discourse, when it becomes purely defensive. That occurs when what motivates the score-keeping individual is not the desire to make an accurate, impartial comparative evaluation of opposing leaders, but rather the desire to deflect criticism of one's own leader. Notice what Jones is doing: he's avoiding acknowledging that Biden has acted wrongly. By shifting attention away from Biden's behavior to Trump's, he's not taking seriously the allegation that his guy did wrong. Shifting the focus from Biden to Trump has another function: it enables the Liberal to avoid being regarded as disloyal to his tribe by admitting that the tribal leader has done something wrong. In effect, he's defending his guy—and signaling his allegiance to him—by attacking the other guy.

If we insist on engaging in score-keeping discourse, we should at least be aware that it has a darker side. Keeping score shouldn't become a purely defensive matter and come at the expense of taking seriously criticisms of our group's leaders and acting as if admitting their culpability is a sign of disloyalty. My worry is that much of the score-keeping discourse we see is purely defensive, that it isn't really aimed at finding out the truth about which leader is best (or least bad) but rather is just an attempt to avoid acknowledging the flaws of our leaders by shifting attention away from their behavior. At any rate, I think that sorting and signaling are more serious when it comes to displacing truth-seeking discourse.

In the next chapter, I elaborate on why it's so important to signal your tribal allegiance and sort other folks into the Us versus Them boxes. By way of preview, for now I'll just say it's because when you're in the tribalistic mode, every political or social issue is seen as inextricably bound up with every other, in a zero-sum, winner-takes-all struggle for the highest stakes.[5] Under those conditions, it's vitally important to know whether someone is one of Us or one of Them. The conflict between Us and Them is seen, or rather felt, as a struggle over which identity will flourish.

If that's your political *Umwelt*, the consequences are momentous. You'll believe we are in a kind of Supreme Emergency that calls for behavior that wouldn't be justified in any other situation. That's especially true if the Supreme Emergency is perceived in identity terms. I'll elaborate on that diagnosis in the next chapter. For the rest of this chapter, I want to focus on the contrast between sorting and signaling and defensive score-keeping, on the one hand, and truth-seeking communication, on the other, and on how harmful it is when the former replaces the latter.

Truth-Seeking Communication

What do I mean by truth-seeking communication? It's a process in which each participant gives reasons for what they assert and expects the others to do so as well. And not just anything counts as a reason. For example, if you say you think Israel is committing war crimes in Gaza (as I write this, it's March 2024) and I reply: "You're just an anti-Semite," I'm not engaging in truth-seeking communication. Taking the content of what the other party says seriously, rather than avoiding engaging with it because you've sorted him into the Them category and assigned certain beliefs and attitudes to everybody in that category, is also part of what it is to engage in truth-seeking communication.

Listening and not interrupting, and refraining from name-calling and other personal attacks is also a hallmark of truth-seeking. Recognizing that factual claims have to be more than mere opinions, that they have to be supported by relevant information from reliable sources, is also crucial to the truth-seeking enterprise.

One of the most important features of truth-seeking communication is a proper attitude toward appeals to authority. Truth-seekers acknowledge the importance of identifying relevant authorities and experts on various matters. They take very seriously the social epistemologists' points about our being social knowers and the difficulty of solving the novice/expert problem. They understand that credentials are important, while acknowledging that some practices of awarding credentials are flawed. They refuse to abuse the concept of authority—to treat what someone has said as if it was beyond criticism just because they are a supposed expert. They don't assume that, for once and for all, they've identified infallible authorities and can ignore all other sources of information.

Truth-seekers are also humble. They are ready to concede that they have been mistaken. What they care about is being right, not having been right. They are committed to revising their views—potentially, any of their views. For them in principle nothing is sacred; nothing is off-limits for critical review. In that sense, they are the opposite of ideologues, because it's a mark of being in the grip of an ideology that you cleave rigidly to some of your beliefs, even in the face of conclusive evidence against them.

They also avoid the temptation of the quest for certainty, the desperate yearning for simple, magic bullet solutions to complex problems. They tolerate complexity, ambiguity, and uncertainty. Because they admit that they may be wrong, truth-seekers deliberately try to avoid what sociologists call confirmation bias: seeking out or attending to information that supports what you believe and avoiding or ignoring information that contradicts it. Truth-seekers play devil's advocate against themselves. And they avoid associating only with those who share their beliefs. The most sophisticated truth-seekers appreciate that our ability to discern the truth and avoid error depends crucially on our environment and especially on the character of our peer group. That's why they are careful not to inhabit belief silos, echo-chambers where everybody thinks the same.

I hope you'll indulge me in another autobiographical example, this time to make vivid the fact that because we are social knowers, the nature of our social environment has profound effects on our ability to know the truth. Appealing to my own experiences is my way of making abstract points concrete and more motivationally effective, I hope.

As I noted in the Introduction, around the age of 14, under the influence of my precocious older brother, I began to sense that a good deal of what I had "learned" growing up in Little Rock, Arkansas, was not just bullshit, but also dangerous racist and sexist bullshit. I hadn't completely unwound the racist ideological shroud I'd been wrapped in, but I had just enough sense to know that I had to get out of there, to relocate to another environment where I wouldn't be subjected to the racist practices and attitudes that had shaped me for my whole life up to that point.

I managed to get a scholarship to Columbia University, and I can assure you that the environment of the Columbia campus in the late 1960s, especially during the "Revolution" of the Spring of '68, was dramatically different from that of Apartheid Arkansas. It wasn't a matter of escaping environmental and peer group influences (that's impossible); it was a matter of replacing one set of influences with another that was significantly better, from the standpoint of truth-seeking about important social and political matters.

There's another feature of my experience that brings home an important characteristic of truth-seekers: they know that seeking the truth can be costly, and they're willing to bear those costs. Cutting loose from my original environment was very costly. It produced changes in me that alienated me from my family and friends and destroyed my relationship with my first love. I also experienced a sense of disorientation in the first months of my new life on the Upper Westside of Manhattan, and serious doubts about who exactly I was. I had to create a new identity, one I hoped I would find satisfying and which would elicit approval in my new environment and wherever I ended up going after I graduated. Doing that was hard and risky.

I found that I had to make a lot of changes, including altering the way I spoke. Because of my Southern accent, I was required to attend, for a minimum of one semester, the language lab for students for whom English is not their first language. People with other regional or ethnic accents were not accorded this gracious benefit. That included the heavy Yiddish-Brooklyn accent of the professor who told me I had to go to the language lab.

Truth-seekers accept such costs. They know that even if the truth shall set you free, it may also make you miserable (while hoping that the misery will be temporary). Truth-seekers are *committed* to finding out the truth. To be committed to something means being willing to incur costs in the pursuit of it.

Truth-seekers acknowledge each other's right to an opinion but also expect opinions to be supported by reasons. Each party proceeds on the assumption that the other is a reason-giver and a reason-taker. Truth-seekers give those they engage with the benefit of a presumption that they are both rational and sincere. They view their interactions as positive sum, not as zero sum, as the cooperative pursuit of something that will benefit both of them, not as a competition for a prize that only one will receive. Their goal is a mutual recognition of the truth, not victory over the Other.

When communication becomes merely or even primarily signaling and sorting, there's an implicit rejection of every aspect of truth-seeking. You view interacting with those you disagree with as a competition, not as a cooperative effort. Your goals are winning and affirming your tribal allegiance, not discovering the truth. You appeal to the authority of those your ideology says are the purest exponents of its beliefs, and you avoid expressing any doubts about their expertise because you know that if you do that you risk being regarded as a defector, as one of Them. Your acceptance of what the leaders of your group say is the truth is absolute and uncritical, as is your total rejection of anything the leaders of the Other say. You're convinced that there is a simple, absolutely correct political view, namely, your tribe's. When the political leaders your ideology endorses act badly, you refuse to acknowledge that and instead try to divert attention from their culpability by focusing on the bad behavior of the leaders of the opposing group (you shift into the score-keeping mode). You stick to your ideological beliefs in spite of serious challenges to them because that's how you signal your unshakeable commitment to your group and its values. You only attend to information that supports your beliefs and scrupulously avoid information that might challenge them. You associate only with those who subscribe to your political beliefs.

How Tribalistic Ideologies Impair the Production of Knowledge

A tribalistic ideology paints the world in black and white, offering a clear and simple solution to all problems: we know the truth, all the truth that matters. When you are in the tribalistic mode, you don't just think you know the truth; you're convinced that your truths are eternal, so there will never be a need to revise your beliefs. That's why you have no patience for ambiguity or uncertainty—and why you won't even consider the possibility that if you took what They said at face value, you might learn something. You don't think you are obligated to treat the Other as a reason-giver and reason-taker, because you think they are unwilling or unable to be either. Your essentialized, deterministic stereotype of Them tells you they are all a mixture of stupidity and insincerity and that therefore they're not the kind of beings you can reason with or learn from. Tribalistic ideology is a formidable obstacle to gaining knowledge, because it systematically undermines truth-seeking communication. When two opposing ideological camps each dismisses what members of the other group are saying, everyone loses potential contributions to knowledge. Those in the grip of this sort of ideology exhibit what philosophers call "epistemic vices," bad habits regarding the formation and preservation of true or justified beliefs.

Human beings have a momentous advantage when compared with the other creatures with whom we share this planet. We needn't just rely on our senses for knowledge about the world. We have the ability to use sophisticated cognitive abilities to gain knowledge of many aspects of reality. More importantly, we have cognitive abilities that enable us to augment what we could know as individuals, seeking the truth in isolation, by cooperating with other truth-seekers.

It is because we are *social* knowers in this sense that we are so successful as a species. We have the remarkable, uniquely human ability to work with others in the pursuit of the truth about the natural and social world we inhabit—*if* we utilize the best cooperative practices for discovering the truth and avoiding or correcting false beliefs. In other words, our success depends upon cultivating epistemic virtues and avoiding epistemic vices. Tribalistic ideologies undermine the epistemic virtues and encourage epistemic vices.

Again, the irony is palpable: when we succumb to tribalistic ideologies, the very cognitive capacities that enable us to be effective social knowers are used to undermine our cooperation as social knowers, to replace the highly beneficial cooperative enterprise of truth-seeking with sorting and signaling and defensive score-keeping.

Sorting and signaling, too, are cooperative enterprises. They're social practices that people engage in together that produce certain benefits for themselves. So, it's misleading to say that tribalistic ideologies destroy cooperation. Rather, they use the abilities needed for cooperation in seeking the truth to construct a quite different cooperative activity, sorting and signaling and score-keeping. All ideologies facilitate cooperation, but tribalistic ideologies facilitate cooperation to destroy one of the most valuable forms of cooperation human beings have developed: truth-seeking communication.

It's also inaccurate to say that tribalistic ideologies replace communication that conveys information with sorting and signaling. Sorting and signaling is all about information. But it's information about who is one of Us and who is one of Them, not about what on the surface it seems to be about (which political positions are most tenable, what the facts relevant to policy choices are, etc.).

Why Do We Persist in Such Self-Destructive Behavior?

How can this be? How can beings as cognitively sophisticated as humans persist in using their most impressive cognitive abilities to undermine one of their most valuable forms of cooperation, the enterprise of seeking the truth together? How can they continue to use the abilities that enable them to be social knowers to impair their performance as social knowers? Why don't they see what they are doing and stop doing it? Why do they simply shrug off the fact that the political leaders they endorse repeatedly exhibit an utter contempt for the truth? Is it that they don't see that the replacement of truth-seeking communication with sorting, signaling, and defensive score-keeping is a disaster, a threat to the production of knowledge, and to productive deliberation about political issues? Or do they see that it is, but just don't care?

Those questions have traction because replacing truth-seeking with sorting, signaling, and defensive score-keeping is very costly. It increases divisiveness, prevents mutually beneficial cooperation, and deprives us of policy-relevant knowledge we could have gained if we'd been engaging in truth-seeking communication. We need to know why people persist in this behavior despite the costs.

I've already suggested the explanation: tribalistic ideologies have convinced people that politics is a zero-sum, winner-takes-all contest for the highest stakes between opposing groups that can find no common ground, who can't even agree on basic facts. If that's your frame of mind, the idea of cooperation with the Other is absurd and that includes cooperation in the form of truth-seeking communication. All that matters is signaling your tribal affiliation and determining who is one of Us and who is one of Them.

It's not that tribalistic ideologues don't see the value of truth-seeking communication—they think they engage in it with members of their own tribe. It's that they think that it's impossible with the Other and that attempting to engage in it with Them simply impairs efforts to defeat Them.

Politics as a Life-or-Death Struggle

At this point it's vital to pause and consider a fundamental question: why would anyone think that, why would they believe that if the opposing group prevails it will be catastrophic, not just an unpleasant second best? Why think we are in a kind of Supreme Emergency where truth-seeking communication with the Other isn't feasible and *should* be abandoned?

The answer isn't that if the other guys win, they will enact bad policies. It's that they will enact partisan policies and engage in other forms of domination that will deprive Us of our most fundamental social identity. The struggle is thought to be for the highest stakes because it's seen, or rather felt, to be a struggle for which identities society will honor and support and which it will scorn and penalize.

If the alien, hostile Others win, they'll use their political power to create a society in which Our identity won't be acknowledged and can't be lived. The current situation is a Supreme Emergency because it poses the supreme threat: a threat to our primary, most comprehensive identity. Because our political identity has become totalizing, which has swallowed up all our other identities, the threat is all the more alarming. It's a threat to who we are. That's the real truth of the slogan that politics now is identity politics. What makes politics the identity politics is not just the prominence of terms like "race," "gender," and "cultural group." It's that even when terms are used that don't explicitly evoke identity, that's the factor driving communication.

The threat is so dire that it is hard for people to talk directly about it. For example, people who want to stop or limit immigration often say they are worried about immigrants committing crimes or being terrorists or gobbling up social services that ought to be reserved for Americans. But what's really driving their sometimes hysterical rants against immigration may be the fear that someday they will wake up in a world that is no longer their own, and that they will be strangers in their own land, because they've lost the identity-domination contest. That's why some years ago, the Right-wing pundit Pat Buchanan asked his radio audience "Do you want to hear bongo drums on the street corner?" I don't think the real issue for him was dislike of Bongo drum music as music. Rather, it's that Bongo drum music in your neighborhood is an emblem of identity-loss; it isn't your neighborhood anymore. You're no longer at home in your home. To talk directly about a perceived threat identity is to acknowledge one's vulnerability, the fragility of that identity. Instead, the anxiety caused by threats to identity is projected onto other matters. This explains why it isn't an objection to analyzes of tribalistic ideologies that emphasize concerns about identity to note that in the rhetoric of tribalistic ideologies, the term "identity" or "threats to identity" is not pervasive.

In some European countries, and especially in France, a very large influx of immigrants from regions with profoundly different cultures, values, and religions is provoking extreme identity-anxiety. Consider the following characterization of how this phenomenon encourages "white flight" from the inner suburbs of Paris, where there are high concentrations of immigrants from North Africa.

> The native French have lost the status of cultural reference point that was theirs during preceding periods of immigration. They no longer influence anything. When the cybercafe is called "Bled.com" and either the fast-food restaurant or the butcher or both are halal, the long-standing inhabitants experience a disconcerting sense of exile. When they see conversions to Islam, they wonder where they are living....they feel like strangers in their own homes.[6]

In my judgment, the identity-anxiety cited in this passage is much more understandable, better grounded in reality, than the structurally similar identity-anxiety fueled by and expressed in the tribalistic conflict between the Right and the Left in America at present. In the American case, there is no prospect of one side becoming a majority through a higher birth rate, as there is in the French case. More importantly, the cultural and religious differences among the opposing groups in America are not nearly as extreme as those between North African immigrants and "native" French people. My diagnosis is that tribalistic ideologies have persuaded many people in America that they are facing a threat to their identity that is as serious as that the French may well be facing, when in fact this is far from being the case.

Unfortunately, what shapes behavior is the perception, not the reality. Accordingly, for some American's whose tribalistic ideology persuades them that their core identity is under serious threat, the response is the same as that of some French people: the abandonment of the commitment to the hard work of democracy in favor of allegiance to a supposedly strong, authoritarian leader.

If you think you are in an actual war for the highest stakes—as was really the case in WWII—you will be willing to accept high costs, including moral costs, if you think they are necessary for victory. You may even think that the bombing of civilians is justified, if that is necessary in order to avoid the great evil that defeat would bring.

Tribalistic political ideologies are extremely dangerous because they encourage that sort of thinking when our situation is not at all that of a life-or-death struggle between good and evil. Stopping with the slogan that all politics has become identity politics doesn't get to the heart of the problem. It's that tribalistic ideologies have made our totalizing political identity so all-important that anything that doesn't affirm it is taken as an existential threat. Even worse, if enough people come to think we have arrived at Armageddon, we'll find ourselves there. Here, too, tribalistic ideologies remake the world in their image.

The problem isn't that our politicians—and many of the rest of us—have become habitual liars. A liar is someone who knows the difference between truth and falsehood and deliberately chooses to utter or write a false statement. People in the grip of tribalistic ideologies aren't like that. They are in the signaling, sorting, and score-keeping mode, not the truth-seeking mode or the truth-denying mode. When they make a statement about some matter of fact, they aren't reporting what they believe, but they're just signaling their tribal allegiance in order to elicit a response that will enable them to sort the speaker into the Us or the Them category. Unfortunately, if the false statements that are used as signals are repeated enough, people may actually come to believe them.

Misunderstanding Trumpian Discourse

Examples of how signaling and sorting replaces truth-seeking communication aren't hard to come by. Trump says that "Mexico is sending their murderers and rapists" to the United States.[7] He also said that if Hilary Clinton were elected president, we would have open borders and in a week there could be 650 million people from Latin America pouring across our Southern border.[8] Both statements aren't just false; they're patently false. Mexico isn't sending anyone; some people from Mexico are deciding to cross into the United States. The total population of Latin America is only 450 million and a lot of them want to stay right where they are.

I don't think that in uttering these falsehoods Trump is lying, deliberately saying what he knows to be untrue. He would have to be a fool to think that his utterances would be successful as lies; that if his audience cared about their truth or falsity, he'd get away with making those claims. He's not a fool. He's a master signaler. Or, more accurately, he's a master identity-cheerleader.[9]

His speech has the grammatical form of statements, assertions about what is the case. But that's just the surface, the deceptive appearance. They are really just signals. They are signals designed to activate his audience's fear that if there are too many of *those* people in our country, then we will not just become a minority but we'll be strangers in our own land, and the dominant culture will not be our culture. In brief, we won't be able to live our identities. The signal both activates identity-anxiety and conveys the reassuring message that *if you support me, I will protect your identity.* Just pointing out that the statements are false completely misses the point. And you're also missing the point if you're baffled as to why Trump's supporters aren't bothered by his uttering patently false statements.

People engaging in ideological discourse may make false statements, but that doesn't mean they're lying. Although their sentences have the form of statements, and as statements can be evaluated as true or false, justified or unjustified, that doesn't reflect their significance or why people utter or write them. The function of a statement is to assert that something is the case; the function of tribalistic speech is to sort and signal, or to keep score, to affirm identities. People in the grip of a tribalistic ideology often literally don't know what they are saying; they think they are in the factual mode when they are in the cheering mode; that's how deep the cognitive disabling goes.

When people lie, they put themselves in the truth-seeking domain. We can challenge what they say by appealing to the facts. When people engage in ideological sorting and signaling, they steer the conversation away from the truth-seeking domain. We'd be better off if there was just lying and no sorting and signaling. We are pretty good at detecting lies and at imposing costs on those who are found to be liars. The problem is that when we are in the grip of an ideology, we aren't paying attention to whether a statement is true or false. If what you really care about is feeling good about who you are, knowing that there are lots of others like you, and that together you can defend your shared identity from threats to it, you won't care enough about what's true or false to ask whether what you hear is true or to deliberately say what you know is false.

If someone we regard as the leader of our group says we are in effect in a Supreme Emergency, a life-or-death, total victory or total defeat situation, we don't do a fact check to see if things are really that bad. We aren't in the domain of truth or falsity or even the domain of lying. We are in something closer to a pep rally for our favorite sports team. But the game isn't your usual sports contest, it's more like The Hunger Games. The stakes are as high as they can be.

Nobody in their right mind thinks that pep rallies are venues for seeking the truth. But we aren't in our right minds when it comes to identity-charged speech. We don't see that once we are in that mode, progress toward agreement is impossible. Cheers in support of our team can't produce agreement, because they aren't assertions, they're cheers. Neither can boos directed toward the opposing team. Ideological utterances are cheers or boos that look like statements.[10]

This explains why pointing out the falsity of ideological "statements" is futile. If you say to a Trump supporter "Mexico isn't sending anybody" or "There aren't 650 million people in all of Latin America and a lot of them don't want to leave their homes," it may have no effect. You don't stop people from cheering and booing by appealing to facts. Cheering and booing aren't in the domain of truth and falsity; they are in a fact-free zone. Don't expect truth-seeking communication at the ongoing pep rally that is tribalistic politics.

When we and those we regard as the enemy act as if we are in a Supreme Emergency—a situation where there's a lethal threat to our social identity—our identity-protecting reactions can *create* a Supreme Emergency. If Sean Hannity is right in thinking that "America is on the brink," that's because we have been brought to the brink by people like him who have convinced all too many people that we are already there. The next chapter probes in greater depth the idea that the idea of an imminent lethal threat to identity, a Supreme Emergency, is key to understanding how tribalistic ideologies work and why they are so dangerous.

Notes

1 Christopher Bail, *Breaking the Social Media Prism: How to Make Our Platforms Less Polarizing.* Princeton, NJ: Princeton University Press, 2021.
2 In Sporting clays, you walk through a series of positions from which you try to hit 3.5-inch-diameter disks traveling at 45–50 miles per hour in random, unpredictable trajectories; different stations present the targets differently. Hundred-yard rimfire benchrest competition is trying to place 20 small holes made by .22 or .17 caliber rifle bullets in a paper target a 100 yards away as close together as possible in the very center of the target, from a seated position, in a limited amount of time. You don't have to hold NRA-type beliefs about a supposedly intimate connection between Guns, (the heterosexual) Family, God, America, and Freedom to enjoy either of these activities. If you doubt that, I suggest you try them, instead of rejecting them because your ideology tells you that people who engage in them are messed up.
3 I first became suspicious of slippery slope reasoning when I encountered "hardshell Baptists" in Little Rock who thought having sex standing up was wrong because it could lead to dancing.
4 In my judgment, in the United States a Fascist revolutionary takeover is more likely than a Communist one, because the former doesn't require neutralizing the power of the wealthy. Fascist revolutionaries coopt the power of capital; Communist revolutionary actors face the formidable task of trying to destroy it. That's part of the explanation why Fascist revolutions, but not Communist revolutions, have occurred in economically developed countries.
5 See for example, Hrishikesh Joshi, "What Are the Chances You're Right about Everything? An Epistemic Challenge for Modern Partisanship." *Forthcoming in Politics, Philosophy & Economics*, n.d. https://philpapers.org/archive/JOSWAT. pdf.
6 Alain Finkielkraut, cited in Introduction, *Enemy of the Disaster*, Renaud Camus. Blowing Rock, NC: Vauban Books, xxxv.
7 Washington Post, "Full Text: Donald Trump Announces a Presidential Bid," June 26, 2015. https://www.washingtonpost.com/news/post-politics/wp/2015/06/16/ full-text-donald-trump-announces-a-presidential-bid/.

8 Sopan Deb, "Trump Says Clinton Could Let 650 Million New Immigrants into U.S." *CBS News*, October 31, 2016. https://www.cbsnews.com/news/donald-trump-says-hillary-clinton-could-let-650-million-new-immigrants-into-u-s/.
9 Eric Funkhouser, "Beliefs as Signals: A New Function for Belief." *Philosophical Psychology* 30, no. 6 (August 18, 2017): 809–31. https://doi.org/10.1080/09515 089.2017.1291929; Neil Levy, *Bad Beliefs: Why They Happen to Good People.* 1st ed. Oxford: Oxford University Press, 2021. https://academic.oup.com/book/38980; Michael Hannon and Jeroen de Ridder, "The Point of Political Belief." In *The Routledge Handbook of Political Epistemology.* 123–134. London and New York: Routledge Taylor & Francis Group, 2021.
10 That's not to deny that it's wrong to make such flagrantly false statements. Though they are functioning as cheers and boos, they are still statements and as such can be evaluated in terms of truth and justification. Engaging in that kind of speech is wrong. Though it isn't wrong by virtue of being lying, it's wrong for the same reason lying is; it shows an utter lack of respect for the truth. Lying is also wrong because it is being deliberately deceptive. They need not be true of identity-signaling booing and cheering.

3

HOW IDEOLOGIES CONVINCE US THAT ARMAGEDDON IS NOW

Existential Threats Everywhere?

The title of Hannity's latest book, *Live Free or Die: America (and the World) on the Brink*, is more than just a statement that we are confronting momentous political choices: it's a prediction that the apocalypse is upon us, a shrill announcement that Armageddon is here and now.[1] In the same vein, at a 2024 Super-Tuesday rally at Mar-a-Largo celebrating primary victories, Trump stated that "If we lose this election, we're not going to have a country left." If we really are faced with a life-or-death, zero-sum total war for the highest stakes imaginable, we are in a Supreme Emergency, and that calls for the most extreme measures.

Political theorist Michael Walzer used the term Supreme Emergency when wrestling with the question of whether there are exceptions to the Just War principle that deliberately harming noncombatants is strictly prohibited. He focused on an actual case: the Allied policy of bombing designed to kill civilians (in hopes of destroying the will to continue fighting) in Germany during WWII.[2] Walzer speculated that Nazi regime was so horrific that this policy was justified—assuming it was necessary for defeating the Germans—that it qualified as a Supreme Emergency. (It probably wasn't necessary after July 1943, because, given their crushing defeats of the Germans at Stalingrad in February and at Kursk in the first week of July, it's very likely that the Soviets would have won the war even if there'd been no Allied terror bombing—and no Normandy Invasion—though it probably would have taken them longer to do it.)[3]

DOI: 10.4324/9781003612469-4

Walzer was rightly hesitant to say there have been any other situations that qualified as Supreme Emergencies. To his credit, he understood that we can believe that we are in a Supreme Emergency and hence that basic moral rules don't apply when in fact our predicament is not nearly so dire. There are all too many examples where this has occurred.

The Genetic Supreme Emergency: Menace of the Morons

Consider the version of the Supreme Emergency framing that was invoked to justify the forcible sterilization of at least 65,000 Americans in the first half of the twentieth century. The eugenics movement of that era pro-claimed, "the menace of the morons."[4] The idea was that better health care, charitable organizations, and the welfare state were allowing the geneti-cally defective to live long enough to reproduce, resulting in an increase in bad genes ("defective germ plasm"). Instead of being winnowed out by the ruthless discipline of natural selection, bad genes were being allowed to proliferate and would eventually destroy not only human health but also civilization itself.

The pseudo-scientific theory of biological inheritance that supplied the premises for the justification of mass sterilization included the belief that virtually all serious social problems—from crime, to poverty, to alcohol-ism and drug abuse—were due to bad genes and that there were packets of bad genes that went together and that resulted not just in physical ail-ments but also serious moral and mental deficiencies (hence the menace of the morons). The moral deficiencies meant that the folks with the worst genes would reproduce in far greater numbers because they lacked moral constraints, especially when it came to their sexual impulses.

Eugenics wasn't just a social and political movement; it was a fairly complex ideology. It's evaluative map of the contemporary social world divided the population into Us, the people with good genes that enabled us to be decent and contribute to society, and the people with genes that made them bad, lascivious people who were a drain on society and who, if allowed to reproduce, would destroy everything of value. You might be interested—and appalled—to know that the architects of the Nazi "racial hygiene" program, which began with the medical murder of disabled Germans and led from there to the Holocaust, publicly acknowledged their debt to the pioneering work of American eugenicists.

The 1927 U.S. Supreme Court decision in *Buck vs. Bell* appeared to rely on the Supreme Emergency framing, at least implicitly, when it approved the forcible sterilization of Cary Buck, a young woman who in fact wasn't mentally disabled, though several "expert" witnesses said she was. The Court noted that in times of war, the state can require the ultimate sacrifice of its citizens, in the form of military conscription that carries the risk of death, and suggested that the mere cutting of the fallopian tubes involved in forcible sterilization was a minor sacrifice in comparison. That conclusion seems plausible if you assume that the cutting of Cary Buck's fallopian tubes was part of a program to stop a catastrophic deterioration of the gene pool and to avoid the unsupportable expenses of carrying for increasingly large numbers of defective citizens. "Three generations of imbeciles is enough," declared the majority opinion written by the lauded American jurist Oliver Wendell Holmes, Jr.[5]

I suspect that it's not a coincidence that Holmes himself had been willing to sacrifice himself for the greater good by serving in the Union army in the Civil War (he was seriously wounded three times). Like many Union soldiers, Holmes may have believed, as Abraham Lincoln did, that the struggle against the Confederates was not just about keeping the United States intact but was also in fact a contest that would decide the fate of democracy and hence the prospects for human progress in the world at large. The idea was that if the United States fragmented, this would be taken as proof that democracy didn't work, and conservative, authoritarian forces around the world would triumph, stifling human progress and robbing individuals of their opportunities for self-improvement. According to this way of thinking, the Southern secession created a Supreme Emergency.

I'm suggesting that Holmes justified involuntary sterilization because he bought into the eugenic idea that bad genes were an existential threat, and that we were facing a Supreme Emergency perhaps even greater than that which the Civil War had posed. Eugenics was so widely popular at the time of the *Buck vs. Bell* decision that the idea of a Supreme Emergency in the form of a cataclysmic decline in the gene pool may well have played a role in Holmes's reasoning. That would explain his tacit reference to the recent emergency of the Civil War to help justify what was done to Cary Buck.

How Patriarchal-Racial Ideology Shielded Eugenic Ideology from Criticism

It's worth noting that ideology played a role in sustaining the bogus science of eugenic ideology. From very early on, at least by the 1920s, there were some scientists who exposed the errors of eugenic "science." But they were ignored. Why? The best explanation is that they were mainly women and Jews (in several cases Jewish women).[6] If a sexist and antisemitic ideology was prevalent in the male Christian-culture-dominated scientific community, you would expect that what women and Jews said would be ignored, especially when it ran counter to the mainstream view. This case is eerily similar to that of a male-dominated ornithology community being blind to the fact that female birds sing.

This is an example of one of the most cognitively damaging features of tribalistic ideologies: they prevent the groups they marginalize or write off as less than rational from contributing to public knowledge. This phenomenon of ignoring or discounting the voices of people we sort into the category of an inferior group is what philosopher Miranda Fricker calls "testimonial injustice."[7]

Ideology-Caused Testimonial Injustice

My more general point is that ideologies promote testimonial injustice, and not just toward members of marginalized minority groups. Opposing groups of roughly equal power and influence inflict testimonial injustice on each other when they operate in the tribalistic mode.

In other words, testimonial injustice can occur and does occur even when there is no power disparity of the sort that exists in Fricker's examples of it. In her examples, a dominant group uses its power to suppress the voices of the less powerful. In tribalism, our ideological beliefs prevent us from hearing opposing voices, even when the speakers have as much social power as we do. Fricker's testimonial injustice is an asymmetrical affair, the result of a pronounced power disparity. Ideological testimonial injustice is in a way more sinister than Fricker's examples suggest, because it can exist in a society in which major inequalities and systematic, heavy-handed oppression of certain groups have already been overcome. To repeat: groups of equal power can inflict testimonial injustices on each other.

Here's an example. On some, perhaps many, U.S. university campuses today, there is a tendency not just to privilege the speech of people who are members of historically disadvantaged groups (and who have been victims of testimonial justice) but also to try to stifle or ignore the speech of Whites or males when it comes to topics regarded as bearing on racial or gender injustice. Several years ago, there was a conference at Oxford University in the U.K. on reproductive rights and the poster for it said that no one without a uterus was welcome to attend. (What about women who've had hysterectomies?)

Once we've sorted a speaker into the Them category, we don't listen. So, tribalistic ideologies don't just impair our ability to process information and to draw sound conclusions from an evaluation of the evidence. They also deprive us of evidence, limit our access to information by making us deaf to what They say.

People who've read Fricker's work and that of various other feminist thinkers, including Katherine McKinnon, will be familiar with the idea of "silencing." For example, feminist thinkers argue that a pervasive patriarchal ideology has created a social world in which when a woman says "no" to a[8] sexual advance by a man, her statement has no effect; in that sense she has been silenced. I think it's more accurate to say that the patriarchal male has been deafened by his ideology and that his deafness is detrimental to women. He simply can't hear the "no." He can detect the sounds, but he can't hear them as a "no."

That's why, at least in the case where there is no significant power asymmetry between the speaker and the person their speech is addressed to, the term "deafening" is more apt than "silencing." The "deafening" language captures the fact that a person's ideology can impair their ability to hear what another person is saying, even if there's not the power asymmetry that makes the "silencing" language appropriate.

Of course, there are power-asymmetries and they often do result in testimonial injustice in Fricker's sense. As I noted in the Introduction, some students and faculty report that they feel compelled to engage in self-censorship—that at least in the campus setting, they simply can't say certain things. They feel this way because they have less power than those who they anticipate will penalize them for their views. Of course, in some cases, people should be criticized for and even stigmatized because of their views. But the problem now is that what counts as unacceptable speech has become too elastic, too capacious.

Ideological Beliefs about Who's Entitled to Talk about What

Sometimes the focus is not on the content of what is said, but rather upon who is saying it. A recent graduate of the University of Virginia, Emma Camp, in an opinion piece in *The New York Times*, reports that she was told that it was wrong for her to say that Sutee, the practice of widow-burning, was wrong, because she was not an Indian woman.[9] Similarly, a friend of mine who is a highly regarded political theorist at a Canadian University was told that she had no business organizing a conference on indigenous peoples' rights because she was not an indigenous person, and this despite the fact that she had affirmed that indigenous people would be included as participants in the conference. In both cases, people who might have made valuable contributions to the pursuit of truth and the production of knowledge were barred from doing so.

Tribalistic ideologies not only over-use the notion of a Supreme Emergency, but they also totalize it. In other words, they present the world of political issues as a kind of seamless web: there are no minor issues, because all issues are interconnected. Everything—from wearing a mask or not, to the kind of vehicle you drive—becomes political, a part of the struggle between Us and Them, and every political issue is important because it is a part of the whole. That means that the extraordinary measures that the Supreme Emergency warrants can be applied even in what might otherwise be regarded as minor political skirmishes.

How Supreme Emergency Thinking Perverts Morality

The result is a race to the bottom, morally speaking. Ideologically primed politicians will lie, break promises, leak confidential information, and voice public support for murderous, authoritarian dictators, in order to achieve what are in fact minor victories because they don't think any victory or defeat is minor. And, what is perhaps even worse, their supporters will accept that kind of behavior for the same reason.

This attitude explains why politicians are apparently willing to sacrifice the common good in order to score points against their opponents. Or, to put it more accurately, why they don't seem to care about the common good, as compared to winning. Consider, for example, Senator Mitch McConnell's announcement, immediately after Barack Obama was elected, that he would lead the Republicans in thwarting every policy Obama attempted to enact. That view only makes moral sense if you think that defeating Obama is an essential component of your larger effort to prevent the loss of what you value most. If you think that way, you'll be willing to block a policy that you admit would be beneficial for many Americans because you think that benefit is dwarfed by the cost of allowing your opponent a victory in the larger life-or-death struggle for the soul of America, a battle that will decide whether the American experiment will succeed or fail. Let's assume, for the sake of charity, that McConnell thought the country was facing something like a Supreme Emergency and that he believed this justified behavior would otherwise be scrupulously avoided.

People frequently complain that our politicians are willing to lie, to cheat, and to play dirty, because all they care about is winning, about gaining or preserving power. That's only part of the story. That diagnosis only scratches the surface. We need to know why otherwise reasonable and morally normal people would act like that. And we need to know why they assume that winning is all-important. We need to know what they think, or rather feel, is at stake, even if they aren't always good at articulating what it is. When they aren't good at articulating their belief about what's at stake, we have to make the case that they do indeed have that belief by showing that their having it plays an important role in the best explanation of what they are doing.

So, my answer to the question "Why do people care so much about winning that they will act in indecent, immoral ways?" is that they are in the grip of an ideology that tells them that every political issue is a part of a life-or-death, zero-sum struggle for the highest stake, and that in such a Supreme Emergency it is permissible and even morally obligatory to do whatever it takes to win. Given that ideological view of the world, the lying, cheating, and playing dirty are not just understandable—*they are morally justified*. That's why saying that politicians are immoral, and leaving at that, obscures just how bad our predicament is. No doubt some politicians have utterly abandoned morality. But the point is that people who haven't jumped into that abyss are violating basic moral rules because their ideologies have coopted morality, turning it against itself. Saying that the solution to the ills of tribalistic morality is to Make America Moral Again misses the point. (A better ballcap inscription would be MATA: Make America Think Again.)

The Supreme Emergency framing doesn't jettison morality; it gives a moral justification for making exceptions to the normal moral rules. The justification is that these exceptions are needed to avoid a much greater evil. This is nothing new. The most cursory knowledge of history reveals that the worst behavior is not committed by amoralists. There simply aren't enough sociopaths to pull off the major, large-scale atrocities. Rather, they are perpetrated by ordinary people who have undergone normal moral development. They haven't lost their moralities; their moralities have been hijacked by ideology. It is an ironic testament to the power of morality that with most people you have to appeal to morality to get them to do grossly immoral things.

Here are three real-life examples. The setting of the first is the French Revolution that began in 1789. Revolutionary forces defeated a counterrevolutionary army in the Vendee region of France and then, over a period of several days, systematically killed the survivors of the army they had defeated. They herded them on to specially constructed barges that were steered into the middle of a wide and deep river and then sunk. At least 4,000 people were killed in this way. Those who perpetrated this atrocity justified it by appeal to their revolutionary ideology, which portrayed the revolution as a struggle, not just for the liberation of the French from monarchial tyranny, but also as a life-or-death contest that would decide the fate of humanity. Given their assumption that the revolution was essential for human progress against the forces of oppression world-wide, the Supreme Emergency framing kicked in. And to meet the threat posed by the Supreme Emergency, measures that in any other circumstance would have been seen as clearly impermissible were embraced without remorse. When we equate the terror of the French Revolution with people being guillotined in Paris over a period of about 18 months, we're profoundly underestimating the horror. Perhaps as many people were killed in a much shorter period of time in the Vendee.

The second and third examples come from the Nazi era. The first is supplied by historian Claudia Koonz in her chillingly insightful book, *The Nazi Conscience*.[10] Koontz gets it: Nazi ideology wasn't an abandonment of morality; it was a morality, in fact a very demanding one. Koontz cites a passage in a textbook for German public school teachers during the Nazi period. Teachers are told that they aren't just to teach their students facts, but also values. Of special importance is the Golden Rule: do unto others as you would have them do unto you—but of course, *with the proviso that it applies only to racial comrades*.

Notice that no moral rule has been abandoned and the teachers aren't being asked to quit being moral or convince their students to do that. Rather, one of the most basic moral rules has been perverted by reframing it in such a way as to exclude millions of people from the protection it provides. Moral motivation hasn't been destroyed; it's been hijacked by an ideology.

There's another way to look at the truncated Golden Rule case: ideology was subverting one of the most powerful resources of the human moral mind, moral consistency reasoning. Here's the first example we know of where someone knew how to use moral consistency reasoning but was aware that it can be subverted, and took precautions to ensure that it wasn't.

> And the Lord sent Nathan unto David. And he came unto him and said unto him, There were two men in one city; the one rich, and the other poor. The rich man had exceeding many flocks and herds: But the poor man had nothing, save one little ewe lamb, which he had bought and nourished up: and it grew up together with him, and with his children; it did eat of his own meat and drank of his own cup, and lay in his bosom, and was unto him as a daughter. And there came a traveller unto the rich man, and he spared to take of his own flock and of his own herd, to dress for the wayfaring man that was come unto him; but took the poor man's lamb, and dressed it for the man that was come to him.
>
> And David's anger was greatly kindled against the man; and he said to Nathan, As the Lord liveth, the man that hath done this thing shall surely
>
> Die: And he shall restore the lamb four-fold, because he did this thing, and because he had no pity.
>
> And Nathan said unto David, Thou art the man.[11]

The point of this Bible story and Koontz's Nazi school teacher example is that although moral consistency reasoning can be a very effective device for determining what's right and wrong, it can be derailed by ideologies. In

Koontz's case it was derailed by Nazi ideology's exclusion of non-Aryans from the scope of the Golden Rule. And the reason Nazi ideology gave for excluding them used the Supreme Emergency framing: non-Aryans fell into two groups: The Jews, who were the instigators of the Supreme Emergency, and other non-Aryans who were at worst dupes of the Jews or at best mere resources to use in the struggle against the Jew.

In the Biblical case, Nathan shows that he was aware of the danger that David's ideology would prevent him from engaging in moral consistency reasoning. If Nathan hadn't concealed the identity of the man without pity, David might well have replied: "I'm the King, God's anointed, and therefore I'm entitled to do what it would be wrong for ordinary people to do." In other words, David might have invoked an authoritarian, divine-right-of-kings political ideology to prevent the application of moral consistency reasoning to his own behavior. Nathan cleverly preempted that ideological derailment of moral consistency reasoning by getting David to make a moral judgment about the type of conduct he had engaged in without being aware that it was his conduct that was under scrutiny.

The second Nazi example is even more disturbing than the first. In 1942, German army special task forces (*Einsatz Gruppen*) were conducting mass shootings of civilians in Poland. Some of the soldiers participating experienced psychological distress (big surprise). To address this problem, Heinrich Himmler, head of the S.S., gave motivational speeches to those troops. He acknowledged the difficulty of killing defenseless women and children, but reminded the killers that it was their moral duty, that the extermination of these people was necessary, not just for the good of Germany, but also for the future of Europe and indeed of mankind. He implicitly invoked the Supreme Emergency framing by appealing to Nazi racial ideology: all that was good and valuable for human beings was threatened by the Jewish–Bolshevik conspiracy and to defeat it any measures were justifiable. What would be morally repugnant in any other context was in fact morally obligatory in this Supreme Emergency.

The French example and the Himmler example show how tribalistic ideologies, by invoking the Supreme Emergency framing, exploit our moral motivation to make us act immorally. The Golden Rule Nazi example and the Biblical example show how tribalistic ideologies can make it easier for us act immorally by disabling a beneficial procedure for determining the right thing to do (putting yourself in the place of those your behavior will affect and asking whether you would find that behavior acceptable). In all three examples, ideologies don't prompt immoral behavior by getting people to abandon their commitment to being moral; they exploit it.

Tribalistic Ideologies Turn the Moral Mind against Itself

In the previous chapter, I showed how ideology can turn our cognitive abilities against themselves. What I've just now shown is that an ideology can also turn morality against itself, re-directing moral motivation to bring about grossly immoral behavior. Irony again: only beings that have a sophisticated moral sense and powerful moral motivation can abandon moral constraints in the name of morality. It's a testimony to the power of morality that people who mobilize others for genocides or for mass compulsory sterilizations don't try to wipe the moral slate clean, but instead channel moral motivation toward immoral ends that are presented as the demands of a higher morality.

In this chapter, I've focused on the way in which tribalistic political ideologies encourage us to believe we're in a Supreme Emergency, that Armageddon is upon us. It's important to understand that the very concept of an emergency, even when it isn't a Supreme Emergency, carries great risks. If you convince people that an emergency exists, they will be likely to accept two very abusable conclusions. The first is that the normal moral rules don't apply (the Emergency Exception idea); that in an emergency it is permissible to do things that would be strictly forbidden in other circumstances. The second is that those in power should be allowed greater power in order to respond to the emergency. Taken together, these two conclusions justify the powers that be exercising great power unconstrained by moral rules. Given the fact that those people, like everybody else, are both fallible and attentive to their own interests, that's a toxic combination.

A supposed Supreme Emergency can involve a high risk of physical annihilation or literal slavery, as in Walzer's case of the threat of Nazi victory in WWII. Or it can involve the risk, not that you will be annihilated or enslaved if (say) the Liberals take over, but that you won't be able to live your identity. The social and political world your enemies will construct will denigrate you and people like you, make it impossible for you to achieve what you think is valuable, and impose on you the choice of repudiating or disguising who you are, on the one hand, or presenting yourself as you are and suffering high costs as a result, on the other. Current tribalistic political ideologies frame the Supreme Emergency chiefly in identity terms, rather than in terms of physical annihilation or literal enslavement, but the logic is the same: if you believe we're in a Supreme Emergency, signaling your allegiance to Our cause and doing whatever it takes to win count more than decency, fair play, and the truth. And remember, as I noted in the Introduction, there is evidence that the brain reacts the same way to identity-threats as to physical threats.

The COVID-19 National Emergency?

The dangers of framing a situation as an emergency were all too vividly illustrated in U.S. COVID-19 policy. Anthony Fauci, the Director of the Infectious Diseases section of the Centers for Disease Control and Prevention, and Deborah Birx, President Trump's chief spokesperson on pandemic matters, have both publicly acknowledged that they lied to the American public and manipulated information because they thought this was necessary for responding effectively to what they considered a national public health emergency.[12]

They also endorsed extremely harmful policies that they didn't come close to justifying. Closing schools had terrible costs, especially for children from disadvantaged families. And those harms were predictable in advance, on the basis of numerous educational and psychological studies showing how vital it is for disadvantaged children to stay in school—studies that were available prior to the pandemic.

Was COVID-19 a national emergency? Well, in one sense, yes: it required a response from officials at the level of national institutions and COVID-19 cases occurred across the nation. But in another sense, it wasn't. Rather, it became clear that it was an emergency for around one to one-and-a-half percent of the population of the country. That's the proportion of Americans who died or had serious negative effects from the virus. So, it wasn't a national emergency in the sense of an emergency that puts everyone at risk. Fauci and company didn't distinguish the two senses of "national emergency" but they clearly encouraged the belief that the pandemic was a national emergency in the sense that everyone was at risk.

It's interesting—and disturbing—to note that when Fauci led the U.S. response to HIV-AIDS, he also presented it as a national emergency in the second sense, falsely saying that everyone was at risk. Of course, not everyone was at risk. IV drug users, people who engaged in anal intercourse, and people who got blood transfusions were at risk, but for people not falling into those categories, the risk was non-existent or at most negligible, a much lower risk than that posed by daily activities like driving or taking a shower.

Why did Fauci exaggerate the scope of the risk of HIV-AIDS? I think for the same reason he exaggerated the scope of the risk of COVID-19: he was worried that if he didn't do that there would be discrimination (especially in the HIV-AIDS case) and/or neglect of those who were at significant risk (in both the HIV-AIDS and COVID-19 cases). In other words, I think he had an ideology that puts such a high priority on preventing that risk that he was willing to lie to avert it by exaggerating the scope of the risk of the diseases. He thought solidarity was essential for an effective response to the pandemic and that you wouldn't have it unless people thought everybody was at risk. He was willing to mislead the public in order to achieve the solidarity he thought was needed to respond effectively to the pandemic.

Framing an event as a national emergency is something one shouldn't do lightly, because it encourages the idea that the normal rules don't apply and that those at the summit of power should be granted even more power. Given these risks, it is important to do things: be clear about the scope of the emergency (in the COVID-19 instance, acknowledging that only a small portion of the population was at serious risk) and be careful not to employ more "emergency powers" than is necessary. Further, you should be sure to take seriously the question of determining when the emergency has ended. In my judgment, the U.S. public health leadership failed on all three counts.

A Massive Public Policy Failure: The Lack of a Justification

Whether I'm right about that or not, there was another, more basic, problem with the Fauci-led response to COVID-19: the public was owed a justification for its harm-causing policies, but it didn't get it.[13] A justification would at minimum have required (1) presentation of the results of a cost-benefit analysis showing that the benefits of the proposed policy would outweigh the costs (all the costs, including the psychosocial costs, not just the financial costs), (2) information about how to access the information employed in making the cost-benefit calculation, and (3) a reply, on the merits, to the major objections to the policy.

None of this was done. Instead, the top public health people simply assumed that closing schools and other public venues would be beneficial and acted as if there either were no costs or that they didn't matter. The closest Fauci came to justifying the closings was laughable, or would have been, if the harms the closings caused hadn't been so great: he said they worked in China. Why did he think that? Because the Chinese government said they worked. That's astonishing, given that the Chinese government lied about the earlier SARS outbreak and refused to cooperate with WHO's request for information about the spread of COVID-19 in China.

For you or I to trust China's word about epidemics, we'd have to be incredibly gullible. Was Fauci really that gullible? Not necessarily. Here's an alternative hypothesis: this was a case of motivated false belief; Fauci believed the Chinese because he wanted to use measures like closings, which conveyed the idea that we were all at risk, in order to achieve solidarity. And his particular brand of public health ideology put a premium on solidarity.

Fauci, Brix, and others didn't just endorse harmful policies without anything approaching a minimally adequate public justification. They also attacked those who objected to them while refusing to engage with them on the substance of the criticisms.[14] They also encouraged discrimination against and even persecution of people who refused to get vaccinated despite lack of evidence that the vaccines prevented infection or its spread. They did that by implying that those who refused to get vaccinated were selfishly putting others at risk and portraying that those who disagreed with them as being anti-science.

One has to wonder, why didn't they feel obligated to provide a decent justification for policies that limited people's liberty and predictably had other harmful consequences? I think the best explanation is that they were in the grip of an ideology that led them to regard the public as less than their equals, as more like minors than adults.

The slogan "follow the science" was deceptive. It suggested that science spoke with one voice, ignoring the fact that respectable, knowledgeable scientists had not unreasonable objections to official policies. In doing so, it grossly misrepresented what science is and then used that misrepresentation to stifle criticism.

Elsewhere, I've argued in detail that this shameful behavior was motivated in part by a strand of public health ideology that focuses exclusively on stopping the spread of a disease regardless of the costs, puts a premium on maintaining or creating solidarity, includes a paternalistic and patronizing attitude toward the public, and thinks in terms of interventions directed toward everyone, rather than targeting interventions toward those at highest risk.[15] One can only imagine what the likes of Fauci and Birx would have been willing to do if they had thought that the pandemic's public health emergency was an inextricable element of a much more comprehensive Supreme Emergency, one sector of the Armageddon battlefield.

Ideological Responses to COVID-19 Policy

In fact, some of those who most strongly criticized Fauci and company did see their COVID-19 policies in just that light. Their tribalistic Right-wing ideology portrayed the policies Fauci and Birx advocated as the first of a series of steps by which Americans would be lulled into acquiescing in the increasing erosion of their freedoms and the expansion of government control. In other words, they didn't regard what they took to be the errors of COVID-19 policy in isolation; they endowed them with the greatest significance by seeing them as part of a larger struggle for the highest stakes. That is the totalizing effect of tribalistic ideologies. While they may have denied that COVID-19 presented a genuine national health emergency, they were convinced that the response to the pandemic was part of a larger, much more consequential Supreme Emergency, the deadly threat to individual freedom posed by those on the Left.

Tribalistic ideologies magnify the risks of framing some condition as an emergency, because they reduce the sense of self to one dimension, a bundled identity in which the political item in the bundle is supreme and what connects all the other identities. When that happens, it isn't surprising that anything that seems to threaten or challenge that primary, all-encompassing identity is going to evoke extreme protective responses. A threat to one identity isn't so frightening if you have other, equally important, independent identities. But if in effect you have only one identity because all your particular identities are tightly bundled together, any threat to any facet of it is an existential threat. That explains why we don't just disagree with people who don't share our totalized identity, but vilify and fear them as well. The very fact that they exhibit a different, opposing identity calls our primary, most encompassing social identity into question. We become convinced that we are in a state of Supreme Emergency. And unlike ordinary emergencies, this one isn't time-limited, it's ongoing.

The Supreme Emergency framing makes our political behavior and discourse more extreme because it amplifies the sense that our social identity is imperiled. If you have non-political identities that are important to you, losses on the political front aren't nearly so threatening. If all or most of your identities are bundled together and tightly bound to your political identity, political losses are all-encompassing and therefore catastrophic.

The Supreme Emergency framing is also involved in the perversion of theory of mind that is characteristic of tribalistic ideologies. For those who thought the response to COVID-19 was just one element of a mammoth liberal plot to destroy individual liberty, no matter what Fauci and Birx said, it was interpreted as insincere: they weren't really concerned about limiting the damage of COVID-19. Everything they said and did was directed toward the goal of getting the public to accept ever greater levels of government control over their lives.

I think it is clear from their own admissions that Fauci and Birx were insincere in some of their statements. Yet I think it's most likely they were insincere because they thought lies and manipulation of information were necessary to protect the public, not because they were necessary for lulling the public into the gradual destruction of their freedom. Making the right inferences from behavior to intentions and goals is crucial if we are to address policy failures and understand their causes. A bogus-ideology-based theory of mind that misunderstands the motivation of government officials is not likely to provide sound guidance for how to make things better. If the real motivation for Fauci's and Birx's deception was the desire to minimize the harms directly caused by the disease combined with a patronizingly dim view of the public's ability to handle the truth, the proper corrective is to convince people like them that if they try hard enough, they can get the public to do the right thing without lying to them and that lying carries a high risk of being exposed and losing their credibility. It would also require convincing them that minimizing the direct harms caused by the disease was not the only thing of importance—that other harms count as well, including those caused by attempts to minimize the direct harms caused by the disease. In contrast, if you think Fauci and Brix were acting to further a mammoth conspiracy against individual freedom, other remedies—if there are any—will be advisable.

The Public Health Ideology That Mangled COVID-19 Policy

When I had the honor of giving the Tanner Lectures on Human Values at Cambridge University in England in 2022, I made the case for a more targeted COVID-19 policy, criticizing the shotgun approach adopted in the United States, especially the closings of schools and other public places. I also voiced doubts about the wisdom of trying to vaccinate and provide a series of boosters to everyone. Those doubts stemmed mainly from the fact that there was growing evidence that the vaccines don't prevent infection or the spread of infection but at most lessen the severity of symptoms in some people—along with the growing evidence that some people, especially young adult males, have had serious adverse reactions to the vaccines, including cardio-myopathy. It was only later that the company that produced one of the vaccines admitted that it had not even tested for efficacy in preventing infection before seeking FDA expedited "emergency" approval for the vaccine. By a more targeted strategy, I meant doing what Sweden did: focusing resources on protecting the people most vulnerable, not acting as if everybody was at serious risk.

After expressing my doubts about closings and mass vaccination, I launched what turned out to be a bombshell: I said that making stopping the spread of the virus the end-all and be-all of policy was a mistake, for two reasons: first, you can't stop the spread of respiratory virus like COVID-19; second, even trying to reduce (not stop) its spread can't rationally be an absolute priority—it has to be balanced against other considerations, including the harms done by efforts to stop the spread. I then went on to suggest that Fauci and company seemed to lack the concept of a trade-off; that they didn't seem to understand that preventing the spread of the disease was not an absolute priority, but rather something that had to be balanced against other considerations.

These remarks provoked an angry outburst from a member of the audience who identified himself as a public health professional. He said "Of course, we've got to stop the spread of the disease!" He ignored what I was saying and just repeated the view I was criticizing. He didn't acknowledge that there was a limit to what we should do to try to reduce (not stop!) the spread of the disease. My point was a simple one: preventing the spread of a disease that seriously affected around one to one-and-a-half percent of the U.S. population was not the only thing of value. And that would be true even if the percentage of those seriously affected turns out to be significantly higher. Costs, not just benefits count, and what counts as acceptable costs depends on just how great the supposed benefits are and how certain we are that we'll attain them.

It was clear to me that the public health guy viewed my remarks as nothing short of heretical and so patently false that he could hardly believe his ears. Another public health professional in the audience chimed in, saying that my proposal for a more targeted approach betrayed a false "individualistic, atomistic" ideology that was inimical to solidarity and contrary to the whole point of public health, which is a matter of promoting population health.

In other words, she attempted to discredit me and thereby my message by saying that a targeted approach was nothing more than an expression of a defective ideology. That enabled her to avoid addressing the targeted approach on the merits. I reminded her that standard public health approaches nowadays sometimes do segment the population into risk groups with different treatment recommendations, for example, in the case of shingles vaccinations and pneumonia vaccinations (the former usually reserved for people who have had chicken pox and the latter for older people). What I was recommending was no more "atomistic" or excessively "individualistic," than those policies.

Stopping the Spread of the Virus Was Not All That Mattered

Here's an analogy to make clear what was wrong with the first public health professional's thinking when he kept insisting that we had to stop the spread of the virus, no matter what. Suppose you thought (mistakenly) that it was absolutely essential to prevent deaths caused by vehicle crashes. Here's one way you could do it: require that all vehicles have the armor of an Abrams tank; be covered on the outside with spongy, marshmallow-like material; and have engines capable of a top speed of three miles an hour. The marshmallow exterior would prevent injuries to pedestrians; the combination of armor and an exceedingly slow top speed would mean that if such vehicles collided with one another, no one would be hurt.

That would be nuts, of course. Anyone who proposed it would be overlooking two important facts. First, that there are other things that are important in addition to preventing deaths from vehicular collisions (like making vehicles an affordable and reasonably efficient mode of transportation and using limited resources to prevent more deaths from other causes) and that therefore there are important limits on what we should do to protect life. In other words, there have to be trade-offs, decisions to balance conflicting goods. Second, almost always, after a certain point, the marginal costs of risk-reduction are rising: the first gains in risk-reduction may be cheap, but eventually each additional increment of risk-reduction becomes more costly, involves giving up more of other things we value.

If you told someone who advocated making cars with marshmallow-coated tanks going at most three miles an hour was not a good idea and they replied, "But we've got to prevent vehicular deaths!" they'd be dead wrong. The public health guy who kept repeating "But we've got to stop the spread of the virus!" was, too.

Framing something as an emergency causes us to focus exclusively on reducing or eliminating the risk that supposedly constitutes the emergency. That framing functions like a bright, tightly focused beam of light that illuminates one risk (in this case, damage from the COVID-19 virus), but obscures all others (including the risks of psychosocial and economic harms resulting from the effort to trying to eliminate that one risk).

If we regard something as an emergency, we tend to forget that there are other, comparable risks that we ordinarily accept or don't take such drastic steps to counter. For example, the risks of economic and health damage and global political instability posed by climate change are certainly greater than the risk for most of us of harm from contracting COVID-19. We also forget that the proper goal is almost always to reduce risks, not eliminate them, and that even for serious risks, reducing them has to be balanced against other goals, that trade-offs are unavoidable and should be openly acknowledged.

The points about trade-offs and the rising marginal costs of risk-reduction are pretty straightforward. They're covered in the first few sessions of Econ 101. Public health people are smart and they're well-educated, so it can't be that they lack the relevant concepts. The only plausible explanation for why they act as if they thought the only important thing in the world is stopping the spread of a virus and as if they never heard of trade-offs and the rising marginal costs of risk-reduction is that they are in the grip of an ideology. We've seen that ideologies can make you stupid. This is yet another example of that.

As I noted in the Introduction, it's not clear to me that the public health ideology I've been criticizing is a tribalistic ideology strictly speaking. Nevertheless, it shares some key features with tribalistic ideologies. To take one important example, my analysis of ideological dumbing down in the public health case has the same structure as my analysis of the immoral behavior of politicians. The best explanation of the monomaniacal behavior of the public health officials is not that they never had or somehow lost relevant concepts and information; it's that their ideology prevented them from applying those concepts and utilizing that information. Similarly, the best explanation of the immoral behavior of our politicians is not that they've suddenly become sociopaths or never developed a sense of right and wrong in the first place; instead, it's that their ideologies have convinced them that we are in a Supreme Emergency in which the ordinary moral rules can be justifiably infringed, for the sake of a higher moral good. Here's another similarity: the public health ideology that I've argued distorted pandemic policy includes a sharp Us/Them distinction, the Us being the enlightened, fully rational, and altruistic public health professionals and the Them being the benighted, less than rational masses.

Emergency Thinking Lowers Moral Standards in the Name of Morality

Once we understand how tribalistic ideologies foster the Supreme Emergency framing of political issues and convince people that Armageddon is here and now, something that is otherwise baffling becomes wholly understandable, namely, the fact that people now tolerate indecent, disgusting, immoral behavior and hateful speech by their political leaders. Not too long ago, a politician who was recorded saying he grabbed women by the genitals or who described immigrants as vermin (employing the standard language of genocide) would have been "canceled," regarded by almost everyone as unfit for office. That would have been the end of their political career.

Today, people who expect and demand decent behavior in other parts of their lives accept the unacceptable in politics because they think victory for their tribe is all-important. For tribalistic types, a person they think is their best leader in the zero-sum, highest-stakes contest against the lethally dangerous Other can do anything. As Trump puts it, they can shoot a man in the middle of Madison Avenue and get away with it. Given our ideologically perverted understanding of what a statesman is, we not only accept what we would otherwise regard as intolerable behavior, but we may even praise it if we think it contributes to Our victory. Our leaders *ought* to play dirty, if that's necessary for victory.

The explanation of why people tolerate behavior that would in the past have ended a political career isn't that suddenly nobody has any standards of decency. It's more specific than that: because of the Supreme Emergency framing and the Armageddon is upon us mentality their tribalistic ideology promotes, they make a special exception to what they regard as intolerable when it comes to people they think are important for the war effort against the opposing tribe. That means their understanding of the nature of a virtuous leader or statesman has been transformed.

Tribalistic ideologies produced stupidity on the Left as well as the Right during the pandemic. I've already mentioned one case: refusing to give any serious consideration to the possibility that the virus originated in a lab in Wuhan because Trump and his supporters do. Here's another: when I've expressed doubts about the proposal to vaccinate virtually everything with a pulse in hopes of preventing the spread of COVID-19, I've been called an "anti-vaxxer," with the implication that I reject all vaccinations, believe they cause autism, and are part of a great conspiracy, etc. That's the sort of misguided sorting that is a hallmark of tribalistic ideologies. It's just plain stupid to assume that if someone is skeptical about the wisdom of mass vaccinations for one particular illness with a new type of vaccine *that hasn't been shown to prevent the disease*, they reject vaccinations across the board and are therefore one of those benighted people who won't "follow the science." The inference "So and so questions the appropriateness of mass COVID-19 vaccinations, therefore so and so is against all vaccines and doesn't believe in science" is patently invalid, but people in the grip of a tribalistic ideology make it, and for them the possibility that it might be invalid doesn't even arise. People of normal intelligence have become stupid, not across the board, but in matters that trigger their tribalistic ideological responses.

In the next chapter, I show that by ruling out serious efforts to bargain or make compromises, tribalistic ideologies undercut the conditions that are necessary for democracy to work. Democracy requires bargaining and compromising. And the willingness to bargain and compromise, like the willingness to accept defeat on particular policy issues today in the expectation that you may win tomorrow, depends on trusting your opponent to play by the rules and to be responsive to reasons. But tribalistic ideologies tell us we shouldn't trust those we disagree with and that they aren't rational. And if Armageddon is here and now, there's no tomorrow if you lose today.

Notes

1 Sean Hannity, *Live Free or Die: America (and the World) on the Brink*. New York: Simon & Schuster, 2020.
2 Michael Walzer, *Just and Unjust Wars: A Moral Argument with Historical Illustrations*. London: Allen Lane, 1978.
3 There's more than a grain of truth in the saying that in WWII "the Soviets beat the Germans, the Americans beat the Japanese, and the British beat the Italians"

(The Soviets inflicted between 80% and 90% of total German casualties.). This is not to devalue the American war effort in general or the Normandy invasion in particular: even if it wasn't necessary for the defeat of the Germans, the invasion of Europe by the Western Allies was a great importance, because it prevented the Red Army from driving into Western Europe and therefore prevented Stalin from establishing Eastern-bloc-style communist regimes there.

4 Daniel Kevles, *In the Name of Eugenics: Genetics and the Uses of Human Heredity*. 1st Harvard University Press paperback ed. Cambridge, MA: Harvard University Press, 1995.

5 Justia Law, "Buck vs. Bell, 274 u. S. 200 (1927)." Accessed May 7, 2024. https://supreme.justia.com/cases/federal/us/274/200/.

6 Elazar Barkan, *Retreat of Scientific Racism: Changing Concepts of Race in Britain and the United States between the World Wars*. Cambridge, GBR: Cambridge University Press, 2011.

7 Miranda Fricker, *Epistemic Injustice: Power and the Ethics of Knowing*. Reprint. Oxford: Oxford University Press, 2011.

8 Alexandra Bacall has an excellent unpublished paper on this topic.

9 Emma Camp, "Opinion|I Came to College Eager to Debate. I Found Self-Censorship Instead." *The New York Times*, March 7, 2022, sec. Opinion. https://www.nytimes.com/2022/03/07/opinion/campus-speech-cancel-culture.html. This is an extremely valuable essay.

10 Claudia Koonz, *The Nazi Conscience*. 1. Harvard University Press paperback ed. Cambridge, MA: Belknap Press of Harvard University Press, 2005.

11 "Samuel 2:12, *KJV*"

12 Deborah Birx, *Silent Invasion*. New York: HarperCollins Books, 2022.

13 For support for my criticisms of U.S. COVID-19 policies, see my 2024 book, *How to Prepare for the Next Pandemic: Avoiding Institutional Failure*. The Tanner Lectures in Human Values. Salt Lake City: University of Utah Press.

14 Thanks to the Freedom of Information act; we now have access to email exchanges between Fauci and Francis Collins, Director of NIH, in which they conspire to besmirch the reputations of the authors of The Great Barrington Declaration, which was a well-reasoned, respectful criticism of the shotgun approach taken by the United States (mass business, entertainment venue, and school closing, trying to vaccinate everybody) and which made a strong case for a more targeted approach of the sort successfully employed in Sweden.

15 *How to Respond Better to the Next Pandemic: Remedying Institutional Failures,* chapter on public health ideology.

4

THE DEATH OF WE THE PEOPLE—
HOW TRIBALISTIC IDEOLOGIES
DESTROY NATIONAL IDENTITY
AND UNDERMINE DEMOCRACY

Peoples versus Populations

The Preamble to the U.S. Constitution begins with the words "We the People of the United States of America...." It doesn't say something quite different: "We, a collection of individuals who happen to live in the thirteen states...." The first characterization conveys an important idea of unity, of shared identity that the second doesn't.

A lot depends upon whether we are a people and, just as importantly, on whether enough of us believe we are. Tribalistic ideologies destroy the unity implied by the idea that we are a people. They split the people into Us versus Them, convincing us that the population divides largely into two irreconcilable groups.

Only a People Can Be Self-Governing

A country that has only a population and not a people is not capable of self-government, because there is no single self to do the governing. Political self-government means government by a collective that is sufficiently unified to make collective decisions. A mere population lacks the unity to be a collective decision-maker and hence to be a self-governing collective. When We the People has died by fragmentation, one of the resulting groups may be a people, but if it governs, self-government is just government by itself, not by a collective self that includes everybody.

Without the belief that we are a people, democracy can't flourish. That's because committing to the hard task of making democracy work requires

DOI: 10.4324/9781003612469-5

the belief that we are working together to govern our collective, inclusive self, and that government is our instrument for doing that, a resource for all citizens, not just some of us.

Two Ways to Think of Political Power

It makes all the difference in the world whether you regard the struggle for political power as a contest over how we (where this includes all of our fellow citizens) are best to govern ourselves or as a fight to prevent some other group that is not Us from using government to dominate Us and destroy what We value. Instead of thinking of political power as a resource for pursuing our common project as one people, we've come to think of it as a weapon to use against radically different creatures who are legally American, but utterly alien. It's one thing to disagree about how best to use a tool in a construction project we are undertaking together; it's another to regard the tool as a weapon that we'd better get control of before the other guys uses it to kill us. The tool is political power. It can either be a shared resource or a weapon we compete to wield. Tribalistic ideologies make it a weapon.

There's no solidarity with those we disagree with on political matters, once tribalistic ideology takes hold. Nor is there trust. Yet solidarity and trust are necessary if we're to cooperate in our democratic processes, in spite of our disagreements. When tribalism takes hold, the idea of a loyal opposition disappears. When you hear Conservatives talk about Liberals or *vice versa*, ask yourself whether they have the concept of a loyal opposition, of people whose hearts are in the right place, people we ought to respect, even though they disagree with us on various policy issues.

Of course, if a democracy is to function, disagreements can't run too deep. There is no We the People, if we intractably disagree on the most fundamental values and on what government is for. In fact, a large part of what defines us as a people is just such fundamental agreement. The problem is not just that tribalistic ideologies represent the Other as disagreeing with us. Nor is it just that they convince us that there is disagreement on fundamental values. It's that they also present the Other as a despicable, untrustworthy, dangerous group of individuals whom we can't reasonably regard as compatriots, as people we can expect to join us in a common project. And because They are irrational, there's no prospect of reasoning with Them in order to lessen the disagreement on basic values.

They Are Not Part of the People

Often the idea of We the People of the United States is understood as our having a shared identity as Americans. That means agreement on some fundamental values, but it also means recognizing that, although some other Americans are different in a number of ways from us, they are the same when it comes to what matters for our being a nation, rather than just a collection of individuals who happen to occupy the same territory. Tribalistic ideologies replace that sense of shared identity as Americans with partisan, tribal identities—and with a characterization of those who are not members of our tribe as having such alien aims and projects that it is impossible to see them as members of a people that includes us.

There's a dramatic historical example of this way of thinking. A man called Abbe Sieyes wrote a pamphlet called "What is the Third Estate?" which was published in 1789, just as the ingredients for the French Revolution were coalescing.[1] He drew on the traditional distinction between Estates or classes or social orders in the France of that day: the First Estate is the clergy, the Second is the nobility, and the Third is everybody else. Sieyes makes a startling claim: the First and Second Estates aren't needed; every service they supposedly provide can be provided by the Third Estate; *and* the First and Second Estates aren't even part of the French nation. They aren't included in the People, but instead are alien parasites feeding on it. This sounds rather like a more explicit, more extreme version of a strain of populist thinking in contemporary America that distinguishes between the People and the "Elites." If the elites are the enemy of the People, with their own interests and agendas, as this populist view holds, then they aren't really part of the People.

What Talk about Red State Secession Really Means

One sure sign that We the People is either already dead or dying is the recent increase in talk about secession. From time to time, secessionist rhetoric surfaces, but throughout the post–Civil War period until quite recently it's been largely a matter of half-serious proposals for a single state (in particular Vermont) or a part of a single state (e.g., the eastern portion of the state of Washington) to become independent.

Now there is talk about all the Red states seceding together to form a new country. I think that's highly unlikely, but that's not the point. Multi-state secession along partisan lines implies a belief that there is no single-American people; that the two separate and mutually hostile Americas each need their own country. The assumption is that the State, the totality of national political institutions, cannot serve the interests of both of the Americas; that it must act on behalf of one or the other. It can't act on behalf of both because there is no common interest.

Taking at all seriously the prospect of partisan multi-state secession implies the judgment that democracy cannot work here. It is an admission that democracy can only be achieved if We can rid ourselves of Them. It's a sign that there is no longer a shared political *Umwelt*.

Here are some remarkable statistics that Lilliana Mason notes in her excellent book on tribalism. They are further evidence of the erosion of the unity implied by the idea of We the People.

> In 2011, 52 percent of American partisans [people who identify themselves as either Republicans or Democrats] said they definitely would not marry a member of the opposing party. As a point of comparison when Bogardus asked these questions of white Protestants in 1928, he found that 10 percent would not marry a Canadian or Northern European, but 90 percent would not marry a Southern or Eastern European. In their suitability for marriage, therefore, outgroup partisans today rank somewhere between Canadians and Italians in the early twentieth century.[2]

In other words, a lot of Democrats feel the same way about Republicans as they do about foreigners and *vice versa*. That's another indication that We the People has fragmented.

I got similar results in a highly unscientific survey with an "n" of one. I asked a rather bigoted acquaintance of mine which he would be most upset about, his daughter coming out as gay or her marrying a Liberal. Though intensely homophobic, he said his daughter marrying a Liberal would be worse. Out of fear of precipitating a stroke or a heart attack, I refrained from asking him how he would feel if his daughter married a Liberal woman.

How Tribalistic Ideologies Transform the Political Vocabulary

Once We the People no longer exists due to the fragmentation that tribalistic ideologies promote, our understanding of institutions undergoes a dramatic sea-change. They are only American institutions in name; in fact, they are either Our institutions or Theirs. The Presidency and the Supreme Court are no longer the common heritage of all Americans; they are spoils that will be captured by Us or Them.

This means that the ideological destruction of national unity, of We the People, entails the abandonment of the belief that our institutions are legitimate. Or, more accurately, it means that our tacit assumptions about what makes them legitimate undergo a profound transformation. Before tribalism became pervasive, the impartiality of an institution, the non-partisan behavior of those who run it, was a hallmark of legitimacy. When tribalism destroys the unity and trust required for there being a We the People, we regard an institution as legitimate if and only if it is on Our side. Partisanship replaces impartiality in our assessments of institutional legitimacy. Of course, we may still mouth the word "impartial" when we describe an institution as legitimate. But our sense of impartiality has been corrupted and with it our understanding of legitimacy. In practice, impartiality just means agreement with Us, with Our ideological stance. The rulings of a Supreme Court or the actions of a President that we would previously have regarded as biased, as partisan, as not impartial, we now see as rightful. If our group doesn't dominate these institutions, we see them as illegitimate and regard everything those who run them do as biased, partisan. When tribalistic ideologies don't cause us to abandon talk about impartiality and the legitimacy of institutions entirely, they systematically pervert it.

Here's a clear example of the abandonment of the idea of impartiality. J.D. Vance, recently chosen by Trump to be his Vice-Presidential running mate, exhibited this feature of tribalistic ideologies when he said that Trump "...should fire every mid-level bureaucrat [and].... Replace them with our people."[3] He didn't say: we ought to replace some bureaucrats with less-biased, better-qualified, and motivated people or less partisan people; he said they ought to be replaced with *our* people.

Tribalistic ideologies destroy an American identity while hijacking the term "American." Those we classify as Other, as not Us, as the political enemy, are not Americans. The very ideological thinking that destroys We the People denies that it is doing so by redefining who the People are, by characterizing what it is to be an American in such a way as to deny that title to half the population or more.

When you hear politicians accuse their opponents of being un-American, it's almost certain that you're seeing a tribalistic ideology at work and that this is just another nail in the coffin of We the People. When you say someone is un-American or not a true American, you don't regard them as someone to engage in arguments with or to try to convince that their views are mistaken. You are sorting them into the category of those who aren't proper parties to discussions about American politics. They are in effect foreigners who have no business talking to Us about what Our country should do. You're making Sieyes's move. Denying someone's membership in the nation is a strategy of exclusion, of casting out, and literally a conversation stopper.

This isn't to deny that the term "un-American" is ever apt. If, for example, a politician says something that rejects a fundamental American value, like the belief in limited executive power, what they have said is un-American. It's more conducive to reasoned discussion, however, to say that—to identify which American value has been rejected—rather than to say that the speaker or their statement is un-American. Too often, the term "un-American" substitutes for reasoned discussion rather than facilitating it. Throwing the term "un-American" around simply obscures the fact that there is and always has been disagreement about what America is or ought to be.

Tribalistic ideologies also pervert the concept of patriotism. A patriot is someone who is willing to bear costs, even to the point of self-sacrifice, for the sake of their country. But now a patriot is thought by many Americans to be someone who defends their tribal values. That's because they no longer are capable of thinking that there might be a difference between their particular values and the good of the country. The unshakeable certainty about being completely right that tribalistic ideologies promote removes any doubt that those two things might diverge. People whom you sort into the Them category can't possibly be patriots. And if someone you've been regarding as one of Us disagrees with your tribe's party line, that's a sign that they aren't a patriot because they aren't one of Us. If you are in the tribalistic mode, you can't even conceive of two people disagreeing about what America is or should be and both being patriots.

In addition, tribalistic ideologies corrupt our understanding of the virtues political figures ought to exhibit, of what it is to be a statesman. We used to think that a true statesman was a person who was above partisan politics and who unified us, who appealed to our shared national identity on the best understanding of it. But nowadays it's just the reverse: politicians are praised for their effectiveness in dividing us, in helping us sort the population into the Us versus Them boxes, in sharpening our awareness of just how different and dangerous They are, and in attacking Them by the most effective means, regardless of whether that means lying, cheating, forsaking decency, or encouraging a mob to invade the Capitol to over-turn the results of an election. This is a complete inversion of the virtues of statesmanship. And along with it goes blindness to any positive traits of politicians who represent the opposing tribe. I'm sure you've seen this feature of tribalistic ideologies in action: Conservatives can't acknowledge that Obama or Biden ever did anything good, just as Liberals cannot admit that Trump or George W. Bush got anything right.

The virtuous politician, the true statesman, becomes one who consistently exhibits unqualified endorsement of Our political views, whose allegiance to our tribe is unquestionable because they never express any doubts about Our possession of the absolute, eternal truths about the realm of the political. This, too, is an inversion of values, because in reality a true statesman is someone who helps us understand who we are on the best interpretation of our identity, which sometimes requires critical revision of our collective self-conception. Think of how Lincoln helped redefine liberty when he spoke, in the Gettysburg Address, of "...a new birth of freedom."

The collective identity implied by the phrase "We the people" is partly descriptive. For example, it includes beliefs about our past, our traditions, and our victories over forces that would dominate or divide us. But it's also partly prescriptive or aspirational: it includes beliefs about who we should be and a confidence that we can move toward the realization of our best collective self. Tribalistic ideologies undercut this potentially progressive understanding of national identity. They entrench a frozen, one-sided, partisan conception of shared identity and disregard any ideas about how we could become our best self if they come from others we regard as not of our tribe. The absolute certainty that we know the unchanging truth about everything that matters destroys the progressive element of national identity.

Creating the national identity that tribalistic ideologies are destroying was a costly affair. In an interview in the Ken Burns documentary series, *The Civil War,* historian Shelby Foote noted that the Civil War made us a singular: instead of saying "the United States are....," after the war, it became common usage to say "The United States is..."

If Foote is right that it took the Civil War to complete the task of creating the We the People referred to in the Declaration of Independence, then that unity came at a high price: six hundred and fifty thousand dead soldiers, not to mention the many civilians in the South who died of diseases of malnutrition and other causes due to the destruction of the economy and infrastructure.[4] Appreciating those costs is important. It may enhance our motivation to try to prevent the total destruction of the national unity that was purchased with so much blood and suffering.

There's another way to look at the ideologically induced demise of We the People. Having a national identity, a sense that there is a We that encompasses all of us, involves the ability to have what philosophers call "we-intentions"—to think in terms of what we want to accomplish, how we ought to live, that isn't reducible to "I want to do X" and "you want to do X," and "He wants to do X," etc. Evolutionary anthropologists have made a good case that the ability to have we-intentions is a distinctively human characteristic, something other animals don't have.[5] And they have also shown that this ability is crucial for the extraordinarily comprehensive and flexible cooperation that is also uniquely human. When we are in the we-intention mode, there's no space between what I want and what you want that can tempt me to be a free-rider on the cooperative efforts of the group, to try to get the rewards of cooperation without contributing to it. When we-intentions are operative you don't ask yourself "Can I do better at getting what I want by cooperating or not cooperating (or feigning cooperation)?" The question isn't "What shall I do?" It's "What are we going to do?"

But if the "we" in we-intentions doesn't include all of our fellow citizens and if it's restricted to membership in our ideological tribe, things are entirely different. Tribalistic ideologies not only restrict cooperation to our group, excluding Them from the scope of our we-intentions, but they also make beating Them our primary we-intention. Instead of being a valuable asset for extending the scope of cooperation to encompass all our fellow citizens, the ability to form we-intentions, when it operates in the service of tribalistic ideologies, restricts cooperation and turns potential cooperators into enemies. Once again, the irony is palpable: a highly valuable, unique human capacity, in this case, the ability to form we-intentions, gets turned against itself.

There have always been disagreements about who we are as a people, about what exactly constitutes our national identity. That's healthy, because it allows for improvements in our collective identity and for reconceiving the nature of the national project that unites us. Reflection on who we are can be productive if it occurs under conditions of freedom of speech and association *and* if everyone is allowed a voice and their contributions to the discussion are evaluated on the merits. But they won't be evaluated on their merits if what people here is ideologically sorted and filtered.

If some potential participants in a productive discussion of who we are as a people are excluded because they are classified as the dangerous, deceitful, stupid Other, there is no reason to be confident that there will be a progressive refinement of our conception of who we are. On the contrary, the ideological straight-jacket will almost certainly magnify and entrench the flaws in its one-sided understandings of who we are and who we ought to try to be.

Every ideological perversion, every inversion of values that I've just described involves fundamental changes in meanings of key political concepts. Patriotism becomes blind loyalty to our tribe's creed. Statesmanship becomes expertise in divisiveness, effectiveness in denigrating Our opponents, and an unwavering commitment to the belief that We have gotten everything that matters right, once and for all. Legitimacy isn't impartiality and dedication to an encompassing shared interest, a common good; it's unalloyed partisanship, harnessing institutional resources for the achievement of Our goals, and above all for the complete defeat of Our opponents, no matter what it takes.

Some terms, rather than undergoing an inversion of meaning, no longer have a referent at all. We have already seen that this is true of "We the People." It's also true of the term "the loyal opposition." If They oppose Us, they can't be loyal; if they were loyal, they wouldn't oppose Us. There is nothing that We and They could both be loyal to; because there is no shared identity, no national project to which we both are committed. We can't learn from our political opponents because we already possess the absolute truth and they are incorrigibly wrong about everything that matters.

The Inability to Agree on Basic Facts

The greater the difference we think there is between Us and Them, the stronger in-group favoritism paired with negativity toward out-groups is likely to be. Tribalistic ideologies magnify the supposed difference between Us and Them when they shatter the unity of We the People. The don't just destroy, however; they also create: they replace We the People with separate political *Umwelten*. And there is no overlap between them. Adherents to opposing tribalistic ideologies live in separate worlds and the gulf between them is unbridgeable. The evaluative maps our opposing ideologies supply feature no common landmarks. Political disagreement is not about which facts are relevant and which policies are best in the light of the facts, because different political *Umwelten* means they can't even agree on the facts. Without agreement on some basic facts, in particular, facts about the history of our country, about its role in the world, and about the way basic institutions are functioning, there can be no We the People.

Two examples of disagreements on extremely important factual matters immediately come to mind. According to some polls, around two-thirds of Republicans believe the official result of the 2020 Presidential election was incorrect, that a massive fraud was perpetrated, robbing Trump of the Presidency.[6] And they believe this in spite of numerous independent investigations of the election and several dozen court rulings, all of which concluded that there was no voter fraud of a magnitude to have determined the outcome of the election. Consider also the fact that less than half of Republicans believe the January 6, 2021, was "very violent," in spite of the fact that there is a clear video recording of many acts of extreme violence and the fact that at least some of those who participated did so with the avowed goal of forcibly preventing the operation of a key democratic institutional process, the certification of electoral college votes required for declaring the winner of the Presidential election.[7] In addition, many Conservatives believe the incursion into the Capitol building was instigated by FBI *agents provocateurs*, even though no one has produced any credible evidence for this claim.

Ideological Fact-Denial on the Left

Fact-denial occurs on the Left, too; especially denial about the facts concerning the history of our country, of the world, and of the place of our country in the history of the world. More specifically, some Leftist tribal ideologies characterize the history of the United States and the world in such a one-sided manner, so replete with false factual claims, as to make the unity of vision and purpose implied by the phrase "We the people" impossible. These ideologies undermine the idea that we are a people by presenting our history as something wholly despicable, rather than as a touchstone of our shared identity. According to this narrative, our population divides into the good people who acknowledge that our country's history is utterly sordid and those who deny that it is. Where there is such a fundamental disagreement, it's hard to see how there can be an American people.

One striking example is an ideology that situates the history of the United States within a more comprehensive history of the world understood as a Manichean struggle between oppressors and oppressed. This ideology includes equal parts of self-loathing and excessive guilt on the part of the "Westerners" who espouse it, on the one hand, and romanticized depictions of the indigenous or pre-modern or non-Western peoples whose idyllic life we "Westerners" wantonly and unnecessarily destroyed, on the other. The films *Dances with Wolves* and *Avatar* are highly effective in disseminating this ideology.

Anthropologist Robert Edgerton and other scholars have debunked the "myths of primitive harmony" that this ideology promulgates: that indigenous or pre-modern people are egalitarian, peaceful, and in harmony with their environment. They have noted that in many cases, indigenous or more generally pre-industrial societies are deeply inegalitarian, featuring extreme gender inequality and slavery. Nor is their violence limited to largely ritualistic martial displays or relatively harmless raids. In many cases they engage in wars of extermination against other indigenous peoples. And there are a number of instances, as Jared Diamond in his book *Collapse* documents, in which indigenous or pre-industrial peoples have devastated their environments, destroying or disastrously depleting the natural resources on which they depended.[8]

Ideological Fantasies about "Premodern Peoples" and How They Divide Us

Until recently, anthropological studies of indigenous and other pre-industrial groups, especially hunter-gatherer societies, have been thoroughly infused with this romanticizing, myth-promoting ideology. This is yet another case in which ideologies not only distort the thinking of ordinary people, but also of a special group of people, scientists, who are supposed to be better than the rest of us at ascertaining the facts and at reasoning from evidence to conclusions (recall my examples of ornithology and early genetics). To their credit, some anthropologists have recently become more critical in their appraisal of indigenous or pre-industrial peoples. As with other scientific disciplines, Anthropology has exhibited the feature that makes science, with all its imperfections, the best way of gaining knowledge humans have developed so far: it is better at correcting its own errors than the alternatives.

False, rigidly held beliefs about indigenous or pre-modern peoples are instances of an ideology-induced cognitive disability noted in the Introduction. The preconception of the idyllic character of the non-Western other led to systematic misinterpretations of their behavior. For example, apparently enthralled by the myth that such people are essentially peaceful, the anthropologist Elizabeth Marshall Thomas wrote a book, *The Harmless People*, reporting the findings of her field work with the San (!Kung) people of Southern Africa. As the title of her book suggests, she portrayed these people as exceptionally nonviolent.[9]

The problem was that her sample of behavior was biased, unrepresentative. The people she studied in fact had a homicide rate among males of around 25%, a figure not uncommon among contemporary hunter-gather or simple (as opposed to ranked clan) tribal groups. That's not exactly harmless. She didn't perceive just how violent their culture was because she only observed a very small group of people for a short period of time. Had she had a larger sample population or observed a small sample for a longer period of time, she would have witnessed many homicides.

People in the grip of this ideology are every bit as much fact-deniers as those Republicans who deny the facts about the 2020 election or the invasion of the capital. I don't see how being one people is compatible with such fundamental—and intractable—disagreement.

The Horror of Whiteness

Another, closely related fact-ignoring ideology of the Left, one that I briefly previewed in the Introduction consists of extreme beliefs about the connection between Whiteness (or Europeanness), oppression, and colonialism. According to this view, all of the problems and disadvantages of people in so-called less-developed countries are due to colonialism, and colonialism is uniquely European and an invention of White folks. This view is in fact a species of racism if it includes the suggestion that to be White is to be guilty, to be an oppressor.

The implication is that all would be well, and peace and justice would reign, if only there had never been White people (or Europeans). Pardon my bluntness, but that's just nonsense. History is replete with examples of atrocious behavior by "non-Whites," "non-Europeans," and "non-Westerners." And today, it is a fact that the majority of the most kleptocratic, human-rights-violating, brutally authoritarian regimes are not led by White people or Europeans or people of European descent.

One extreme version of this anti-Western, Wokish ideology is that when the victims of oppression, including those subjected to the supposed "settler colonialism" of Israel, commit what is rightly regarded as an atrocity; they are blameless and that it's their oppressors who are culpable. This latter view was on full display when some American college students voiced unreserved, unqualified support for Hamas in the wake of the murder of Israeli civilians, including 300 young people at a music festival, on October 7, 2023.

Ideological Misunderstandings of Colonialism

Europeans didn't invent colonialism, if colonialism means invading someone else's homeland, displacing, killing, or subjugating them, expropriating their land and resources, and exploiting them. Groups around the world have been doing that for as long as human groups have existed. The Iroquois and Zulus and Comanches did that, as did the Islamic warriors who surged out of the Arabian Peninsula in the 640 C.E. and colonized the Middle East, displacing or subordinating Jewish and Christian communities that had been there for centuries, expropriating their goods and commandeering their labor, imposing special taxes on them because they were "infidels," and replacing their temples and churches with mosques.

Nor are all the problems faced by formerly colonized peoples due to colonialism. Some are due in significant part to bad government supported by cultural acceptance of kinship network-nepotism and other forms of corruption that pre-date colonialism. Kinship network-nepotism may have been somewhat less harmful and even in some ways beneficial in simpler, smaller-scale societies where there was no centralized coercive power. But under the conditions of the modern state, it is extremely destructive when unaccountable leaders use public resources to favor their kin.

Furthermore, some of the most serious problems of formerly colonized countries are due to the fact that international law treats any group of thugs who can control a territory and the people in it as a legitimate government, with the right to use resources and incur debts—rights that it is free to exercise in ways that are harmful to the majority of the people. That empowers awful people to enrich themselves while utterly disregarding the good of the people.[10] And it's worth noting that non-Western peoples have been among the most vigorous proponents of this conception of state legitimacy and of the use of international law to affirm virtually unlimited sovereignty in the name of the right of collective self-determination. The problem is that in many cases sovereignty isn't an exercise in self-government but rather the misgovernment of everybody else by an authoritarian leader for the sake of enriching himself and his family.[11]

There's another aspect of this White-Western-European–bashing ideology that is quite troubling—and quite demeaning in its attitude toward those it presents as the victims of colonialism. The picture it paints is one of helpless peoples—passive, pure victims. In fact, in all of its main instances, colonialism was a cooperative enterprise; some of the "natives" cooperated with the colonizers. The motives for cooperation varied. Paradoxically, this kind of anti-colonialist view shares with the colonial mentality it attacks a rather negative and patronizing view toward colonized peoples.

We shouldn't assume that all who cooperated were "collaborators" in the pejorative sense. Here's one example where that negative label doesn't seem to fit the "collaborator" label.

When Cortez invaded what is now Mexico, he had only about 400 Spaniards under his command. But he eventually gained the support of perhaps as many as 200,000 indigenous people, many of whom were Tlaxcalans. Only in the last few years, the descendants of those people have begun to protest against the pervasive view that their ancestors were collaborators in the pejorative sense, guilty accomplices in the Spaniards depredations, people who betrayed other indigenous people to curry favor with the conquerors. Spokespersons for this group have another interpretation: their ancestors thought an alliance with the Spanish was their best prospect for overthrowing the brutal, mass human-sacrificing rule of the Aztecs, who had invaded and colonized their territory only rather recently.[12]

At a philosophical conference I noted that this was not an isolated case, that cooperation of some of the colonized with the colonizers is quite common. In response, a philosopher in the audience said, "Of course, there are always collaborators." Her anti-colonialist, anti-Western ideology apparently prevented her from hearing what I was saying, namely, that not all cooperators are collaborators. When I described a case of cooperation that didn't warrant the pejorative term "collaboration," her ideology deafened her to what was saying. She literally couldn't hear me when I went to considerable pains to distinguish between collaboration and cooperation. That's a classic case of an ideology impairing a normal cognitive function, in this instance the ability to process the content of what someone is saying.

I've emphasized that the essentialized, deterministic stereotyping typical of tribalistic ideologies can impair theory of mind, causing one to misinterpret what another person says, once you have sorted them into the Other category. In the present example, the same result occurs simply because of a substantive ideological belief, in this case, the belief that the colonized are all either passive victims or collaborators in the pejorative sense. That belief disabled the woman's ability to comprehend the distinction between cooperation and collaboration in the pejorative sense. When I said "cooperate," that belief caused her to substitute "collaborate." I'm sure she was a highly intelligent person, but her ideology had a dumbing-down effect. It made her unable to understand a simple distinction between cooperators and collaborators.

The trans-Atlantic slave trade was also a cooperative effort. Africans forcibly rounded up other Africans, driving them to the coast where they were sold to Europeans. And slavery, as well as the buying and selling of slaves, was a feature of life in Africa, and India, and many other regions before the incursion of Europeans.

What I have just said about slavery is not disputed by anyone with a minimum of historical knowledge. Yet I have encountered students at elite universities who don't know these facts. And because they don't know them, they are more receptive to ideologies that blame all the ills of the world on White people. Since (fortunately) not everybody buys that view, the result is divisiveness that undermines We the People, a shared American identity.

When I made the observation that the Atlantic slave trade involved the cooperation of Africans, a student said: "Yes, but that was because of colonialism." I replied that this cooperation occurred before the Western African region from which most slaves were taken was colonized. My surmise is that her response was due to the fact that she had swallowed an ideology that attributed all bad things to White people or to colonization by White people.

The point is that this type of White Devil or European-bashing ideology is inherently divisive; it contributes to the death of We the People, dividing the American population into those who recognize that the history of America is nothing more than the story of White oppression and those who deny that history and thereby remain complicitous in "social injustice." It directly attacks the idea that there is a history of our country that we can all take some measure of pride in (even while recognizing its negative aspects).

Ideologically Induced Stupidity about History

I had a personal encounter with this one-sided, Western-culture-bashing, self-loathing ideology at a meeting of the American Philosophical Association. I was giving a talk on moral progress and cited the abolition of slavery in the British Empire as an example. In the discussion period a middle-aged White fellow, presumably a Philosophy professor, said "Yes, but Europeans invented slavery."

This public display of gross ignorance left me speechless for a moment. I recovered and asked him if he'd ever read an old but still popular book called the Bible in which such thorny questions as "May one sell one's daughter as a slave?" are considered. I went on to point out something that every minimally educated person should know, namely, that freedom, not slavery, has been the "peculiar institution" throughout history, until quite recently.

Many non-Western people had slaves. That includes Native Americans. The Commanche Empire, for example, was built on raiding and trading, including trading and selling human beings captured in raids conducted primarily for that purpose.

Understanding the nature of Commanche society is important for resisting the myth that things were just fine until Whites invaded the territory of indigenous peoples. In fact, given the facts about the Commanche way of life, it's a bit misleading to say that Whites invaded traditional Commanche territory, as if there was some clearly bounded locale where they resided and where they engaged in non-parasitic, non-exploitive, peaceful cooperation. That's misleading because Commanche territory, if you can call it that, encompassed all areas within the limits of Commanche raids (which sometimes covered several hundred miles), all of the areas in which they could forcibly steal other people and other people's goods and engage in their practice of torturing people to death.

An accurate understanding of European colonialism and of the treatment of Native Americans by White people is damning enough. There were genocides and other atrocities. There is no need to exaggerate the horrors or to pretend that nothing remotely like them has ever been perpetuated by non-Whites or non-Europeans—especially when doing so erects obstacles to achieving the kind of unity that democracy requires.

Ideologically Distorted Views of History and Identity

What accounts for this kind of ideological distortion and this utter obliviousness to basic facts? Surely, the explanation must be quite different from that of ideologies that portray the Other in a negative, rather than an overly positive light, and that portray Europeans or Whites as the source of all that is good. How could standard ideologies that demonize the Other and praise Us and ideologies that demonize Us and praise the Other have the same cause?

Strange as may seem, they have the same cause. The explanation at bottom is the same for both Other-bashing and self-bashing tribalistic ideologies: identity drives both kinds of misperceptions, one-sidedly negative and one-sidedly positive.

Why for so long did anthropologists and many ordinary people romanticize and idealize pre-modern cultures and by comparison denigrate their own? One part of the explanation may be that they felt that their own culture was deficient and that they were dissatisfied with their identity as modern people or, more specifically, people living in a capitalist society. If you lament the breakdown of community, the prevalence of hyper-individualism, the mania for consumption goods, and the lack of agreement on basic values that are said to be characteristic of modern, capitalistic societies, you may naturally look to pre-modern societies with longing. If you feel that sense of alienation or what the sociologist Durkheim called "anomie" that is supposed to be uniquely modern, you will yearn for a world in which there was no such thing. In other words, the falsified, overly rosy perception of pre-modern societies that we project onto them may largely be a case of motivated reasoning: believing something because you want to believe it, because believing it makes you feel good (or in this case less bad), not because the preponderance of evidence, impartially considered, supports it.

This identity-based explanation of the psychological roots of mistaken factual beliefs about pre-modern societies has an important advantage. It explains why the romanticized, idealized pro-indigenous ideology is more prevalent among people on the Left. It's because they are especially critical of capitalism, a fundamental feature of modernity. My suggestion, then, is that for people on the political Left, their broader political ideology makes them receptive to the bogus pro-indigenous ideology—or rather that the latter is one aspect of the former.

Of course, Conservatives also have their own complaints about modern society—its disregard of tradition, its lack of agreement on basic values, and its tendency to not take authority seriously. So, it may be that the prevalence of the myths of primitive harmony among anthropologists wasn't just due to the preponderance of Liberals in academy in general. Maybe it was the result of a rare convergence: the shared belief on the part of Liberals and Conservatives in the discipline that pre-modern societies had to be superior in some respects, because they weren't afflicted by the maladies peculiar to modern societies. In other words, both Liberals and Conservatives tend to be dissatisfied with their identities as modern people or people living in capitalistic societies and that may have led them to idealize pre-modern, non-capitalistic societies. And that may be the case despite the fact that Liberals and Conservatives have different views about what's wrong with modern societies.

Why have I gone into considerable detail to show that there is egregious fact denying on the Left as well as the Right? I've done that to make it clear that *there can be no We the People if there are intractable ideological disagreements regarding the basic facts about the country, its history, and its role in the history of the world.*

Two Opposing Tribalistic Ideologies That Help Destroy National Unity

More specifically, to be a people we must have enough agreement on those facts to feel that we have a common heritage in which we can take some measure of pride and a future that will have some features we all will regard as valuable. Tribalistic ideologies are undermining that agreement. Consider two radically different understandings of the history of the United States and its role in the world.

Tribalistic Ideology No. 1: The Extreme Wokish **Umwelt**

The history of this country is little more than the story of a massive experiment in social injustice. America has always been and continues to be a single-minded, key player in the world-wide oppression wrought by White people. All you need to know about our institutions, all that really matters, is that they are racist. If we are to take rightful pride in our country, it will not be pride in its history; it will be pride in overcoming its history.

Tribalistic Ideology No. 2: The Extreme Conservative **Umwelt**

American history is the story of a glorious experiment in freedom. America is, and always has been "the land of the free." Its unique role in the world has been that of a beacon of hope, encouraging the expansion of freedom in other countries, and defending freedom against its enemies. The problem of racial injustice, the one significant departure from the ideal of freedom for all, was solved, if not by the abolition of slavery, at least with the passing of the Voting Rights and Civil Rights Acts of 1964–1965. There is no such thing as systematic, institutionalized racism in the United States. People of color and women are no longer subjected to serious discrimination; instead, they are given special privileges and accorded advantages in employment and admission to universities that violate the core American values of merit and equal opportunity. Liberals are threatening to demolish the freedoms Americans enjoy and to make America incapable of continuing to play its unique role as the exemplar and defender of freedom in the world.

The point is that both of these visions of America are grounded not just in false factual claims, but also in factual claims whose falsity is not hard to determine—if you can see the world without a tribalistic ideological lens.

In the extreme Leftist political *Umvelt*, nothing is visible in the history of the country and the current functioning of institutions but racism (or racism and sexism); in the equally extreme Rightist political *Umvelt*, nothing is visible but the triumph of freedom (and the threat Liberals pose to it).

Such a profound disparity in perceived realities—such a disjuncture of political *Umwelten*—makes the idea of a single American people a fantasy. In other words, it's hard to see how there can be one American people if Americans disagree so profoundly about what their country is and what it's role in the world has been. How can we be one people if half of us think we are living in the land of the free, a beacon of hope for all mankind, and the other half think we are living in the land of thorough-going racism, the most potent example of global oppression?

Those who live in these starkly opposed realities have ideologies whose maps are so different that they contain no common landmarks. There's no ground on which to agree to meet to try to reach principled agreement or even a *modus vivendi*, a begrudging peace or at least a cease fire between parties who both regard it as a second-best when they've concluded that victory isn't possible.

How Tribalistic Ideologies Erode the Commitment to Democracy

So far, I've described the ways in which tribalistic ideologies destroy We the People and I've identified some of the consequences of this loss of national unity. There's another, related harm the destruction of We the People inflicts on us that I haven't noted so far: it undermines the *commitment* to democracy. If democracy is to work, enough people must be willing to bear costs to make it work. If they regard themselves as parts of a people, they will be willing to bear costs; that they wouldn't be willing to bear if they didn't think there was a people, but instead only a permanently divided population or two different peoples locked in mortal combat with one another. For example, if you're committed to democracy, to helping We the People (all of us) govern ourselves, you won't try to foster division; nor will you lie or cheat to achieve victory on disputed political issues, even though this is costly, even though it disadvantages you, even if you could achieve more political success if you didn't constrain yourself in these ways and incur the costs that entails. And you will accept the cost of not always getting your way. One reason you'll accept those costs is that you will believe that if you lose on this issue today, you'll win on something equally important tomorrow. It's hard to sustain that belief if you don't trust your political opponents to behave decently and think they are incapable of playing the political game fairly. It's also hard to sustain the "we'll win on another day" attitude if you think Armageddon is here and now and there won't be another day if you lose.

If you think that the opposition is not part of the people, or that there is no one people, but rather two inherently opposed peoples locked in a zero-sum, winner-take-all conflict for the highest stakes, you won't just think that lying and cheating are justified; *you'll think they are morally mandatory*. You won't be willing to bear the costs of refraining from lying and cheating because you'll regard lying and cheating as necessary if your tribe is to prevail in this Supreme Emergency situation.

If enough people are like you, unwilling to bear the costs of moral restraint that must be borne if democracy is to work, democracy will fail. Being committed to your tribe's total political victory, no matter what that takes, is incompatible with being committed to democracy.

How Tribalistic Ideologies Undermine Democracy by Destroying the Psychological Conditions for Bargaining and Compromise

There is one more, equally serious blow that tribalistic ideologies strike against democracy. As I suggested earlier, their essentialized, deterministic stereotype of the Other combined with their Supreme Emergency framing make bargaining and compromise impossible. But bargaining and compromise are necessary for democracy. If all of the members of the opposing group are the same and their behavior is rigidly determined by their shared essence, and that behavior is utterly unacceptable to us and diametrically opposed to our good, then there is no prospect for finding common ground, no hope of a mutually acceptable and beneficial compromise. And because the war that politics has become is all-encompassing, any concession made for the sake of a compromise or to strike a bargain might be fatal.

What I've said in this chapter leads unavoidably to a grim conclusion: unless the grip of tribalistic ideologies is broken, it is unlikely that democracy can survive. It's a gross understatement, then, to say that tribalism has lowered the standard for political behavior and made people acquiesce in the most indecent behavior by their political leaders. If that was all there was to it, democracy might survive, though in a rather seedy form. The more serious problem is that tribalistic ideologies systematically destroy the necessary conditions for democracy, including preeminently the sense that we are one people, engaged in a project of self-governance where the self includes all of us.

It's often been said that democracies typically fail from internal causes, that they don't succumb to attacks from without, but instead rot from the inside. In this chapter, I've explained how tribalistic ideologies can destroy democracy without an invasion, but also without a coup, and without abandoning the legal forms of democracy. The death of democracy doesn't begin with a deterioration of our institutions; that comes later, after we first corrupt ourselves. Our democracy is failing because, by turning our most admirable cognitive abilities against themselves and making our moral motivation the engine of immorality, we have become the kind of creatures that are no longer capable of making democracy work.

You might think that the growing might of China is the greatest threat to democracy, at least so long as that country continues to reject the very idea of human rights and to embrace authoritarian rule. Perhaps, but we won't have a chance of countering that threat if we are no longer a people. That's one more reason why the enemy within us is the most dangerous enemy of democracy.

Notes

1 "Internet Modern History Sourcebook Abbé Sieyes: What Is the Third Estate?, Excerpts." Fordham University, n.d. https://sourcebooks.fordham.edu/mod/sieyes.asp.
2 Lilliana Mason, *Uncivil Agreement: How Politics Became Our Identity*. Chicago, IL: The University of Chicago Press, 2018.
3 "Jack Murphy, "Jack Murphy Live." JD Vance – JML #070, 2021.
4 *The Civil War*. Directed by Ken Burns, Documentary Series, 1990.
5 Michael Tomasello, *A Natural History of Human Morality*. First Harvard University Press paperback ed. Cambridge, MA: Harvard University Press, 2018.
6 Jérôme Viala-Gaudefroy, "Why Do Millions of Americans Believe the 2020 Presidential Election Was 'Stolen' from Donald Trump?" *The Conversation*, March 3, 2024. http://theconversation.com/why-do-millions-of-americans-believe-the-2020-presidential-election-was-stolen-from-donald-trump-224016.
7 Farnoush Amiri, "Less than Half of GOP Say Jan. 6 Was Very Violent, AP-NORC Poll." *PBS News*, January 4, 2022. https://www.pbs.org/newshour/politics/less-than-half-of-gop-say-jan-6-was-very-violent-ap-norc-poll.
8 Jared Diamond, *Collapse: How Societies Choose to Fail or Succeed*. Harmondsworth: Penguin Books, 2006.
9 Elizabeth Marshall Thomas, *The Harmless People*. Revised ed., 2nd Vintage Books ed. New York: Vintage Books, 1989.
10 Leif Wenar, *Blood Oil: Tyrants, Violence, and the Rules That Run the World*. Oxford and New York: Oxford University Press, 2017.
11 Nothing I've said should be taken as denying the wrongness of European colonialism. In my view, there were many wrongs, but the most serious were these: severe economic exploitation and practices of humiliation. Both were rooted in the belief that Europeans were superior beings.
12 Christopher Minster, "Cortez and His Tlaxcalan Allies." *ThoughtCo.* Updated October 1, 2019.

5

SOCIAL MEDIA AS A MASKED IDENTITY FASHION SHOW

Is Social Media the Main Culprit?

For any book on tribalism, bemoaning the pernicious effects of media is obligatory. I'm not going to blame the media; I'm going to blame us for how we use it. And I'll say some new things not only about how we use it but also about why we use it in the way we do. First, let me relate an incident that led me to think harder about how the internet, especially social media, fuels tribalistic ideologies, and made me appreciate just how hard it is for people to limit their use of social media.

Studies show that, when college students have their devices open during class, a substantial percentage of the time (over 20%) what they are viewing has no connection to the lecture or course material. Just as disturbingly, a study at a liberal arts college found that female undergrads spend an average of ten hours a day on their cell phones, while males "only" spend eight hours.[1] I think it's unlikely that they are talking about course material most of that time.

Because I was worried by these statistics and thought that in-class internet surfing meant that the parents of my students weren't getting their money's worth (being an undergraduate at that university costs around $90,000 a year), I did an experiment. In the middle of a lecture, I asked my students to raise both hands above their heads and keep them there. I then went around the room checking out what was on their screens: one case of internet porn, four cases of Facebook, two of Instagram, two emails, three Tweets, two Amazon shopping expeditions, one case of a Wikipedia search for a term I had just used in the lecture, eight

DOI: 10.4324/9781003612469-6

cases of notes on the lecture or texts from the course reading list, and five screen savers.

After reporting the results of the experiment to my students, I announced a new policy: for the remainder of the semester, you can keep your devices open during class, but if you do, at the end of each class, before you leave the room, you have to send me an email attachment with detailed notes on what went on in class. I will randomly inspect these notes and if they are deficient, your semester grade will be lowered by as much as 40%.

All but one student elected to keep their devices closed. She produced excellent notes. And by the way, several students thanked me for forcing them to escape their social media prison, if only for three hours a week.

Why Are We in Voluntary Servitude to Social Media?

What makes people so willing to spend so much time online when they know it's not good for them? Why do they persist in a condition of "voluntary servitude" to social media? Why do a lot of students squander their educational opportunities by cruising the internet in class or devoting more time to social media than to their studies? I'll try to answer those questions in this chapter, but first I want to note some rather obvious facts about social media and then reject the common wisdom about the media and their role in polarization and tribalism.

The most obvious point about the role of the media in the destruction wrought by tribalistic ideologies is quite simple: media—I mean primarily current electronic, web-based social media—allows for the rapid and wide dissemination of ideological beliefs. In terms of spreading the word, current media is as superior to print media as print media is to smoke signals. Another obvious point: that type of media allows you to choose what "information" you are exposed to and avoid what you don't like, and that means that your choices can simply reinforce your ideological biases. But there is a lot more to it than that.

In fact, the media exacerbate all the negative features of tribalistic ideologies I've described in the preceding four chapters. How do they do that? Mainly by allowing people to engage in communication that looks like the sharing of information about things unrelated to identity, but is really all about sorting and signaling, affirming their identities, and presenting themselves in ways that they think will elicit approval, which in turn will help them feel good about themselves. In brief, a great deal of internet traffic is the verbal equivalent of sharing "selfie" photographs.

Before explaining how that works, I want to ponder the limitations of a very common explanation of the media's contribution to tribalistic ideology. The story goes like this. Current media allow individuals to choose their political reality by electing to inhabit information "silos," internet sites frequented by people who have the same political views they do. When they do this, some research purports to show that two things happen: their political beliefs become more extreme and they become more inflexible, even less responsive to disconfirming evidence or experience.[2]

As an explanation of *why* ideological beliefs are so inflexible, this is not very convincing. If we are always in a silo, we will seldom hear any challenges to our views and therefore never have to develop any rejoinders to them, since they wouldn't be needed. But we aren't always in our silos and silo walls aren't impenetrable. If some challenging information does reach us, we'll be at loss for how to counter it because we'll have had no experience in defending our views against criticism, and that could result in doubting the belief rather than vigorously affirming it, as the silo story says.

We've already seen that there's a much more convincing explanation of the rigidity of certain beliefs. Beliefs are extraordinarily rigid when challenges to them are perceived to be threats to one's most important, most encompassing identity.

There's another respect in which the emphasis on identity is superior to the standard silo story: it explains why people inhabit silos. They do so because being in the company of those who share your identity affirms your identity, in two ways. First, by making you feel that you are not alone, which is very important because the kind of identity we are talking about is a "we-identity," one that involves membership in a group. Second, by providing an environment in which your identity will be valued, where how you present yourself will be approved of and even admired.

The identity-affirming property of silos explains why people who inhabit them continue to do so even when they know about the studies that show that doing so makes their views more extreme and irrationally rigid. In Chapter 3 we saw how people abandon the pursuit of truth in favor of the sorting and signaling behavior that is motivated ultimately by the need to protect and affirm identity. Staying in a silo when you know damned well you shouldn't is just another case where the desperate need to protect your identity and have it affirmed by others wins out over the commitment to truth.

There's another account of the role the media plays in the flourishing of tribalistic ideologies that's also worth stating—and debunking. It's the view that most people are extremely gullible, and that modern media provide powerful resources for exploiting that vulnerability.

In a fascinating and well-argued book titled *Not Born Yesterday*, Hugo Mercier marshals solid evidence to refute the claim that people in general are highly gullible.[3] In addition to listing many instances when people aren't gullible, he argues that "The logic of evolution makes it virtually impossible for gullibility to be a stable trait." Why? Because "Gullible individuals would be taken advantage of until they stopped paying attention to messages" and that would be the end of gullibility. In other words, widespread, extreme gullibility isn't an evolutionarily stable trait.

Mercier goes on to describe what he calls the "mechanisms of open vigilance," defenses humans have developed to prevent being duped. The open part means we don't try to avoid communications from others; the vigilance part means we are smart enough to be on our guard.

I think Mercier's argument is compelling. But it's compatible with there being an important limitation on our tendency not to be gullible. More specifically, it's compatible with our vigilance mechanisms being switched off or becoming less effective when tribalistic ideological beliefs link what we are hearing or reading to our identity. If we interpret what someone says or what we read on some internet site as a signal that they are one of Us and if what they say counters perceived threats to our identity, we are likely to believe them, even if what they say is quite implausible. That's compatible with our vigilance mechanism generally being effective across a wide range of other contexts. Notice that this fits the general point I've been making about tribalistic ideologies: they disable normal cognitive functions, but in a selective way. In this case the normal cognitive function is the operation of our open vigilance mechanisms when our identity is threatened, not across the board.

Selfie-Mania and Identity-Anxiety

A recent experience I had while waiting at the gate prior to boarding a flight produced a eureka moment in my attempt to understand the connection between tribalistic ideologies, identity, and social media. I noticed a young woman sitting across from me. She kept taking selfies with her Iphone, more than a dozen of them in a period of just 20 minutes, posing in various ways, sometimes seductive, sometimes cheerful, sometimes playful, and sometimes pensive. After each push of her cell phone camera button, she would scrutinize the result. When it met her approval, her face lit up with a combination of pride and satisfaction, and she immediately posted that selfie. She was clearly experimenting with how she wanted others to see her, with the visual presentation of alternative selves. But she was also trying hard to determine which self, which identity, *she* found most satisfying.

There was a whiff of desperation in her behavior. It seemed as if she would have continued to take selfies indefinitely had she not hit on some she approved of—and thought others would approve of. I was reminded of a famous experiment in which rats who have been conditioned to press a bar to stimulate their pleasure centers continued to do so until they collapsed from exhaustion or died of a heart attack.

Here's a hypothesis: self-esteem, and more specifically, feeling secure about your identity, and frequency of selfies are inversely correlated. The less secure you are, the more selfies you take, other things being equal. In other words, I doubt that people who are secure in and satisfied with their identity are likely to take selfies as frequently as those who have anxieties about their identity. The fact that so many people take so many selfies suggests that identity-anxiety is pretty prevalent. The key point is that social media have become a venue for trying out identities to see how those whose approval matters to us respond and whether we ourselves find them satisfying.[4]

We now have an explanation of why using web-based technologies to post literal "selfies," carefully posed, flattering photographs of oneself, is so popular. The explanation *isn't* that we are experiencing an epidemic of narcissism. It's that for a variety of reasons people are experiencing identity-anxiety and are desperately seeking assurance that the identity they've opted for is optimal, from their own standpoint and in the eyes of others. Tribalistic ideologies respond to that desperate need and the media provide the mechanism by which they satisfy it. Social media have one huge, unique advantage when it comes to experimenting with identities: they make it virtually costless, almost risk free.[5]

Here's how selfies, literal or otherwise, relate to tribalistic ideologies: ideologies guide the choice of "try-on" identities and the choice of venues to exhibit them. If you have a particular tribalistic ideology, certain identity options will be salient because they fit well with the ideology and others will be excluded because they aren't consistent with it or are devalued by it. And since ideologies help form group identities, in part by providing cues for distinguishing Us from Them, they supply guidance for which media sites are frequented by your group and hence are likely to approve of your try-on identities.

The Social Media Fashion Show

Think of social media as a venue for a vast fashion show in which we can all tread the various runways multiple times, wearing different outfits, seeing how we look in mirrors all along the walls, and noting how others respond to the various outfits.

But here's the crucial difference between the social media fashion show and your ordinary fashion show: in the social media case, you can wear a mask. You can control how the audience sees you, or rather which you they see. You can choose among multiple masks. You can also choose your audience is, by doing your identity try-ons on certain media sites and not others. But in any case, you'll be making choices, deliberate or not, as to how you will present yourself. In that sense, masks are inevitable, even when not deliberately chosen as masks. More importantly, you can shape the sort of response you're likely to get to the way you present yourself by choosing which internet audience to present yourself to, where you post your literal and figurative selfies.

If your costume doesn't elicit approval from the audience (or the segment of the audience whose approval matters to you), you needn't suffer a reputational loss. Social media give you the option of shielding your real-life identity when you try on alternative internet identities.

There's another unique feature of internet identity experimentation: the range of alternative identities you can try on is not limited in the way identity experimentation in real life is. In real life, I can't convincingly present myself as a Black NBA star, but I can do it on the internet, at least for a while.

Anyone who's tried online dating will understand what I'm talking about. But notice that there is a difference between online dating self-presentations and ordinary social media self-presentations. In online dating there's the expectation that if you find a good match you will eventually meet them in person. That sobering prospect limits the misrepresentations of yourself you're likely to indulge in. Not so with your Facebook or Twitter self-presentation or with Instagram if you are adept at photoshopping. You may never meet most of your followers.

A Fashion Show where Moral Restraints Are Disabled

The fact that you can wear a mask on the internet fashion runway also explains why some people say nasty, hurtful, outrageous things online that they would never say in person. The mask shields you from disapproval and from experiencing shame. And the fact that you can choose a runway where the audience shares your values and beliefs means you can be nasty without being disapproved of by people whose opinion matters to you, so long as the nastiness targets those your group regards as the enemy.[6]

Anthropologists and psychologists who think in evolutionary terms tell us that disapproval and shame are extremely powerful forces for making us conform to moral rules and rules of etiquette, good manners. Conscience is important, too, of course, and so is the threat of punishment. But no society would work very well if people didn't care when others violate moral rules and if the disapproval of others didn't make us feel ashamed. (If that's so, it's worrisome that current Wokish ideology seems to be saying that shaming is always wrong—except when you are shaming people you classify as among the oppressors. But that's a subject for another book.)

The option of anonymity (or a false identity) and the ability to choose your audience in internet self-presentations make shaming less effective. That's serious, because shaming is one of the most powerful forces for making morality work and for the cooperation it facilitates. The reduction of the risk of being shamed means that online we can be as morally unconstrained as our remote primate ancestors whose bad behavior was not held in check by shaming practices.

Chimpanzees are much worse at inhibiting violent impulses than humans are. One reason for this is that they can't make each other feel ashamed when they act badly. As they are, so lacking in violent impulse control, chimpanzees are very dangerous. If they maintained their inability to control violent impulses but became as intelligent as we are and had speech, they'd be a lot more dangerous (that's the plot of *Planet of the Apes*). Online, we can behave the way chimpanzees would if they'd been re-engineered to have speech and sophisticated cognitive abilities but weren't constrained by the shaming practices humans benefit from in real life.

There's good reason to think that our remote ancestors were as bad as chimps are, so far as violent behavior goes—until they eventually developed various means of "self-domestication," including shaming. Social media turn back the evolutionary clock by neutralizing some of our means for moderating violent or nasty behavior, including shaming.

One way you can avoid being shamed is by steering away from social media sites populated by those who would find your behavior shameful. Shaming is only one of several social practices humans have developed to constrain morally wrong or nasty behavior—and that are less effective when we inhabit social media.

I want to emphasize that anonymity or using false identities aren't the only, or the most important, ways social media allow us to avoid shame. You can say shameful things and not be shamed if you choose your internet audience in the right way. On sites where most everyone agrees with you, you can say things you ought to be ashamed of without being called out. My main point is that, in less than a generation, we've developed communication technology which, in the context of tribalistic ideologies, reduces the effectiveness of beneficial, morally justified shaming, a powerful "moral technology" that took eons of evolution to develop.

Now we can see why it's incorrect to say, as most theorists of tribalism do, that people behave especially badly online because they inhabit silos that make their political views more extreme. That diagnosis is seriously incomplete; it overlooks a crucial fact: even strong motivation to act immorally can be neutralized, if the costs of behaving immorally are high enough. The core of the explanation for why behavior online is often so nasty, ill-mannered, and aggressive is that the normal constraints on immoral behavior that took hundreds of thousands of years to evolve, including shaming, can be removed or made less effective the moment you go online. In other words, the problem with the internet is that it renders negligible the costs that humans have developed to inhibit bad behavior. To act worse than we did in pre-web days, we don't have to have abandoned morality; we just have to be subjected to fewer constraints. In economic terms, the internet has drastically lowered the costs of bad behavior—and when the cost of something goes down, people can afford more of it.

Please don't misunderstand me! I'm not saying that social media eliminates shaming. On the contrary, people use it to try to shame those they regard as the dangerous, unreasonable Other. In fact, social media make it easier and less costly to engage in shaming behavior. My point is that people in the grip of tribalistic ideologies can use social media in ways that make shaming a less effective means for restraining their own bad behavior. One consequence of this is that they can engage in shameful shaming of other people, without being subject to appropriate shaming themselves.

Escaping the Burdens of Acting Decently

There's something else the internet does for us—or rather something else we use it to do: it frees us of the psychological burdens of behaving morally and with good manners. At times the moral constraints of real life are burdensome for most of us. So are the demands of good manners.

The socially enforced moral rules say you can't do this and you must do that—in spite of the fact that the voice of self-interest tells you to do otherwise. In fact, morality is so good at facilitating cooperation and reducing destructive conflicts among people who share a morality precisely because it constrains self-interest.

The Seventh Commandment tells you not to commit adultery even if you have a burning desire to do so. Like other moral rules, it demands that you not do what you want to do; in that sense it prohibits self-interested behavior. It's less obvious, but equally true that manners impose constraints on self-interest that are burdensome. The brilliant sociologist Norbert Elias (whom Steven Pinker described as the smartest guy you never heard of) argues that table manners are meant to inhibit greedy self-interested behavior and, more importantly, to signal to those around you that you can constrain your greedy impulses. That's why you pass the food on to others before taking your portion, don't take seconds till everyone else has been served, and consume your soup by moving your spoon outward in the bowl instead of toward you, eagerly shoveling the liquid into your gaping mouth.[7]

Elias's big point is that it's very important not just for people to inhibit their self-interested impulses, but also to signal to others that they can do so. Failure to give a convincing signal that you follow rules that constrain your self-interest can result in your being excluded from cooperation or even in preemptive violence against you. Think about the custom of shaking hands with strangers. When your arm is extended and your palm is open, it is clear you are not in fighting mode. Depending on the circumstances, the costs of inhibiting your self-interested impulses and effectively signaling to others that you are doing so can be fairly substantial. If those costs were very high and the costs of not inhibiting your self-interested impulses were very low, most of us would probably act quite differently.

So far, so good. Now we understand how the option of internet anonymity (or false identities) and the ability to choose your tribal audience unleash self-interest and aggressive impulses that shaming and other social practices constrain in real life. And we've seen that this has its attractions, including relief from the burdens of morality and good manners. We also now understand that the internet provides an ideal venue for affirming and exploring identities, because it has become the site of a masked identity fashion show. But we still don't know the answer to the billion dollar question: why are so many people so anxious about their identities that they spend remarkable amounts of time and energy constructing and projecting them?

Disappointingly, though a lot of books on tribalism or polarization claim that the quest for identity and identity-approval is the heart of the matter, they typically don't pose much less answer this fundamental question. I won't pretend to give a comprehensive answer, but I will offer what I think are the two most important parts of an answer. The first is an evolutionary account of why identity, especially identity that includes a prominent moral element, is so important to us. The answer has to do with the connection between moral identity and cooperation and the fact that people need to be accepted as cooperators in order to survive; it explains why identity is so important to us. The second part is a history-based explanation of why so many people today experience anxiety about identity.

Why We Care about Our Identity

Let's begin with the evolutionary explanation of why our identity is so important to us. Cooperation requires restraining self-interest. Being seen by others as a reliable potential partner in cooperation, which requires the ability to restrain your self-interest, is vital for dependent beings like us. In contemporary forager (aka hunter-gatherer) groups and presumably in our remote ancestors who had that same way of life, exclusion from cooperation usually means death.

So, there were selective pressures to develop ways of behaving that effectively signaled that you were a reliable cooperator, that you could be trusted. It enhanced your reproductive fitness to be seen that way. A big part of being a reliable partner in cooperation is being someone who predictably follows the moral rules, especially those that facilitate cooperation by constraining self-interest. That means people had to see you as a moral person, someone who is committed to doing the right thing. If they didn't, you'd be excluded from cooperation, and that would generally be fatal. We evolved to care deeply about how others perceived our identity.

So far, we have an evolutionary explanation of why humans want to be *perceived* as being moral, in particular as beings who can keep their self-interest on a leash by following the moral rules. That accounts for why it is so desperately important for us to present ourselves to others as having not just an identity, but also a sound moral identity—as being someone who is committed to acting morally, even when that entails costs, in terms of the advancement of their interests, the satisfaction their desires.

There's one piece of the puzzle still missing: why do I care, not just whether others regard me as having an identity that features a commitment to morality but also about whether *I* can see myself that way? Why do we want to be moral, not just look like we're moral?

The answer has two parts. First, societies that flourish or even just survive are good at instilling a commitment to morality in their members. The individual's process of development, guided by the cultural practices of their society, results in the vast majority of people (sociopaths aside) wanting to be moral, not just to be perceived by others to be moral. Second, human beings have evolved pretty effective ways of detecting whether someone is trying to deceive them, in this case trying to appear to be moral when they aren't. And the costs of being unmasked as someone who is merely talking the talk but not walking the walk can be really high. In the forager groups where human morality originally evolved it can mean exclusion from cooperation, which was in effect a death sentence. Even today, where people have the option of moving from one cooperative scheme where they've been unmasked to another in hopes that people will mistake their feigning for the real thing, there's a risk in being exposed, because of the unlimited range of social media and easy internet access to public records.

Why Most of Us Should Want to Have a Good Moral Identity, Not Just to Seem Like We Do

Because humans are pretty good at detecting people who try to convince us that they are moral when they aren't, the best strategy for being regarded as someone with a wholesome moral identity and hence as a trustworthy partner in cooperation is not just to consistently do the right thing, but also actually to be moral, to do the right thing because its right. At least that's the best way for most of us. And being moral enough to be viewed as trustworthy isn't too terribly hard for most of us, most of the time, given that our development has been shaped by cultural practices that make us care about being moral for its own sake, not just because it makes us look good.

When you think about it, at least if you live in morality-friendly conditions, that is, where the costs of being moral aren't too high and you get rewarded for being moral, life is a lot easier than it is when you have to be constantly presenting yourself as something you aren't, feigning being moral when you aren't. Also, to have a good reputation, to be regarded as having a wholesome moral identity, you don't have to be a saint. You just have to be generally reliable, not perfect.

A person who is dedicated to feigning morality but acting in violation of the moral rules when it's in their interest to do so and they think they can get away with it has to live what might be called the thoroughly strategic life. The point is that being purely self-interested while appearing to be moral is a formidable task, one that requires being constantly in the calculating mode, always trying to figure out how to be immoral without being detected.

If you want a vivid fictional portrayal of the thoroughly strategic life, and how it drives out the pleasures of spontaneity, as well as the satisfaction of revealing yourself to others as you really are and being valued for who you are rather than for who they wrongly think you are, read Stendhal's wonderful novel, *The Red and the Black* (*Rouge et Noir*). The main character, Julien Sorel, idolizes Napoleon, has as his goal rising in the class structure of France in the 1830s, and accordingly approaches every aspect of his life, including his romantic endeavors, as if it were part of a well-planned military campaign. He turns out to be so good at presenting himself as something he's not and hiding his true motivations and feelings that he eventually becomes alienated from them. He no longer knows what he wants, only what he should want given his campaign plan. His attempt at the purely strategic life instrumentalizes everything and robs him of pleasure when he does achieve his strategic goals.

He becomes an object to be manipulated by himself and thereby loses any hope of having an authentic self, a genuine identity. One lesson to be drawn from this novel is that to have a genuine identity—a sense of yourself that is coherent and fulfilling—you have to present yourself to others in a way that reveals what you're really doing, what you're really about, what you're actually trying to achieve, and who you really are. If you dedicate yourself wholly to constantly wearing a mask, the risk is that the person behind the mask will disappear—you'll become the mask. That's Stendhal's point.

This literary illustration was chosen to support my claim that, for most of us, the best way to be regarded as a moral person is to be one (at least a good deal of the time). For most of us, that's more fulfilling than a life of deception. We've seen why it matters so much to us whether other people think we are moral, that we can be relied on to follow the moral rules. It's also important to most of us that we regard ourselves as morally sound. That's why tribalistic ideologies that present us as the good guys and sharply distinguish us from those awful other people are so appealing.

Given the evolutionary story about the connection between moral identity and being accepted as a cooperator, we now know why we care so much about our identity. But now need an answer to our second question: why is there nowadays so much anxiety over identity? Why do adults, not just adolescents, need to experiment with alternative identities, and why do so many people feel their identity needs affirming? Why aren't they confident enough, secure enough, that they don't need this constant affirmation?

The Causes of Identity-Anxiety

The first part of my answer is this: our society doesn't do as good a job of assigning and sustaining clear-cut, unambiguous identities—and limiting the options for identities—as societies used to. It doesn't have widely followed, prescribed practices, like rituals of manhood in tribal societies, that give you a definite, easily recognized identity and that reinforce that identity throughout your life. And, just as important, unlike traditional societies, our society has an expanding set of identities to choose from. In traditional societies, identities were largely assigned, not chosen; there was a limited number of them, and shifting from one to the other was either impossible or very costly.

Think about the numerous anthropological studies describing complex social practices that enable people to transition from childhood to adulthood or that make a young man a warrior or a young woman a wife. Often these rites of passage involve serious costs: ritual scarification, fasting, circumcision, etc. They do so in order to mark a strong and enduring distinction between those who have been initiated into a particular identity and those who haven't. But they also convey the message that the new status is so valuable that a painful admission ticket to it is warranted.

I don't know about you, but I made the transition from childhood to adulthood without anything approaching adequate social guidance. More specifically, neither my parents nor my teachers nor my pastor gave me much guidance for how to express my sexuality—and how to treat females respectfully in doing so. I think that's generally true in American society.

There are two extremes: effective social practices that assign and sustain a very limited number of well-defined, in some central cases mutually exclusive, identities, on the one hand, and a largely unstructured individual quest for identity with lots of options, on the other. Each arrangement has its pluses and minuses. The former is very hard on people who don't fit any of the clear-cut, limited options. The latter produces a lot of floundering and anxiety. The optimal arrangement would strike the right trade-off between social guidance and individual freedom.

I'm not suggesting that our society doesn't assign identities at all. I started out self-identifying and being identified by others as a White, Southern, protestant, German-American, for example. It's just that modern societies lack the resources for instilling durable identities in which people feel secure and for limiting the options for identity choices.

That's compatible with some of the identities it assigns being not chosen and irrevocable. I think that's true with being classified as an African American. Nonetheless, apart from ethnic exceptions like that and at least until recently, gender, I think it's accurate to say that, at least compared to traditional societies, contemporary American social practices exhibit a conspicuous absence of identity-assigning and -sustaining practices and allow for a good deal in the way of changing one's identity.

In traditional societies there are clear roles and orders of rank, and social status hierarchies that allocate identities. If you were a serf in Medieval Europe, there wasn't much in the way of identity options. (You remained a serf or you became an outlaw or you joined a monastery or a convent, but whatever you did you'd remain a commoner.) In societies that aren't that deterministic regarding identity assignment, but where religion is very powerful, the range of options for identity will still be highly constrained. If you are a devout Christian or Muslim or Jew, only some identities will be compatible with your faith. But in a society like ours, where powerful social practices for assigning and sustaining identities are lacking and many people are not religious, determining who you are or want to become is a real issue. And the fact that there are so many options and that exiting one identity to enter into another is no longer so costly means that any identity you opt for will be more fragile than the identities that traditional societies assigned. The possibility that there's a superior alternative out there somewhere can undermine your commitment to and satisfaction with the one you now have.

There may be an even more important source of identity-anxiety: the decline of communities, that is, real-world, face-to-face (not virtual) communities where people interact in physical proximity. In spite of their differences on other matters, some of the best thinkers on tribalism agree that a major factor in the spread of tribalistic ideologies is the fact that community-based identities and the satisfactions of community involvement are less available.[8]

There's a way to elaborate this hypothesis. Sociologists have made much of the breakdown of various communities in modern, advanced capitalist societies. Karl Marx was the first to make this point, but as with much else he typically doesn't get credit for it. His view was that "monetization" or the "commodification" of everything, which came with the spread of capitalism, dissolves traditional obligations and communal ties.[9] A classic contemporary work in this vein is *Bowling Alone* by Robert D. Putnam, which you've probably read or at least heard of. Putnam documents the decline of communities in America—and by "communities" he means face-to-face associations in which people interact in physical proximity to one another.

Community Membership and Identity Security

This is all relevant, because communities foster and sustain identities. When they break down, a sense of who you are and the perception that you are approved of by others whose opinion you care about can be seriously damaged. When you are in that predicament, you are ripe for being recruited into a tribalistic ideological group because that will give you a sense of shared identity.

For many people, their religious affiliation provided a valuable source of community, especially at the level of their membership in a particular church, a physical structure with a definite location in space where they regularly interacted face-to-face with people with whom they shared basic values. The decline of religion or at least of church going may therefore be a significant source of the identity-anxiety.

There may be a still deeper connection between the decline of religion and the spread of tribalistic ideologies: the latter for some people may have become a kind of substitute for religion, at least for the sort of religion that presents the world in Manichean, good vs. evil, saved versus damned terms. One indication that this may be so is the fact that the cognitive impairments that tribalistic ideologies cause, including rigid adherence to beliefs in the face of disconfirming evidence and the various forms of dumbing down discussed in the Introduction are manifested in extreme religious belief-processes.

Although I won't pursue the idea further here, I think it is worth asking whether tribalistic ideologies are in fact either a type of religious ideology or a close relative of religious ideologies. Whether that idea is plausible depends on how broadly you define religion or religious ideologies. If they need not feature belief in a supernatural being, then I think the case for saying that tribalistic ideologies for some people function as substitutes for religion or religious ideologies is quite strong. (Many consider Buddhism a religion, though on most interpretations, the major forms of Buddhism do not include clear references to a deity.) Some people may find that tribalistic ideologies satisfy some of the needs that religions formerly satisfied, but without the onerous obligations of traditional religions.

Another term for the breakdown of community, or rather, a consequence of it, is "social isolation." Because we are inherently social creatures, social isolation—lack of participation in meaningful communities—is distressing. Social media provide a kind of sham, or at best second-rate substitute for lost community, a seductive apparent antidote to the malady of social isolation. If, as I suspect, the "communities" in which one participates using social media are generally not as fulfilling as face-to-face communities, then the damage that social media do is far from being outweighed by its benefits, at least in terms of the yearning for community. It may be an exaggeration to say that virtual communities are to face-to-face ones like masturbating to internet porn is to sex with another person, but there's more than a grain of truth in that quip.

I'm not saying that virtual communities are worthless. Some are extremely valuable. Human rights activists scattered around the world are able to work more effectively because they can form communities on the internet. Here's a more humble example: I participate once a week for an hour and a half in each of two different book clubs that meet using Zoom. I find them very fulfilling. My point is not that virtual communities are bad; I just worry that virtual communities will become dominant, displacing face-to-face communities.

It's not just social media that can substitute for relationships in physical space with real, unmasked persons. Because of cheap, easily used electronic media, people can choose to stay at home and watch the sports channel rather than attend games with friends, and they watch excellent drama on Netflix or Amazon Prime Video or Britbox, rather than go to theaters where they will mingle with people they otherwise wouldn't meet. They can also take courses online and never sit in a classroom with other human beings. Electronic media has made us less dependent on community, not just for our sense of identity, but also for our entertainment, recreation, and even our education. That, too, has contributed to the decline of community and opened a space for promoters of tribalistic ideologies to enlist us in virtual communities in which the dominant identity is political.

Virtual versus Face-to-Face Communities

As you've no doubt noticed, I've sometimes contrasted traditional, face-to-face communities with the kind of group-membership constituted, largely through the use of social media. I've yielded to the temptation to describe the former as "genuine communities" and the latter as "sham communities" or "pseudo communities" or "second-rate communities." Those phrases imply what many people believe, namely, that real-world, offline, face-to-face interactions are generally more fulfilling or in some other way superior to the relationships that people who never physically encounter each other have online. Now, without denying that virtual communities can be valuable, I want to support that belief by highlighting some of the differences between these two quite different kinds of interactions and making the case that the differences make face-to-face interactions in physical space better, other things being equal. The purpose of this comparison isn't to show that virtual communities are worthless; it's to support my claim that we would lose a lot if virtual communities largely replaced face-to-face communities.

To identify relevant differences between the two kinds of communities, I'll draw on evolutionary theory and on the fact that human sociability, until very recently, has been overwhelmingly "embodied"—that it has been the interaction of beings with bodies who encounter one another in physical space. For embodied beings, physical proximity and physical contact are important for sociability. If you are active in a particular community, say one centered on a church or constituted by a voluntary group of the ordinary, traditional sort, you will interact physically with other members. You will greet them with a handshake or a hug. You will pat them on the back. You will handle objects together. You may literally rub shoulders with them while performing various practical tasks together. The embodied, physical nature of your interaction will be important for creating and sustaining communal bonds and it will contribute to the satisfaction you get from participating in the community. I find that virtual communities, including, Zoom groups, are more satisfying if they were preceded by face-to-face encounters. The fact that I have had lots of face-to-face interactions with the graduate students I mentor enriches my online interactions with them.

In fact, much of the communication that builds the trust and solidarity that are essential for community is not verbal. When you are in face-to-face relationships with people, your theory of mind has a wealth of material to work with, from the expression on people's faces, to the timbre, volume, and pace of their speech, to their posture and other body language. None of this is true of the vast majority of interactions on the internet.

The kind of socializing that builds community depends not just on our being embodied beings, but also upon some very special features of our bodies. Evolutionary anthropologists have noted an unusual physical trait of humans: the white sclera, that portion of the human eyeball surrounds the pupil. Most mammals don't have this. When you see another person's eyes, the white sclera enables you to see where they are looking. That can tell you a lot about their mental state, their intentions, whether they are averting their gaze because they are lying or ashamed, etc. If your whole eyeball was a dark color, I wouldn't be able to tell whether you were looking at me, at someone else, or just gazing distractedly into space. You don't have the cues that white sclera provides when you read someone's re-Tweet or their comment on a political internet site.

Scientists, especially those who specialize in the evolution of primates, also emphasize the importance for bonding and solidarity of certain forms of physical contact, and in particular, grooming behavior. Nowadays, literal grooming behavior among humans is largely limited to family members and particularly the behavior of parents toward children (combing their hair, washing them, etc.). But shaking hands, patting someone on the back, helping them carry a heavy object, all of these sorts of behaviors, are grooming from a functional point of view. They all serve to signal benign intentions and caring, and they all contribute to solidarity. They help to establish the bonding, the special attachments that are part of what it is to be a community.

What I am suggesting is that evolution has made us the kind of being that tends to experience the most robust and satisfying kinds of group relationships when we interact as embodied creatures, in physical proximity to one another. If that is so, then there is a very concrete sense in which, for humans, real-world, offline group associations are superior to the disembodied, anonymous, virtual group membership you experience on the internet. And that's why we need to think long and hard about how to structure our society in ways that encourage the kind of community that our evolved nature suits us for. Doing that will mean providing alternatives to tribalistic identities, so far as the latter are largely creatures of the "communities" constituted by electronic communications generally and social media in particular. In Chapter 6, my list of possible strategies for combatting tribalistic ideologies will include efforts to build new, face-to-face communities where people interact in physical proximity to one another, with actual physical contact. The hope is that eventually we will recognize the importance of face-to-face communities and make them a priority.

Too Many Choices

Another source of identity-anxiety is the plethora of available identities. Quite recently, advances in medicine have expanded the range of possible identities enormously: a person assigned the identity male at birth can now choose to transition to become a woman and *vice versa*. If genome-based biotechnology continues to develop, and is augmented by the power of synthetic biology, there will be more options. In the not-too-distant future, people may be able to choose identities, not just for their offspring, but also for themselves, that we wouldn't recognize as human identities. (I've explored this possibility in two books, *Beyond Humanity: The Promise and Perils of Biomedical Enhancement* and *Better than Human*.) More identity options will mean more choices we have to make, and more choices may mean more anxiety about making the right choices. And so far as the choices aren't limited or irrevocable, identity-anxiety will become a persisting fact of life.

There's another way to look at it. Our society is much freer than traditional societies. People aren't assigned rigid identities according to who their parents are and what class they are members of. They have the freedom to choose among many identity options. But with this freedom comes great uncertainty and the potential to make costly mistakes.

There's another, less obvious reason why many people today are anxious about their identities. Our world is rapidly changing, in unpredictable ways, and the rate of change seems to be accelerating, due in part to the rapid development of technologies. These technologies not only help create new economic relationships, but they also create new roles and occupations while making others obsolete. In doing so they also create some new identities and make others either infeasible or unsatisfying.

To put it differently, identities are relational in the sense that they are typically defined relative to a particular social environment or type of social environment. But if technological innovations are rapidly and unpredictably changing social environments, that means there will be increasing identity instability. And for some people that will mean severe anxiety. For example, in destroying some types of occupations, technology-driven globalization is threatening identities that are defined at least partially in terms of those occupations. Ideologies are adept at attributing such threats to deliberate predatory behavior by identified groups, rather than to structural changes.

Ironically, moral progress, not just technological progress, can contribute to identity-anxiety, too. At least in cases of moral progress involving the reduction of injustices grounded in the domination of some groups over others, progress lessens the status, social influence, and often the wealth of those in the dominating group. And these losses are rightly felt as threats to their identity. The victories of the civil rights movement lowered the status and reduced the social influence of Whites, just as improvements in women's rights lessened the power and prestige of men. It is not surprising that those losses of social status are often experienced as threats to identity, because that's precisely what they are.

Finally, as Jonathan Haidt, in *The Anxious Generation*, and many others have observed, the internet may exacerbate identity-anxiety by making it impossible to avoid the fact that there are people smarter, better looking, better dressed, more successful, and more popular than you are. Those largely unavoidable comparisons can make you dissatisfied with who you are.

The Sociability Hypothesis

I'm not alone in thinking that the obsession with identity is the most important driver of the current widespread, extremely time-consuming engagement with social media (and that constant engagement with social media makes one vulnerable to tribalistic ideologies). That's the perhaps the single most widely endorsed hypothesis among analysts who otherwise have quite different takes on tribalism. But there is another, simpler hypothesis worth considering: evolution has made us creatures who have a strong desire to socialize, and social media enable us to act on that desire cheaply and non-stop. Call this the sociability hypothesis. It's advanced in a marvelous book by Sinan Aral entitled *The Hype Machine*.[10]

The basic idea behind the sociability hypothesis is that the forces of natural selection have made us find interacting with other human beings very pleasurable. Because it's pleasurable, we spend a lot of time socializing and always have. The difference is that now we have technology that allows us to socialize with so many more people, so much more frequently, with so much less effort and costs.

Why was there selection for this trait? The answer is simple: socializing is good for us from the standpoint of reproductive fitness. Humans only do well enough to succeed in reproducing themselves if they cooperate with one another. Socializing fosters the trust and solidarity needed for cooperation and cooperation enhances reproductive fitness.

I think the evolutionary story is a plausible explanation of why we like to socialize. I think it has a big drawback as a hypothesis to explain how we actually use social media and why we spend so much time on social media sites. It doesn't explain the particular kind of sociability that dominates social media use, namely, sharing the ubiquitous verbal and video selfies, participating in the great masked fashion show. Sociability can take many forms. So, the sociability hypothesis by itself isn't capable of explaining what may be the most important feature of social media use: the obsession with identity. Of course, those who emphasize the basic desire for social-izing, like Aran, can acknowledge that the hypothesis needs to be modified, made more specific, by adding that the chief kind of socializing we do on social media revolves around the presentation of identities.

Not Just Grooming

That's still not enough, however. We also need to explain why there's so much nasty, aggressive, tribalistic socializing. Among primates, grooming is a major form of socializing. But if social media use is akin to human grooming, it's quite anomalous. When chimps groom, they pick lice and debris off of each other, thereby exhibiting concern for and approval of the one they groom. Social media grooming, if that's the right metaphor, includes analogs of that in our behavior toward members of our group, but in far too many cases, it's more a matter of throwing lice or debris (or feces) at the Other. The grooming metaphor, as an elaboration of the socializing hypothesis, helps explain nice behavior in social media use, but not nasty behavior.

That's where the idea that this sort of behavior is a reaction to per-ceived threats to identity comes in. That idea explains why social media socializing is often bashing the out-group, not just stroking our group. The bottom line is that the hypothesis that evolution made us enjoy socializing explains why we find a powerful technology for socializing attractive, but it doesn't explain why we use that technology the way we do. To explain that we need the concept of identity-anxiety. That concept helps explain both positive, grooming-like behavior and nasty behavior.

Now we know why identity is so important to us (the evolutionary story about cooperation explains that) and why there's currently so much identity-anxiety (there are several explanatory factors, including the loss of communities that previously provided satisfying, stable identities; the plethora of identity options; and threats to identity caused by technologi-cal or moral progress). But here's what we still don't know: why, for so many people, are their various identities bundled together in such a way that their political identity is in charge? Or to put it differently, why do so many of us react as if challenges to our political beliefs are challenges to everything important about ourselves? I began to answer that question in the Introduction, when I noted how the two-party system and the first past the post electoral arrangement give politicians incentives to foster identity bundling. I want to fill that explanation out now by exploring a related question: why is the political aspect of identity-bundles so important to people; or, why do tribalistic political ideologies tie the elements of the bundles together in a way that makes the political aspect of one's complex identity so salient and important?

I don't pretend to have complete answers to those questions, but I think I do have a significant part of them. In my view, there are at least two factors contributing to the pervasiveness of identity-bundles in which political identity is dominant: (1) most everyone has more than one identity or, if you prefer, has a multi-dimensional identity (you may think of yourself as a business person and as a parent, etc.), and (2) tribalistic ideologies, by promoting the idea of an all-encompassing zero-sum, highest-stakes struggle for political power, subordinate all identities or dimensions of identity to the dominance of the political. Tribalistic ideologies don't create multiple identities or multiple dimensions of identity, but they unify them under the dominance of the political. They transform identities that are not essentially political into facets of political identity by linking them to the no-holds-barred, highest-stakes, zero-sum struggle.

Political identity entrepreneurs exploit and magnify this tendency of tribalistic ideologies. In a two-party system like that of the United States, politicians in both parties have an interest in getting people to connect their various identities into a package and make all of the bundled identities political or at least connected to a political identity. That's because politically dominated and connected bundled identities have two advantages from their standpoint. First, they make a person's political identity more motivationally powerful by enabling it to combine the motivation attached to all the various identities subsumed under it. Politicians want the members of their party to be motivated, so that they will vote for them, invest in campaigning activities, donate money, etc. Second, a bundled identity, especially if one's ideology makes set of identities look like they go together naturally, may be more satisfying for many people than a disconnected set whose members may be in tension with one another. In other words, a bundled identity may give the individual a sense of a more unified self.

If party affiliation facilitates that sense of unity, of wholeness, then it will be in the interest of politicians to compete with each other in offering ideologies that create coherent, connected bundles. Savvy politicians are good at promulgating ideologies that foster reasonably coherent and to that extent satisfying identity-bundles. They don't start from scratch. They notice, for example, that some people who are conservative are more likely to value patriotism, to be in favor of relatively unrestricted private gun ownership, and to be especially concerned about crime. So, they create print ads and videos that associate patriotism, the use of guns for self-defense, and voting for candidates of their party. An example is a full-page ad in a shooting sports or outdoor magazine depicting a man in an American flag tee-shirt brandishing a handgun to defend his wife and children from a hooded figure climbing through the bedroom window. National Rifle Association (NRA) ads often explicitly link gun ownership, crime prevention, and patriotism. And the NRA magazine, *The American Rifleman*, actually publishes lists of political candidates who are described as patriotic, law and order oriented, anti-abortion, and gun ownership friendly, urging readers to vote for them.

Such methods of identity-bundle creation foster the illusion that certain things go together naturally, that you can't have one without the other. In other words, when deployed skillfully by politicians and partisan pundits, tribalistic ideologies not only project stereotypes on the Other, but they also produce stereotypes of their own adherents. The result is that if you disavow one or more of the items in the identity-bundle, you run the risk of being regarded as a traitor, or as an enemy who all along was disguising himself to infiltrate the tribe.

Tribalistic ideologies put a premium on conformity, partly to facilitate a clear distinction between Us and Them. Once ideology-promoting politicians and partisan pundits have made a particular bundle of identities salient and identified them with *bona fide* tribal membership, the pressure for conformity makes tribal members more likely to adopt them.

Whatever the full story on why tribalistic ideologies feature political-identity-dominated bundles turns out to be, the fact that they have this feature has momentous consequences. The most important one is that any challenge to one's political beliefs is an existential threat, an assault on you, not just a criticism of your beliefs about public policies. And the you that is threatened is you as a member of a group, a group that partly defines itself in terms of its opposition to another group.

This chapter described the features of social media and the motivations for our particular uses of it that foster tribalistic ideologies. The next chapter moves from description to prescription. It identifies several different forms of resistance to tribalistic ideologies.

Notes

1 James Roberts, Luc Yaya and Chris Manolis, "The Invisible Addiction: Cell-Phone Activities and Addiction among Male and Female College Students." *Journal of Behavioral Addictions* 3, no. 4 (December 2014): 254–65. https://doi.org/10.1556/JBA.3.2014.015.
2 There's now controversy as to whether this is really so. Nothing I say depends on how that dispute is resolved, because I focus on other ways in which social media use contributes to tribalism.
3 Hugo Mercier, *Not Born Yesterday: The Science of Who We Trust and What We Believe*. First paperback printing. Princeton, Oxford: Princeton University Press, 2022.

4 Christopher Bail, *Breaking the Social Media Prism: How to Make Our Platforms Less Polarizing*. Princeton, NJ: Princeton University Press, 2021.

5 Christopher Bail, *Breaking the Social Media Prism: How to Make Our Platforms Less Polarizing*. Princeton, NJ: Princeton University Press, 2021.

6 Maeve Duggan, "Online Harassment 2017." Pew Research Center, July 11, 2017. https://www.pewresearch.org/internet/2017/07/11/online-harassment-2017/; John Suler, "The Online Disinhibition Effect." *CyberPsychology & Behavior* 7, no. 3 (June 2004): 321–26. https://doi.org/10.1089/1094931041291295.

7 Norbert Elias, *The Civilizing Process*. Oxford: Blackwell, 1994.

8 David Brooks, *The Second Mountain: The Quest for a Moral Life*. 2020. Random House trade paperback ed. New York: Random House, 2020; Francis Fukuyama, *Identity: The Demand for Dignity and the Politics of Resentment*. 1st ed. New York: Farrar, 2018; Yuval Levin, *The Fractured Republic: Renewing America's Social Contract in the Age of Individualism*. New York: Basic Books, 2016; Robert D. Putnam, *Bowling Alone: The Collapse and Revival of American Community*. A Touchstone Book. London: Simon & Schuster, 2001.

9 I hope you won't take my favorable reference to Marx as a signal that I'm a member of the communist tribe. I can agree with some things he said and disagree with others, because I don't treat his claims as an indivisible bundle. In that sense, my approach to Marx is decidedly not tribalistic.

10 Sinan Aral, *The Hype Machine: How Social Media Disrupts Our Elections, Our Economy, and Our Health—And How We Must Adapt*. 1st ed. New York: Currency, 2020.

6

DE-ZOMBIFICATION

What Works, What Doesn't, and What's Ethically Permissible

Are We Condemned to Tribalism?

There is a view about our evolved moral nature that, if true, appears to make the search for solutions to the problem of tribalistic ideologies futile. It's the view that we are tribalistic by nature. The problem is that the phrase "tribalistic by nature" is ambiguous. It could just mean that we are essentially groupish critters or that, in addition to being groupish, we tend to have inflated views of the goodness or our group and rather negative views about other groups. If that's all it means to say we are tribalistic by nature, it doesn't follow that we are condemned to the extremely nasty, exclusive kind of groupishness that characterizes tribalistic ideologies.

Some people who reflect on the evolution of human beings as moral creatures draw a more pessimistic conclusion: that we are by nature tribalistic in a more extreme, nasty, exclusive sense. And if that is so, then it looks like we're stuck with tribalistic ideologies—and all the damage they do.

Why would one think that the correct understanding of how we became moral creatures implies that we are tribalistic by nature in the extreme, negative sense that condemns us to tribalistic ideologies? The answer is straightforward. It's an account according to which the environmental pressures to which the development of human moralities developed resulted in those moralities being extremely tribalistic, exclusionary. The core idea here is that this formative environment, what evolutionary anthropologists call the Environment of Evolutionary Adaptation or EEA, included conditions that selected for moralities

DOI: 10.4324/9781003612469-7

that featured very robust obligations among people within the group (the hunter-gatherer band) but which relegated out-group individuals to a grossly inferior moral status or to no moral status at all. The most important of those conditions were these: (1) there was intense competition between human groups for the means of survival; (2) because human groups were widely scattered, they had different immune histories and strangers posed a threat of exposure to diseases to which members of one's own group were completely vulnerable; and (3) there were no institutions or practices (such as markets) that allowed peaceful, mutually beneficial interactions among groups. The idea is that under these conditions natural selection would have produced a moral nature that is thoroughly tribalistic, groupish in the extreme, exclusionary, nasty sense. To put it differently, the idea is that the risk management strategy that would be selected for in these harsh conditions would be to act on the maxim that the best defense is a good offense—to do unto others before they can do unto you. A mindset that regarded the Other as dangerous and untrustworthy is what one would expect, if this is the right description of the EEA.

I've devoted the better part of a whole book to showing that the best account currently available about how we came to be moral creatures doesn't show that we are tribalistic by nature in the extremely negative sense. What that account shows is that evolution produced a moral mind that is highly flexible, that can be expressed either in extremely tribalistic moralities or in more inclusive ones—and that the nature of the environment plays a large role in determining which of these possibilities is realized.[1]

I won't rehearse my argument about how a plausible understanding of the evolution of human morality doesn't support a pessimistic conclusion about the prospects for combatting tribalistic ideology. There's no need to do that because there's a more direct way to show that we aren't extremely tribalistic by nature, hard-wired for it, unable to be anything else but nasty, exclusionary tribalists. We just need to open our eyes to two facts: first, some people's moralities—and I'm sure this includes you—are much more inclusive, less tribalistic, than those that were probably dominant in the EEA. They are more inclusive in two ways: they acknowledge the basic equal moral status of all persons, not just members of one's own group; and they believe that at least some nonhuman animals have moral standing, that there are limits on how we may treat them; that they count, morally speaking, in their own right. I call these two moral sea-changes the Two Great Expansions. They are expansions of the circle of moral concern. And they warrant the adjective "Great" because they are among the most momentous examples of moral progress.

Second, the Two Great Expansions aren't just a matter of beliefs or aspirations without practical effects. They're implemented in law and social practices, often at great costs. The first Great Expansion at present is most fully articulated and institutionalized in the modern human rights movement, which has produced major changes in international and domestic law and institutions. The second is much less fully realized, but in some countries, including the United States, it's implemented in laws concerning the use of animals in medical research and in the practices of major corporations involved in producing or marketing animal flesh for food. Further, we have no reason at present to think these changes can't persist, that they won't become entrenched and durable, by being institutionalized and backed by law.[2]

The fact that the Two Great Expansions are more than a change in beliefs, not just aspirational, is a refutation of the claim that we are tribalistic by nature in the extreme sense. Whatever the full evolutionary story turns out to be, evolution didn't produce a moral mind that was rigidly extremely tribalistic. It produced a moral mind that was flexible enough to get expressed in quite different kinds of moralities, depending on the nature of the environments in which it operates. The big point in my two books on this topic is that only fairly recently, humans have constructed environments quite different from the EEA; environments in which the costs of being more inclusive are lower and the benefits higher.

Once we've debunked the thesis that we are tribalistic by nature in the nasty, exclusive sense, we can see that the attempt to combat tribalistic ideologies isn't futile. We are free—and I would say obligated—to consider strategies for reducing the damage that tribalistic ideologies are causing.

Avoiding False Comforts

To begin to understand how we can reverse the damage tribalistic ideologies are doing, or at least avoid further damage, we need to know what doesn't work. Time is of the essence, so we can't afford to tread paths that lead to dead-ends.

To know what doesn't work, we need to remember a basic fact about ideologies: they include a belief immune system, a set of mechanisms for sustaining ideological beliefs in the face of disconfirming evidence. Once you understand how effective the belief immune system is, you'll see that merely providing corrective information and pointing out how damaging tribalistic ideologies are isn't likely to rid us of them. Nor will it have much effect to tell people to pull up their moral socks, to quit lying and besmirching the character of those they disagree with and start acting like they knew the meaning of the word "decency." That won't work, because, as I have shown in some detail, tribalistic moralities hijack our commitment to morality. They encourage immoral behavior in the name of morality. And once immoral behavior has become pervasive, anybody who unilaterally abstains from engaging in it will be at a severe disadvantage.

The Main Options for Combatting Tribalistic Ideologies

If providing corrective information, rational persuasion, and moral exhortation don't work, it looks like there are ten main alternative strategies worth considering. Obviously, they aren't mutually exclusive. Several or all of them could be employed in combination.

1 Combat the tendency of tribalistic ideologies to exaggerate the scope of political disagreements. Mount an information campaign to highlight just how much agreement there actually is on a wide range of issues and how relatively minor disagreements are in some other areas. On an individual level, this would mean actually finding out what the other folks think about a wide range of issues and not just focusing on points of disagreement. So, this strategy goes beyond the mere provision of information; it requires changing our behavior, generating new experiences of what the Other is like.

2 Re-orient public education in such a way as to equip people with the skills they need to avoid forming tribalistic beliefs.

3 With an understanding of tribalistic ideologies in hand, monitor our own personal behavior and when we see that we are going tribalistic, back-off. And we can monitor the behavior of our friends and loved ones, letting them know when they are behaving tribalistically. (I've done this with a friend, pointing out to him that he was frequently engaging in defensive score-keeping rather than arguing about political issues on the merits. So far, it hasn't worked, but I'm still trying.)

4 Unbundle the identities that tribalistic ideologies make so salient and dangerous. That way, a threat to one identity won't be perceived as a threat to you.

5 Create an environment where opposing ideologically bundled identities can somehow co-exist peacefully and not undermine democracy.

6 Transform social media platforms so that they aren't the kind of masked identity fashion show venues in which tribalistic ideologies thrive.

7 Limit our exposure to media that foster tribalistic ideologies.

8 Assuming that tribalistic ideologies thrive in good part by fostering substitutes for the loss of traditional, face-to-face communities, develop strategies for creating or, if they still exist, sustaining the latter. Make our social environment more community friendly.

9 Legally prohibit or exclude from First Amendment protection the most divisive or dangerous forms of tribalistic discourse.

10 (Most controversially) develop and deploy nonconsensual, coercive measures designed to dismantle tribalistic ideological beliefs—something like forcible de-programming.

Emphasizing Agreement

1 The strategy of combatting exaggerations of the scope and intractability of political disagreements is in my judgment very promising. We will need to think hard about how to implement it and we must be willing to devote considerable resources to making it effective. As individuals, apart from any organized efforts, we can work with individuals we know to try to discover what we agree on, rather than assuming that we disagree on every matter of importance.

Reforming Education

2 The educational strategy seems obvious and appears to have great potential. Students would be taught to become aware of tribalistic behavior in themselves and others, to understand how destructive tribalistic ideologies are, and to develop skills of critical thinking to combat the formation of tribalistic ideological beliefs.

The problem is that in American society at present, the education system is one of the most important sites of tribalistic ideological conflict.

The very divisions which educational reform would aim at overcoming are the greatest impediment to educational reform. The conflict is chiefly about the content of what is to be taught and especially content regarding American history and current social conditions in this country. Tribalists on the Right want public education to portray American history as the triumph of freedom and equal opportunity; those on the Left want it to include a major emphasis on racism and sexism. Education could be a major force for combatting tribalism, but where tribalism has infected the debate about what education should be, that's not an option.

I can offer no prescription for freeing discussions about what the goals of public education ought to be from the tribalistic maelstrom. My hope—and it's only a hope—is that a shift away from the debate about content to a focus on the development of critical thinking skills might work. The assumption is that people on the Right would want their children to have the resources to resist Leftist indoctrination and *vice versa*. Unfortunately, there has been some resistance to introducing critical thinking into public education on the part of some people on the Right on the grounds that it is a veiled partisan tool for undermining respect for authority.

In most countries, public education, for most of its history, has been more of a tool for instilling tribalism—more specifically, nationalistic versions of tribalistic ideologies—than a resource for resisting tribalism. Whether the battle against tribalistic ideologies can be won may well depend on whether a major re-orientation in public education is feasible. Given how problematic the educational strategy is, we need to consider all the other options.

Self-Help by Self-Awareness

Strategy (3) would work like this. If you find yourself responding to a criticism of your candidate by saying that the critic's candidate is guilty of the same thing, you know you are in the tribalistic score-keeping mode. Be on the alert to avoid purely defensive score-keeping. Try to steer the conversation toward the truth-seeking mode by addressing the criticism, not dodging it. Think about what you are about to say: are you really stating what you believe to be the case or are you just signaling your tribal allegiance and probing your audience to see what their allegiance is? Don't say it if you don't mean it, aren't willing to stand by it. Whether this strategy would make much of a dent in the tribalistic juggernaut will depend on how many people use it. But quite apart from that, if you use it, at least you can take a certain amount of pride that you aren't participating in the festival of mutual destruction. You might also succeed in limiting your associates' indulgence in tribalistic behavior by making them aware of it.

How Could We Unbundle Identities (And Would It Be a Good Thing)?

Number (4), unbundling existing ideologically constructed identities, would be a good thing. The idea is to somehow convince people that a threat to one of their identities isn't necessarily a threat to all the rest. As far as I can tell, the psychological literature doesn't shed much light on how this might be done.

There's an alternative to unbundling that's worth considering: encouraging people to form bundles of identities that cross partisan lines. That would require giving people incentives to develop interests that put them in contact with people their tribalistic ideology may have already written off as stupid or perverse. It's hard to construct good relationships with people you distrust and don't respect. Sometimes, however, personal contact, in the right sort of setting, can begin to break down your negative stereotype of the Other. That's happened to me, because, as I explained in the

Introduction, I inhabit two different worlds. My dual citizenship has led me to be more tolerant of those I disagree with and reduced the tendency to engage in simple stereotypes. We need more information about how to do this on a very large scale, constructing such settings and incentivizing people to come together in them.

As I noted in the Introduction, there is reason to believe that the problem of tribalistic ideologies is exceptionally serious and pervasive in the United States and that one reason that this is so is that the two-party system, along with the incentives politicians and political influencers are subjected to, leads to a situation in which many people believe that which party becomes dominant in the political system will determine whether their (bundled) identity fares well or ill. If that is so, it may prove necessary to change the political system: to break out of the polarizing two-party only system and transition to a multi-party system in which people aren't confronted with an all-or-nothing choice as to their political identities. How this could be accomplished is far from clear. The problem is that the two-party-only system seems to be exceptionally stable. Perhaps if enough people become dissatisfied with both parties—and become aware of how polarizing and toxic the two-party-only system is—the formation of viable additional parties might become feasible.

Notice that strategies (4) and (1) are complementary in this sense: combatting the exaggeration of political disagreement would make it easier to avoid politically charged bundled identities and to foster identities that cross partisan lines. In a multi-party system in which political control requires building coalitions across party lines, it might prove easier both to reduce substantive political disagreements through compromises and bargaining and to enable people to think that politics is not a zero-sum contest for the highest stakes. Taken together, those changes might result in complex identities that are not so starkly oppositional.

Little Prospect for Peaceful Co-Existence

Solution (5) doesn't look promising, because the bundled identities at play today are inherently oppositional, held together by Supreme Emergency, Armageddon is-here-and-now thinking. Being inherently oppositional and existing in the zero-sum framework, they can't tolerate one another. Peaceful co-existence isn't an option at Armageddon.

How Can We Separate the Profitability of Social Media Platforms from Their Facilitation of Tribalism?

Number (6) looks like a good idea, but there's a problem. I don't think the social media platform owners are likely to voluntarily make the needed changes, because that would reduce profits. The profitability of the platforms currently depends on their ability to attract advertisers and they attract advertisers by using algorithms that reinforce and amplify whatever preferences people happen to have, including their tribalistic biases. I don't think anyone has come up with algorithms that don't have this feature but are profitable enough to be adopted by those who control the platforms. And I don't trust a bunch of geriatric congressmen who can't use their devices without help from their grandkids to regulate the platforms. That leaves options (7), (8), (9), and (10).

Help from Ulysses

Let's start with (7). My suggestion is that the best prospect for limiting our exposure to social media that encourages tribalism is to devise *group self-binding strategies*. Our first recorded account of a self-binding strategy is one used by an individual, not a group. It occurs in *The Odyssey*. Odysseus (aka Ulysses) is on his way home to Ithaca from the Trojan War. He knows his route will take him near the island of the Sirens: nonhuman creatures that sing beautiful, seductive songs to lure sailors to their death. Odysseus wants to have his auditory cake but not be eaten by the Sirens: he wants to hear their songs but not follow the music to his death. So, he has his crew put beeswax in their ears (but not his) and instructs them to sail close enough to the island of the Sirens to hear their songs, with him lashed to the mast so he can't jump ship and swim ashore.

I knew a modern-day Ulysses: a fellow graduate student. He just couldn't seem to buckle down and write his dissertation, kept procrastinating. So, he contacted a behavioral therapist. The therapist had him write a dozen personal checks made out to the Re-elect Richard Nixon Campaign Fund. Unless my friend turned in five pages of dissertation text a week to the therapist, the therapist mailed a check to the Nixon campaign. My friend loathed Richard Nixon, so it worked. He only failed to meet the deadline once.

We've seen how the masked identity fashion show of social media provides the perfect setting for a competition for identity that unleashes the worst in us. If that's the case, then perhaps the single most important step to take in combatting tribalistic ideologies is to limit our exposure to social media. So, if you understand that visiting certain social media sites is making you stupid and shameless, why not do what my friend and Odysseus did? Get an app that blocks access to those sites and/or limits the amount of time per day you can spend on social media.

My students admit that they over-use and abuse social media. When I suggest they use an Odysseus strategy, they invariably reply: I'd be happy to do that, but if I do and people I care about don't, I'll be forgotten, excluded. This is what game theorists call the assurance problem. You'd be willing to do something—in this case, contribute to the collective good of curbing the damage social media does by limiting exposure to it—but only if you are assured that others will do their bit.

There are ways of solving the assurance problem. Understanding how that works comes from an unlikely quarter: the battle to end female genital mutilation (FGM). Human rights activists have had success in reducing the incidence of this harmful practice by bringing the mothers of young girls together at the village level, encouraging them to publicly pledge to each other that they won't allow their daughters to be cut, and also encouraging the mothers of young men to pledge to each other that they'll make sure their sons marry uncut girls.[3] Before this strategy was employed, mothers tended to reason as follows: I'd like to refrain from having my daughter cut, but if I do so and others don't, my daughter will be a pariah. No one will want to marry her.

A conversation I had with a student prompted me to think about how something similar might be done to reduce social media use. The university at which I was then working had the wonderful practice of funding lunches that brought students and faculties together outside the classroom. A student invites a professor to lunch and the university foots the bill. I used these lunches to learn more about my students. (In fact, I used them to conduct informal social science research, without approval by the university's Human Subjects Committee, i.e., Institutional Review Board.)

At one such lunch I asked a student about her cell phone use. She showed me the screen of her phone: there were about dozen dots on it, some moving and some stationary. This was her circle of close friends: they all had an app that allowed each to know where all the others were at any given time. I found this very creepy.

Jokingly, I asked "How do you cheat on your boyfriend?" After a pause, she replied: "It's difficult, but not impossible." When I recovered from the realization that her answer, unlike my question, was apparently quite serious, it occurred to me that it should be possible to develop a similar app that would keep track of whether your friends were sticking to an agreement to limit social media use. In other words, this meta-app would alert everybody if anybody had turned off their first-order app, the one that limited their access to social media. If that could be done, it would solve the assurance problem. The app would tell you and everybody else in your circle of friends whether any of you had turned off the app that limits your exposure to social media. If your group found out you had violated the collective commitment to using the app that limits social media time, you would be subjected to criticism and stigma imposed by your close friends, the people whose opinion of you matters the most to you.

The meta-app is just one means of achieving group self-binding. There are no doubt others. I won't attempt to canvass the full-range alternatives for group self-binding. I simply want to emphasize that this type of arrangement can solve the assurance problem and overcome collective action failures. And this is important: group self-binding is voluntary and consensual, not forcibly imposed by some external agent. It's autonomy-respecting.

In my judgment, the first line of defense against tribalism-fostering social media should be group self-binding—the analog of what's been done with FGM. I would be very grateful, if anyone reading this book who has a lot more IT savvy than I do would think about developing the needed group self-binding software, meta-app, and all.

Building (Offline) Communities

Suppose that the group self-binding strategy isn't adopted on a sufficient scale to be effective in combatting tribalistic ideologies. That brings us to strategy (8) building traditional, face-to-face communities in the hope that they will provide satisfying, less tribalistic-group-based identities that people will prefer to the sorts of identities involved in tribalistic ideologies. This strategy is based on the plausible assumption that the loss of traditional communities is a major factor in the rise of tribalistic ideologies.

If that's the case, we need to think long and hard about how to structure our society in ways that encourage them. That will mean providing alternatives to tribalistic identities, so far as the latter are largely creatures of the "communities" constituted by electronic communications generally and social media in particular. It will mean fostering genuine, face-to-face communities so that people who feel the need for a sense of group-membership identity won't have to resort to membership in the tribalistic political communities.

How might we foster genuine communities, the kind of associations that satisfy the need for a sense of belonging but not by identifying Us as those who are the enemies of Them? One intriguing suggestion, offered by the philosopher Travis Quigley, is to undertake a massive institutional change: to create what he calls "Exit Federalism."[4] The idea is to provide incentives and resources to people so that they can sort themselves into different jurisdictions within an over-arching Federal polity. That way, people can be freer to live their own chosen group identities. They can locate in an environment that's friendly to their favored identity, surrounded by and forming a community with people who share that identity. They'd be more secure and less vulnerable to tribalistic ideologies.

In contrast, when we all have to live under one government, in one jurisdiction, if there are deep differences in values and identities, politics can become a zero-sum contest to see which identity-group can capture political power and use it to further their flourishing. In those circumstances, tribalistic ideologies thrive.

In the Exit Federalism scheme, political power is dispersed, distributed among a plurality of communities in their own jurisdictions. In this arrangement, the Federal Government would guarantee basic rights for everyone and provide security against hostile acts by other countries, but the people in individual units would be free to adopt quite different policies within that basic framework. The Federal Government would also provide people with resources, perhaps in the form of a guaranteed basic income, to help them bear the costs of exiting one community and entering another.

The idea is that this sort of arrangement would be more community friendly than what we have now, and that the availability of (face-to-face) communities would reduce the risk that people will invest heavily in virtual communities that define their identities through tribalistic ideologies. Quigley thinks that Exit Federalism would be an effective means of combating tribalistic ideologies because it would undercut one of the major contributors to them, the loss of genuine communities.

I'm not trying to sell Quigley's proposal. For one thing, I don't know how politically feasible it is, and I worry that it might lead, not to healthy pluralism in a stable federal system, but to the breakdown of the system through secession. I do think, however, that it's a good example of the need to think about how to provide favorable conditions for communities that are not tribalistic.

Extending the Concept of Hate Speech

Now consider option (9). It is often said that in American law, hate speech does not enjoy the protection provided by the First Amendment's right to freedom of expression. That claim, however, is rejected by some constitutional lawyers. The disagreement may be due to differences in how "hate speech" is defined, or it may be due to differences in how the First Amendment is understood.

For the sake of argument, let's assume that the claim is true, that hate speech is not covered by the protective mantle of the First Amendment. The concept of hate speech has chiefly been applied to speech that targets individuals or groups on the basis of race, gender, religion, ethnicity, or disability, rather than on the basis of political affiliation. Including political groups is problematic, because there are good reasons to protect political speech in general, and singling out some forms of political speech on the grounds that it counts as hate speech might be subjected to partisan bias. It is better, some would argue, to draw a bright line and refuse to classify any political speech as hate speech, if it is assumed that hate speech does not enjoy First Amendment protection.

That line of argument has its own difficulties. In particular, it relies on the assumption that we can clearly determine which cases of speech are political and which are not. Perhaps the best solution is not to try to use the concept of hate speech to combat tribalistic ideologies, but rather to make it clear that First Amendment protection does not extend to any speech that, given the circumstances in which it occurs, can reasonably expected to incite violence.

Applying that standard to tribalistic discourse may prove difficult. In many cases, a good deal of information about causal connections between particular instances of speech and acts of violence may be needed and just what the causal connections are may be in dispute—especially in just those contexts in which there is an attempt to determine what the causal aggregative effect of many instances of speech that vilifies a group that a particular tribalistic ideology characterizes as an enemy. No particular instance may meet the standard of being reasonably expected to incite violence.

The main limitation any strategy for combatting tribalistic ideologies that focuses on a connection between speech and violence, however, is the fact that the features of tribalistic ideologies I have identified in this book, though extremely harmful, do not involve clear incitements to violence. They include the replacement of truth-seeking discourse with sorting, signaling, and defensive score-keeping, the disabling of theory of mind, the destruction of the conditions for democracy, the loss of national unity, the acceptance of indecent behavior by politicians, and ideologically motivated immoral acts undertaken for the sake of victory in a supposed Supreme Emergency situation. Restrictions on free speech are most plausible in the case of incitements to violence; further restrictions are more subjected to abuse. My conclusion, then, is that the strategy of using the concept of hate speech to combat tribalistic ideologies is not very promising.

The De-Programming Alternative: Justified Paternalistic Intervention?

Suppose that none of the preceding nine strategies, either singly or in combination, provide effective means for combatting tribalistic ideologies. Then, we have to consider next a more problematic and disturbing approach: option (10), nonconsensual, coercive interventions to dismantle pernicious ideological beliefs—something like the forcible re-programming that's used to free people from allegiance to whacky cults. In case less problematic measures like group rational persuasion and group self-binding don't work, I want to advance a bold hypothesis: under certain conditions coercive, nonconsensual measures can be justifiable in principle. That's a claim about what's ethically permissible. As far as I know, other books on tribalism don't explore or even acknowledge the need for an ethics of combatting tribalistic ideologies. I aim to begin to fill that gaping hole in the literature.

We've seen that the belief management processes that ideologies contain include powerful cognitive dissonance resolution mechanisms that make the core beliefs of the ideology rigid, recalcitrant to correction in the face of apparently disconfirming testimony or experiences. (Hence when we say someone is an ideologue or in the grip of an ideology, the implication is that they are dogmatic, too prone to sustain their beliefs, despite significant evidence against them.) It is the power of these belief-preserving mechanisms that limits the effectiveness of rational persuasion and raises the prospect that nonconsensual, coercive measures to combat ideological beliefs may be the only effective remedy.

Would it ever be ethically permissible for a friend or a family member or the parents of a teenager to use such measures? Even if the answer to that question is "yes," allowing government officials to do so would be much more problematic, for pretty obvious reasons. Any augmentation of the state's already staggering coercive power ought to be subject to the strictest scrutiny. Our default stance should be: no new coercive powers for the state, a weighty presumption against giving it still more opportunities for abuse and error.

It's important to keep in mind the fact that there are also options that lie between government action and private, individual action. For example, a religious group—either the governing body of a particular congregation or the leadership of a whole denomination—could require members to limit social media use or refrain from it altogether. Noncompliers could be banned from membership, publicly denounced, etc. This would also have the potential for abuse or error, but the risks presumably wouldn't be as great as with state action.

To my way of thinking, the least problematic case, from an ethical standpoint, would be where parents, having failed to persuade their teenager that they should use a self-binding app or in some other way voluntarily limit social media use, force them to do so. Yet even in this case, there could be an ethical objection: treating your offspring in this way could be seen as a denial of their competence or a devaluing of their autonomy. How serious this objection is would depend, of course, on the age of the child or rather the extent to which they had developed the capacity for autonomy.

Some Help from Moral Philosophy

To make any headway on the question of whether coercive, nonconsensual interventions are ethically okay, we need to get clear about why you might think they are problematic, morally speaking. To do that, we need some distinctions. More precisely, we need to do a bit of Moral Philosophy, and that will take a certain amount of patience on your part. I don't think that's a reason for complaint, because I think it's naïve to assume that you can tackle tough moral problems in sound bites. We'll need to engage in extended reasoning—the kind of thinking that social media use has driven out by its emphasis on constantly changing stimulation. Sound bites or memo-type thinking won't do the trick. So, please, bear with me.

A nonconsensual, coercive intervention can be either paternalistic or other-regarding or both. An other-regarding intervention aims to dismantle a person's ideological beliefs that put others at risk of harm. A paternalistic intervention aims to a person's ideological beliefs for the sake of preventing harm to the individual or to promote their well-being or autonomy. A paternalistic intervention is some action or omission that limits an individual's freedom, or constrains their options for choice, or prevents them from recognizing that there are options, for their own sake.

What's (Usually) Wrong with Paternalism

Paternalistic interventions are morally problematic because they typically infringe the individual's autonomy, either by imposing on them a conception of their good that's not their own, or by preventing them from pursuing their own good in their own way. Accordingly, paternalism is deemed disrespectful of the person as agent. Here's yet another story from my racist past that will make clear why people who are treated paternalistically feel insulted, not treated with due respect.

My maternal grandfather owned a construction company in Little Rock. Among his long-term employees was a Black man whom my grandfather called "Shorty" (despite the fact that he was a bit taller than Grandpa and had a name). My grandfather decided to do a good deed. (One aspect of his racist ideology was the idea of *noblesse oblige*—superior types should exhibit the virtue of beneficence toward their inferiors.) He gave Shorty a pay raise but didn't tell him about it. Instead, he opened a bank account for him and deposited the additional dollars from the raise in it. After a considerable amount of money accumulated in the secret bank account, my grandfather proudly presented the bank account book to Shorty, no doubt expecting a response of profound gratitude. Well, Shorty didn't react as anticipated. Without uttering a word, he took the bank account book, walked off the construction site, and was never seen again by my grandfather.

My grandfather's response? He wrote Shorty off as just another ungrateful n____. I have another interpretation of Shorty's behavior: he was deeply offended that my grandfather was treating him like a child, as someone who lacked the self-discipline to put a raise to good use. He felt disrespected and rightly so. That's why paternalism is morally problematic: when it's directed toward a competent adult, it's (almost always) disrespectful. More precisely, it fails to acknowledge that the supposed beneficiary is a being capable of autonomy, of making their own decisions, running their own life.

If you don't find this example compelling, I suggest you think back to your own teenage years and recall episodes where your parents, "for your own good," stopped you from doing something. I'm betting that when you were really disturbed by their paternalism, it wasn't just because you were prevented from doing something you wanted to do. (Having a tattoo might not have been all that important to you—until your parents said you couldn't have one.) It was what your parent's paternalistic act implied about their view of you that bothered you. Some of the most bitter disputes between parents and adolescents are really disagreements about when the child is no longer a child, and when paternalism becomes disrespectful.

Acceptable Paternalism?

There's one type of paternalistic intervention, however, that promotes, rather than denies, autonomy: an intervention that aims to restore an individual's competence or capacity for voluntary action, and hence for autonomy. Here's what I hope is a relatively uncontroversial example. Your teenage son has been diagnosed as schizophrenic. You know that it is vital for him to take a certain medication every day. He won't take it voluntarily because his mental illness has convinced him it's poison, so you force him to take it, for his own good. You reason, quite plausibly, that his mental illness has made him incompetent to determine whether to take the medication. You don't do this out of disrespect for his autonomy; you do it to restore his autonomy.

The most plausible justification for paternalistic intervention to combat pernicious ideological beliefs, then, is this: paternalistic intervention (intervention for the individual's own good) is in principle justified if it's reasonably calculated to *remedy cognitive disabilities that render a person incompetent in some morally important domain(s) of agency or judgment and that incompetence puts the individual at risk of serious harm.* I added the qualifier "in principle" to acknowledge that, depending on the circumstances, there may or may not be some person or institution that you could trust to do the intervention.

The basis of the paternalistic justification for nonconsensual interventions is the fact that having an impaired theory of mind or other cognitive disabilities caused by tribalistic ideologies can be bad for an individual and therefore that intervening to remedy that impairment can be good for them. That point merits elaboration.

The impairment of theory of mind that tribalist ideologies cause can damage or prevent the formation of valuable relationships with people you disagree on political matters, even causing painful conflict between and alienation of lovers, spouses, siblings, and other family members. In extreme cases, it can lead you to act violently and aggressively toward people to whom you wrongly attribute malevolent, aggressive intentions.[5] In that way, it can contribute to wrongful behavior that is inconsistent with being the person you want to be. When that occurs, the ideologically induced cognitive disability results in an especially serious harm to the self.

Ideological beliefs can also lead you to act imprudently, to do things that are harmful to you in more concrete ways. For example, if your ideology convinces you that some other group is dangerous, you may undertake preemptive action against them, to your own detriment, either because they retaliate or because you run afoul of the law. Think of the people who stormed the Capitol building on January 6, 2021, who are now serving prison terms.

As the schizophrenic son example shows, the case for nonconsensual paternalistic intervention to remedy an ideology-induced, competence-impairing cognitive disability is strengthened if the same ideology that causes the impairment also makes it difficult or practically impossible for the individual to understand that their ideology is causing a cognitive disability. If the harm to you that your ideological beliefs are causing is serious enough and if consensual measures aren't sufficient, there's at least a strong case for nonconsensual ones—something like the "de-programming" that's done with young people who've been seduced into allegiance to a harmful religious cult. In the case of ideological de-programming, parents or friends might forcibly prevent the individual they are trying to help from meeting with certain people, communicating with them, etc.

So far, I've tried to make a preliminary ("in principle" or prima facie) case for paternalistic nonconsensual interventions to combat pernicious ideologies. If we focus instead, not on preventing harm to the individual, but on harm to others that can occur because the individual's behavior is driven by a tribalistic ideology, the case for nonconsensual, even coercive interventions is all the stronger. There are many cases where we think, quite reasonably, that it's permissible to intervene, nonconsensually and even coercively, if necessary, to prevent someone from harming other people. That's what enforcement of the criminal law is about in many cases.

A Real-Life, Successful Example

Until now, I've been proceeding hypothetically, asking under what conditions would coercive, nonconsensual efforts to combat tribalistic ideologies would be morally permissible. I now want to describe an actual case that looks like one in which paternalistic, nonconsensual, coercive intervention to combat a pernicious ideology was justified.

The policies of the Western Allies occupying roughly half of Germany at the end of World War II (WWII) can be seen as manifesting just the sort of intervention I'm claiming to be justifiable in principle. These policies included nonconsensual, coercive interventions to expunge Nazi ideological beliefs in order to make it possible to create a culture that would support the formation of a liberal, constitutional, rights-respecting democracy. The motives of the policy-makers were no doubt mixed, but presumably one aim was to improve the lot of the German people for their own sake by dismantling the distorted thought-processes, misguided practices of deference to supposed experts and authorities, and misinformation that had been instilled in them by 12 years of relentless and systematic Nazi propaganda.

The process of compulsory re-education (or de-programing) was quite reasonably thought to be a necessary step toward building a society that would benefit the Germans. If that is so, then the intervention was at least in part paternalistic: it involved restricting the liberty of Germans to engage in certain behaviors (by prohibiting Nazi salutes, the display of the swastika and images of Adolf Hitler, dissemination of Nazi propaganda, etc.) and by featuring compulsory compliance with various re-education initiatives and doing all of this for their own good. The Allied leadership may also have thought that there was a powerful other-regarding reason for their coercive re-education program: to prevent a persisting Nazi ideology from fueling a resurgence of German aggression.

In my judgment, independently of whether the other-regarding (preventing harm to others) justification was valid, it was permissible and perhaps even obligatory for the occupiers to try to eliminate or reduce the pernicious effects of Nazi ideology on the capacity of Germans to build a new, democratic, nonaggressive, and human-rights-respecting society. That is, intervention for the sake of the German people, paternalistic intervention, was justified. And if compulsory re-education and coercive suppression of behavior expressing allegiance to Nazi ideology were necessary for expunging Nazi ideology, they were morally permissible.

If you find the German example less than fully persuasive, consider the Herculean task that would face the liberators of North Korea, where the regime has had a much longer time-period and the advantage of more sophisticated communication technologies to instill an oppressive, dangerous ideology and to block the penetration of information or counter-ideologies that challenge it. Then ask yourself whether an exceptionless prohibition on nonconsensual, coercive means of dismantling ideological beliefs is plausible.

The German example is only invoked to show that nonconsensual, coercive paternalistic intervention to dismantle pernicious ideological beliefs can be justifiable in principle. I recognize that the circumstances in which the example occurred are quite different from those that obtain currently in the United States. So, I am not suggesting that a similar intervention would be justified in this country, at least not in this time. The biggest problem is that in the circumstances in which this last resort strategy would be most needed, the very problem it is designed to solve would make it very unlikely that anyone could be trusted to implement it in a non-partisan way. I'm only asking you to think about the possibility and perhaps explore the options for reducing the risks to tolerable proportions. I just think that our predicament is so dire and the more obvious options for extricating ourselves from it are so limited, that we have to consider the full range of strategies. In contrast to government action, nonconsensual, coercive interventions by family or friends to prevent the harmful effects of tribalistic ideologies may now be justifiable, depending on the facts of the particular case.

Fighting an Ideology with an Ideology

In the German case, the effort to combat a pernicious ideology included the attempt to instill a counter-ideology, a liberal-democratic, constitutionalist political ideology. A comprehensive account of the ethics of combatting ideological beliefs should address this question: is it morally permissible to try to neutralize a pernicious ideology by instilling a counter-ideology? I think the German case indicates that it can be.

The ideology of liberal-democratic constitutionalism that the Western Allies tried to inculcate in Germans may well have included misrepresentations, painting an exaggerated picture of the virtues of actual democracies and down-playing democracy's deficiencies. My claim is that if the moral case for dismantling the Nazi ideology was strong enough, recourse to the counter-ideology was nonetheless justified.

I don't pretend to have advanced a fully worked out, bullet-proof justification for nonconsensual, coercive intervention to alleviate the damage of pernicious ideological beliefs, much less to provide a comprehensive account of the ethics of combatting tribalistic ideologies. Instead, this chapter had two more modest main goals. The first was to explore several ways of combatting tribalistic ideologies and to make a case for group self-binding measures as perhaps the most plausible among them. The second was to explore the ethical dimension of combatting pernicious ideological beliefs in enough depth to make it clear that nonconsensual and even coercive intervention shouldn't be ruled out—at least without a more thorough ethical investigation.

Another goal of this chapter was to prompt an expansive rethinking of what the enterprise that philosophers call "ideology critique" encompasses and a corresponding reconsideration of the role of the ideology critic. Regarding this goal, my chief conclusion is this: if nonconsensual, coercive means for dismantling pernicious ideological beliefs are sometimes permissible, the proper role of the ideology critic isn't limited to being a teacher or cognitive psychotherapist who reveals the distortions of an oppression-supporting ideology by discursive argumentation or rational persuasion. It also requires the ideology critic to be willing to be a political activist, to consider seriously the option of using or advocating the use of nonconsensual coercion to combat pernicious ideologies.

In reflecting on the de-Nazification example, I've suggested that the best way to combat a bad ideology may be to foster a good (or at least less bad) one. There's a more general question that needs to be addressed: can we do without ideologies?

That's a topic for another book (or perhaps a multi-volume set). But I'll say something here about why I think ideologies may be necessary, at least in large-scale, complex, ethnically, culturally, and religiously diverse societies. I think they may well be necessary if two very plausible claims are in fact true. The first is that that sort of society requires some kind of hierarchy, that is, a structure of institutionalized authority that gives some people power over others that others don't have over them. The dominant view in organization theory is that hierarchy in that sense is necessary for the complex coordination that modern societies require if they are to function reasonably well. The second claim, the second premise in the argument for the conclusion that ideologies are necessary in modern societies, is that hierarches don't work in that sort of society unless enough people support them, not just out of fear of punishment if they don't, but also because they regard them as legitimate—and that a widespread belief in their legitimacy can only be achieved by a pervasive ideology.

Imagine that that line of reasoning (if filled out a lot more carefully) is cogent. If it is, then the task isn't to free people of ideologies but it's to liberate them from the destructive kinds of ideologies. And doing that may require fostering an ideology that not only repudiates the wrong sort of ideologies, but also plays a more constructive role in enabling a modern society to function. Efforts to foster more benign ideologies that would provide an attractive alternative to tribalistic ones might be a valuable adjunct to the other strategies I've already discussed.

Two More Options

We've now worked our way through a list of ten strategies for combating tribalistic ideologies. Some are more promising than others, but they all face significant hurdles. Suppose none of them, singly or in combination works. Is our situation hopeless?

Not necessarily, because there are two additional alternatives worth considering: bottoming-out or achieving unity in the face of an external threat. First, consider the bottoming-out scenario. Perhaps, if the damage that tribalistic ideologies inflict becomes obvious to enough people, they'll conclude "We can't go on like this!" and devise some way to break out of the tribalistic mode, perhaps through some fundamental institutional changes or by virtue of something motivationally like a mass religious conversion.

Call this the bottoming-out scenario. This isn't a strategy, not a plan we would deliberately adopt. It's just something that could happen, whether we want it to or not.

Beneficial change in response to bottoming-out has occurred before. Here are two instances: the Peace of Westphalia and the founding of the modern human rights movement. Let me elaborate.

The Peace of Westphalia consisted of two treaties, one signed at Munster and the other at Osnabruck, both in 1648. They ended the Thirty Years' War, the most destructive conflict in European history prior to WWI.

Religious disagreement between Protestants and Catholics was one major source of the war, because many people were in favor of forcibly spreading their faith or at least prohibiting alternative faiths. More precisely, efforts of Catholics to force their views on Protestants and *vice versa* were an important source of the conflict. The treaties acknowledged that. They specified that the ruler of a particular polity could determine the official religion and that no one else could forcibly overturn that decision. They also specified certain rights for minorities.

Historians generally describe the Peace of Westphalia, not as a breakthrough in morally progressive thinking, but as a *modus vivendi*, a way of getting along. The idea is that the warring parties were exhausted and came to the realization that they couldn't count on a stable victory. So, they settled for what was for each side an acceptable second best. But to get to that agreement, they apparently had to hit rock bottom. The carnage had to reach unprecedented levels.

A similar story can be told about the radical change that occurred within a few years of the end of WWII. Sovereign states did something unprecedented: they committed themselves in international law to limiting their own sovereignty, by pledging to observe certain standards, framed mainly in terms of human rights, for how they were to treat those within their jurisdictions. This was nothing short of a rejection of a fundamental tenet of international law and traditional political theory, namely, that it was a state's business as to how they treated its own people. The best explanation of why they did this is that there was a widespread sentiment, in the wake of the horrific destruction of the war and the Holocaust, that things had to change, and change fundamentally. The assumption, a quite reasonable one, was that unlimited state power was one of the causes of the war, or at least a condition that enabled the other causes to operate.

What's the point of these historical excursions? It's quite simple: we may have to bottom-out before we get serious about reducing the power of tribalistic ideologies over us. The problem is that things may have to get very bad indeed before we reach that point. There may have to be a lot of bad news before there's good news, and it's not a sure thing that there will be good news. We may reach rock bottom and not be able to climb up to a better elevation. In addition, sometimes bad situations don't produce unity: the recent pandemic is an example.

There's an alternative to the bottoming-out scenario. We might overcome our tribalism if we were confronted with a potentially lethal external threat. The need to come together to counter a dire threat can make for curious bedfellows. Recall Churchill's statement: "If Hitler invaded Hell, I'd make an alliance with the Devil."

During the Cold War, the threat of a militaristic, aggressive Soviet Union may well have helped unify the American people. The growing threat of China might do the same. Sadly, the recent pandemic didn't foster unity; quite the contrary, it became a site of tribalistic conflict.

Sometimes I think the only thing that could overcome our tribalistic divisions would be the necessity of providing a united front against an invasion of creatures from outer space. Liberals might not seem so strange and menacing to Conservatives and *vice versa* when compared to weird-looking aliens bent on colonizing Earth and raising humans for food.

Let me consider one last hopeful scenario: what if a recognition of the destructiveness of identity-anxiety driven tribalistic ideologies led enough people to reconceive their identities in ways that led them to reject tribalistic ideologies? Something like this has happened before. The British Abolitionist movement was initiated mainly by nonconforming (i.e., not Anglican) Protestants who came to believe that being a true Christian required active opposition to slavery. This was a big change in how they conceived their identity as Christians, because prior to that time, Christianity, like the other major religions, had accepted slavery. We don't know exactly how this happened, but apparently the spread of Enlightenment ideas about natural rights played a role in causing these people to reconceiving their religious identity as Christians in a way that mobilized them in opposition to slavery and to reject the tribalistic ideology that was invoked to justify slavery. Perhaps such a transformation of identities could occur again. At least the possibility is worth thinking about. Unfortunately, I haven't seen much evidence that the religious leadership in America is doing much to transform religious identities in ways that would combat tribalism successfully. In fact, in America, a good deal of the tribalistic behavior on the Right comes from people who describe themselves as Christians and is apparently grounded in their conception of their identity as Christians.

I'll end this chapter with a bit of well-deserved self-criticism. Remember the fellow at the gun club who declared that if Biden is elected, the United States will become a communist country? I thought it was pretty clear that he was just signaling and hoping to elicit a response from me that would indicate whether I was one of his tribe or belonged to the opposing tribe. So, I didn't engage with him on the content of what he said, because I thought it most likely would have been futile.

That means that I didn't treat him with respect, as a person who could be reasoned with. And I didn't treat him as an individual rather than as a member of a group. I shouldn't have done that. Even if the probability was pretty low that he would respond in the truth-seeking mode, I should have tried. I should have said:

> With all due respect, I think that's really unlikely. Biden isn't even a socialist, much less a communist. Quite apart from that, there are entrenched powerful interests and institutions, like the Constitution and the private property rights legal regime, that are big obstacles to a communist takeover. And it's worth noting that there has never been a successful communist takeover in a developed country. All the successful communist revolutions occurred in less-developed countries. They were all to a large extent, peasant revolutions.

I didn't do that; instead, I reacted to his tribalism in a thoroughly tribalistic manner, assuming that he fit my stereotype of Right-wing tribalists. In doing that, I was helping to perpetuate tribalism. I should have resisted the urge to stereotype him and dismiss what he said. Sometimes resistance is morally mandatory, even when it's unlikely to be effective.

The point is that tribalistic behavior tends to elicit tribalistic responses. That's why, when tribalism is pervasive, we are in what economists call a stable equilibrium. We'll have to work very hard to break out of that straight-jacket. We won't break out of it if we respond to tribalistic behavior in a tribalistic way.

Notes

1 Allen Buchanan, *Our Moral Fate: Evolution and the Escape from Tribalism.* Cambridge, MA: The MIT Press, 2020.
2 The Second Great Expansion is in its infancy. Though cat burnings are no longer a recreational activity in Paris today as they were in the Thirteenth Century, modern factory farming inflicts suffering on an enormous scale.
3 Christina Bicchieri and Annalisa Marini, "Female Genital Mutilation: Fundamentals, Social Expectations and Change." University Library of Munich, Germany, No. MPRA Paper 67523 (2015).
4 Unpublished manuscript.
5 Robert Jervis, *Perception and Misperception in International Politics.* New ed. Princeton, NJ: Princeton University Press, 2017.

CONCLUSION

Rhinoceroses vs. Humans, Despair vs. Hope

Alienation That Was Emancipating, but Fatal

The six-decade-long journey that resulted in this book began when my older brother, Steve, goaded me into questioning the beliefs I'd unthinkingly absorbed in the racist society he and I grew up in. You may be wondering whatever became of Steve. Life didn't go well for him. At first, he was amazingly successful. Puberty and a rigorous weight-lifting regimen transformed the sedentary fat kid into an athletic Adonis. He graduated with honors first from Columbia University and then from Columbia Medical School. He married a lovely woman and fathered a son. He seemed destined for a brilliant career and wonderful life.

Then it all began to unravel. He was fired just as he was about to be appointed chief resident in psychiatry at a highly regarded medical center for having an affair with a schizophrenic patient. He became addicted to several drugs as well as alcohol, and went from job to job, staying just ahead of the medical licensing police. His physical health deteriorated because of a belatedly diagnosed hereditary illness, hemochromatosis, which I also have.[1] The combination of physical disability and psychological deterioration led him to end his life with a .45 caliber bullet to the heart.

I've often wondered whether the skepticism and alienation, the sense of not belonging, that led him to resist drinking the cultural Cool-Aid in Little Rock was also his undoing, that it played a role in the bad choices that eventually led him to suicide. He seemed to think that he was an exception; that the rules that applied to the rest of us, including those that apply to risk taking, didn't apply to him, and that he could get away with doing

DOI: 10.4324/9781003612469-8

things that would be disastrous for the ordinary person. Be that as it may, I like to think that he would have approved of this book or at least of the effort I put into writing it. I just wish I had made clearer to him how much I owed him. I didn't realize the full extent of my debt until he was gone.

Summing Up Our Results

Here's my attempt to summarize most of the main results of the conversation my brother initiated. I present them while acknowledging that you may think the results were different. If you do, I would love to hear from you at allenb@duke.edu (I don't use social media).

- Tribalism is a type of political ideology. To understand it, we need to take advantage of the best social science work on ideologies. Doing so indicates that certain ideologies play a crucial role in fueling and guiding the quest for identity that is at the heart of tribalistic behavior.
- Tribalistic ideologies commandeer key evolved normal cognitive functions and re-purpose them into defenses against perceived threats to identity, and they do so in ways that show an utter disregard for the truth or for compliance with moral rules or the requirements of good manners. They turn the mind against itself, hijacking our most impressive, distinctively human cognitive abilities, using them to undermine our cognitive performance. They also turn the moral mind against itself, causing moral disabilities, impairing our moral judgment, and encouraging immoral behavior in the name of morality.
- The most important fact about the role of social media in tribalism is that they are venues for masked identity fashion shows: people can try on different identities to see whether they make them feel better about themselves and elicit the approval of others, but without the risks they would run if they weren't able to shield their real-life, offline identities. The masks enhance freedom, but they also reduce the costs of acting badly.
- Many people feel insecure about their identities and use the online identity masked fashion show option because our society is not as effective as traditional societies in assigning and sustaining clear identities and in limiting the options for identity. Another source of insecurity is the fact that social media continually make you aware of people who are better looking, more popular, smarter, and richer than you are. In addition, because identities are social environment dependent, technological change that produces rapid and continuing changes in the social environment can fuel identity-anxiety. Perhaps most important of all, the loss of traditional, face-to-face communities, which provided secure identities, has also contributed to identity insecurity.

- Human psychology apparently has always included an in-group/out-group distinction, with favoritism toward Us and bias against the Other. The tendency to divide the human world into Us versus Them was originally a response to the threat that was posed by literal outsiders, members of another society. Under those conditions, the distinction helped sustain the unity of the group so that its members could cooperate effectively in competition with other groups. At present, tribalistic ideologies draw the distinction between Us and Them *within* society. Such ideologies provide secure group-based identities. They do unify Us, but at the cost of dividing Us from Them.

- Political discourse has become so violent, rude, and nasty because any political view that is different from ours is felt as a personal attack of the most profound sort: an assault on one's identity.

- Tribalistic ideologies replace truth-seeking communication with sorting, signaling, and defensive score-keeping.

- Tribalistic ideologies destroy national unity; they are the death of "We the People," that is, the state can only serve one people or the other, but not both.

- The kind of democracy that is worth working hard to sustain is deliberative democracy, a political process where citizens engage in the give and take of reasons regarding what We should do and what Our collective goals should be. Tribalistic political ideologies make such engagement difficult if not impossible, because they present the Other as beings We can't reason with and with whom we share no basic values.

- The worst political behavior isn't the result of our politicians or ourselves suddenly abandoning morality: it occurs because our tribalistic ideologies have convinced us that we are in a Supreme Emergency, an Armageddon struggle between Us and Them, where the only alternative is total victory or total defeat. If we believe that, we'll violate moral rules for the sake of the higher moral good.

- Even if we have a tendency toward extreme tribalism, we are not condemned to it. The moral mind is flexible enough to accommodate more inclusive, less extremely tribalistic moralities. What sort of morality is pervasive in a society depends upon the environment. The more we learn about which environments promote less tribalistic moralities, the better we will be at avoiding the damage that tribalism inflicts.

- We probably can't do without ideologies in modern, complex, diverse societies—unless we are willing to hold things together solely by sheer force. But not all ideologies are as damaging as the tribalistic varieties. The task is not to try to eliminate ideologies, but to promote those that are progressive and suppress those that cause us to regress morally and cognitively.

- There are at least ten strategies for combatting tribalistic ideologies that are worth considering. Determining whether they are feasible and if so how to implement them will require a lot of thinking as well as social science knowledge that we don't have at present but must develop. If none of these strategies, individually or in combination, work, then there are two alternatives: bottoming out and overcoming tribal divisions in response to an external threat.

Solutions to the Puzzles We Started with

In the Introduction, I promised that by the end of this book, I'd provide answers to some puzzling questions. Here are the questions and my answers.

1 Why are politicians today so prone to lie, cheat, and engage in such nasty attacks on their opponents? Because they think we're in a Manichean struggle, a Supreme Emergency, where it's moral to violate normal moral rules. Or they think their constituents believe we are in a Supreme Emergency, and they have incentives to encourage that belief.

2 Why do their supporters accept such behavior? Because they also have come to think in Supreme Emergency terms and expect their leaders to do whatever is necessary for Our side to win.

3 Why do people make such outrageously, patently false statements about political matters? Because they aren't in the truth-seeking mode; they're in the pep rally mode, where speech is used to boo and cheer.

4 Why do people keep using social media to criticize the views of people on the other side of the ideological divide when they know doing so won't change anybody's mind? Because the point of their criticisms isn't to change the minds of members of the opposing tribe but it's to signal allegiance to their own tribe and to affirm how different We are from Them.

5 Why is there so little respect for the truth nowadays? Because truth-seeking communication is being increasingly replaced by sorting, signaling, and defensive score-keeping.

6 Why can't people in different political tribes even agree on basic facts? Because their tribalistic ideologies have created disparate political *Umvelten*, with no shared factual beliefs to serve as landmarks accessible to both of the opposing groups and as sites for compromise, bargaining, and truth-seeking communication.

7 Why is there not just "polarization," disagreement on policy, but also "affective polarization," which involves regarding those you disagree with as despicable, devious, dangerous, insincere? Because the political

has become the personal, due to tribalistic ideologies' linking political identities to other items in a bundled, compound identity. The result is that political disagreements are felt to be threats to the self, to one's identity. The focus is then on those who pose a threat to Our identity; disagreement on issues only matter so far as they connect with the perceived struggle between opposing identities.

8 Why do people who are civil and well-mannered in real life become so nasty when they go online? Because they're expressing their extremely tribalistic conception of the Other in a medium in which the major evolved mechanisms for constraining nasty behavior, including shaming, aren't very effective.

9 What happened to the idea of the common good? Its extinction is one aspect of the death of We the People. Part of what makes a population a people is a shared conception of the good.

Why I Think My Motivation Matters

Those are intellectual results of the journey I've invited you to accompany me on. Merely listing them doesn't capture the emotional impact that writing the book had on me or tell you anything about my motivation for writing it.

Why would I want you to understand my motivation? Well, I suppose it's because I, too, care about my social identity; it matters to me how you perceive me. Although I'd be flattered if, after reading this book, you sort me into the box labeled "intellectuals" or "smart people," or "good writer," I want you to know that's not all there is to me. I want you to know what I care about and what motivates my intellectual efforts. Maybe that's a bit narcissistic, but that's how I feel.

There's another, more important, less self-centered reason for my attempt to explain what motivated me to write this book: I hope that if I make my motivation clear, it may help stimulate your motivation, that revealing my emotional connections to the subject matter may make them contagious. I worry that if they are presented just as intellectual items, with no emotional background, they won't be motivating and won't really produce any change in how you act or who you are. I don't just want you to agree with what I've said; I want it to matter to you. That's why I'm taking the risk of being branded a narcissist by telling you about my motivations and using recollections of my past to make them clear.

If you allow yourself to come face to face with these same feelings in your own case, the book may make more sense to you. Maybe by expressing my emotions, I will have made it easier to express yours.

That's not a crazy idea. One of the things that makes novels so valuable is that by vividly portraying the emotions of fictional characters; they can help readers become more in touch with their own emotions. They typically do this by enabling the reader to identify with one or more of the novel's characters. After all, to identify with someone is not just to hold similar beliefs, but also to empathize with them, to feel as they do, and to have similar emotions in response to similar stimuli. I hope to have revealed some aspects of myself that you can identify with. If that identification occurs, you will experience the emotions I experience and be motivated by them, as I have been, to think hard about ideologies and have the patience to do that job well.

My main motivation wasn't intellectual curiosity, a desire to find out the truth about tribalism. There was intellectual curiosity, but there was also a toxic combination of fear, disgust, and alienation, pushing me toward despair. I fear we are destroying our democracy. I am disgusted by the stupidity and brutishness of our politicians and even more disgusted by the fact that we accept such behavior, and I feel alienated from my own society—and even from some of those I care deeply about.

Perhaps my dominant motivation for writing this book was alienation: I can no longer recognize the country I live in; I feel like a stranger in a foreign country, unable to speak or understand the language. Sometimes it feels like there has been an invasion of the body snatchers, that malignant beings have taken over the brains and hijacked the bodies of a substantial part of the population. In biological terms, our situation is eerily like that of creatures suffering from the host manipulation I described in Chapter 1 using the zombie spider, ant, and fly examples.

Waking Up to a World Where Humans Have Become Less Than Human

The feeling of alienation prompted me to reread Eugene Ionesco's disturbingly relevant play, *Rhinoceroses*, in which more and more people are transformed overnight into huge, aggressive, thickly armored beasts.[2] Ionesco was trying to convey what it was like to live in a society in which Fascism, one particularly dangerous instance of tribalistic ideology, was becoming the dominant political view.

His play superbly captures four central aspects of tribalistic ideologies I've identified in this book. First, the damage they do doesn't begin with changes in institutions; it begins with a transformation of ourselves. Second, tribalistic ideologies provide formidable defenses against challenges to their constitutive beliefs (in the play, the beasts people become are covered with the armor-plate-like tissue characteristic of rhinoceroses). Third, tribalistic ideologies transform humans into something less than human, impeding the exercise of some of their most distinctively human cognitive and moral abilities. Finally, the play also captures the sense of alienation: the narrator realizes that he is no longer living in a world of humans. He is shocked to find that close associates have been transformed into beasts.

I recently had the same experience, and it was extremely personal and painful. I was talking with a dear friend about the growing evidence that Trump conspired with others to overturn the results of the 2020 election by creating bogus members of the electoral college. My friend shrugged this off, saying "Politics is war." He didn't dispute the allegation; instead, he apparently accepted it as a fact that Trump had conspired to undermine a basic democratic process. Instead of condemning it, he implied that it was justified because "politics is war." That is, he seemed to invoke the idea that the ordinary moral rules don't apply in a state of war. It wasn't clear whether he meant that politics has always been war or whether he meant it is war now. I replied that there are rules even in war and that some people actually comply with them. He made no response.

Reluctantly, I concluded that my friend had gone full tribal; that he had bought into the idea of a total war, a zero-sum contest in which the ordinary moral rules don't apply because it's victory or death. If you think that deliberately subverting the democratic process is acceptable, then your over-riding commitment is to winning. You either don't value democracy or you think it isn't feasible. You'll continue to endorse the leader of your tribe even if he makes a direct assault on the democratic process. That's tribalistic ideology pure and simple.

There's another interpretation of my friend's not expressing any hint of disapproval of an apparent attempt to subvert the electoral process. Maybe he just thought that we have sunk so deep into the tribal abyss that it is naïve to expect anything better. Maybe he meant, not that politics is (always, inevitably) war, but that it has become war for us—and that there's no point in morally condemning behavior that in our current situation is inevitable.

I've two responses to that interpretation. First, if that's what he meant, that's what he should have said; he shouldn't have said politics is war as if it was the eternal essence of politics to be conducted without constraint. Second, even if he was right in thinking that politics has become war, he shouldn't just accept that as an unalterable fact; or at least he should have expressed sadness or dismay that we've come to that. By not doing either of those things, he tacitly approved of the wrongful behavior in question or at least didn't acknowledge that it was wrong. We'll never extricate ourselves from the tribalistic swamp or get better leaders if we don't at least denounce such awful behavior. We've got to preserve our sense of right and wrong, and of what political behavior is acceptable and what is not.

In the past, I had seen signs of tribalism on his part, in particular, a tendency to engage in what seemed to me to be purely defensive score-keeping behavior in discussions about various political leaders. But his refusal to condemn acts designed to subvert democracy was much more serious. If enough people feel as he does and act accordingly, politics *will* be war, war without constraints. And democracy will be doomed.

His transformation into a tribalistic warrior wasn't as rapid as the change from human to beast in Ionesco's play, and the transformation was far from total. He continued to be the honest, good person I've known so well and for so long. His transformation only affected his political self, and his political self is not all there is to him; but there the transformation was momentous.

This episode hasn't diminished my commitment to the friendship. I still regard him as one of the most admirable, multi-talented, intelligent people I have ever known, and I cherish our relationship. But the fact that someone as bright and morally upright as my friend can succumb shows just how seductive tribalistic ideologies are.

Hope, In Spite of Everything

Neither the feelings that motivated me to write this book nor those I experienced on having finished working on it were entirely negative. I also felt and still feel hopeful that if we can truly understand tribalistic ideologies, we can devise ethically permissible ways to combat them effectively.

That hope may well be the result of my subscribing to an Enlightenment ideology of optimism—a belief in the improvability (not the perfectibility!) of humans and the possibility (not the inevitability!) of moral progress. If that's how people categorize me after reading this book, so be it. For reasons I've already noted, I don't think having an ideology is necessarily a flaw. It depends on the ideology.

Nor do I think the Enlightenment was a mistake, an attempt to shape the world according to a Eurocentric, parochial moral vision. In my judgment, the biggest problem about the Enlightenment in its best form is that its values still haven't been fully realized. My view about the Enlightenment and its ideology is like what Mohandas Gandhi said when asked what he thought about Western civilization: "Sounds like a good idea; at least it's worth a try."

One last point about Enlightenment: it's not the kind of thing we can achieve once and for all. There are always new enemies of the light, new shadows cast over the human scene. There will always be a threat of tribalistic ideologies, because the in-group/out-group distinction that is part of our evolved human nature provides a rich soil for their growth, and there will always be people who have an interest in cultivating those poisonous plants and an intuitive grasp of human psychology that makes them master gardeners.

Tribalistic ideologies are like a perennial, toxic, highly invasive weed that has to be eradicated, over and over again, because it is rooted in the soil of our primordial in-group/out-group mentality. You can cut down the plant, but the roots will remain intact, ready to sprout into a new plant, given the right combination of environmental conditions.

Just as the struggle against domination by other people is perpetual, so is the struggle against the enemy within.[3] These two struggles converge when those who seek to dominate us promulgate ideologies that turn our cognitive and moral powers against themselves, making us ripe for being dominated, first by our own distorting thinking and then by those who exploit it.

At the beginning of this book, I confessed that my struggle against my own racist ideology didn't end with a conclusive victory over it when I transformed myself by moving from Little Rock to the Columbia University campus. I tried to capture the idea that that struggle won't end by saying I am a recovering racist. Given how deeply rooted in human psychology the tendency toward tribalism is, I think it's fair to say that we are all at best recovering tribalists: we can never vanquish the tribalistic outlook completely and for good. It's always latent, lying in wait, ready to be activated by the right combination of perceived threats to our identity and entrepreneurs of identity ready to exploit the desperate longing for emersion in a group that those threats provoke. We can only hope to constrain it, disempower it, and above all, to avoid the conditions in which it comes to life.

Sadly, it's true that tribalistic ideologies are in some ways like parasites that manipulate their hosts. But they needn't be as effective as the fungi and larvae that invade spiders, ants, and flies. That's because their human hosts have immune systems that, if properly developed, can neutralize the invader; cognitive and moral resources that can prevent or even possibly undo the damage tribalistic ideologies do. Making our immune systems strong enough to prevent tribalistic ideologies from disabling our most admirable cognitive and moral capacities requires, first of all, understanding what the brain-invader does to us. This book has been an attempt to do that.

Notes

1 Once again, I was indebted to him. Because he developed heart failure and was finally—much too late—diagnosed with hemochromatosis; I was tested for it, because it's a genetic disease. Unlike Steve, I was diagnosed early enough to avoid most of the damage from the disease.
2 Eugène Ionesco, *Rhinoceros: A Play in Three Acts.* Translated by Derek Prouse. New York: Samuel French, 1960.
3 Allen Buchanan, *Ideology and Revolution: How the Struggle against Domination Drives the Evolution of Morality and Institutions.* Cambridge: Cambridge University Press, forthcoming.

WORKS CITED

Allen, Garland E. "Eugenics and Modern Biology: Critiques of Eugenics, 1910–1945." *Annals of Human Genetics* 75, no. 3 (May 2011): 314–25. https://doi.org/10.1111/j.1469-1809.2011.00649.x.

Amiri, Farnoush. "Less than Half of GOP Say Jan. 6 Was Very Violent, AP-NORC Poll." *PBS News*, January 4, 2022. https://www.pbs.org/newshour/politics/less-than-half-of-gop-say-jan-6-was-very-violent-ap-norc-poll.

Aral, Sinan. *The Hype Machine: How Social Media Disrupts Our Elections, Our Economy, and Our Health—And How We Must Adapt.* 1st ed. New York: Currency, 2020.

Bail, Christopher. *Breaking the Social Media Prism: How to Make Our Platforms Less Polarizing.* Princeton, NJ: Princeton University Press, 2021.

Barkan, Elazar. *Retreat of Scientific Racism: Changing Concepts of Race in Britain and the United States between the World Wars.* Cambridge, GBR: Cambridge University Press, 2011.

Baumeister, Roy F. "Tribal Hostility in Political Conflict." In *The Tribal Mind and the Psychology of Collectivism*, edited by Joseph P. Forgas, 1st ed., 271–85. New York: Routledge, 2024. https://doi.org/10.4324/9781003395836-18.

Bicchieri, Christina, and Annalisa Marini. "Female Genital Mutilation: Fundamentals, Social Expectations and Change." University Library of Munich, Germany, No. MPRA Paper 67523 (2015).

Birx, Deborah. *Silent Invasion.* New York: HarperCollins Books, 2022.

Bowles, Samuel, and Herbert Gintis. *A Cooperative Species: Human Reciprocity and Its Evolution.* 1. Paperback print. Economics, Anthropology, Biology. Princeton, NJ: Princeton University Press, 2013.

Brooks, David. *The Second Mountain: The Quest for a Moral Life.* 2020 Random House trade paperback ed. New York: Random House, 2020.

Buchanan, Allen. *Our Moral Fate: Evolution and the Escape from Tribalism.* Cambridge: The MIT Press, 2020.

Buchanan, Allen. *Ideology and Revolution: How the Struggle against Domination Drives the Evolution of Morality and Institutions.* Cambridge: Cambridge University Press, forthcoming.

Buchanan, Allen, and Rachell Powell. *The Evolution of Moral Progress: A Biocultural Theory.* New York: Oxford University Press, 2018.

Camp, Emma. "Opinion|I Came to College Eager to Debate. I Found Self-Censorship Instead." *The New York Times*, March 7, 2022, sec. Opinion. https://www.nytimes.com/2022/03/07/opinion/campus-speech-cancel-culture.html.

Camus, Renaud, *Enemy of the Disaster.* Blowing Rock, NC: Vauban Books, 2023.

Carnegie Endowment for International Peace. "Polarization, Democracy, and Political Violence in the United States: What the Research Says," n.d. https://carnegieendowment.org/research/2023/09/polarization-democracy-and-political-violence-in-the-united-states-what-the-research-says?lang=en.

Carothers, Thomas, and Andrew O'Donohue. "How Americans Were Driven to Extremes." *Foreign Affairs*, September 25, 2019. https://www.foreignaffairs.com/articles/united-states/2019-09-25/how-americans-were-driven-extremes.

Dawkins, Richard. *The Selfish Gene.* Oxford: Oxford University Press, 1976.

Deb, Sopan. "Trump Says Clinton Could Let 650 Million New Immigrants into U.S. - CBS News," October 31, 2016. https://www.cbsnews.com/news/donald-trump-says-hillary-clinton-could-let-650-million-new-immigrants-into-u-s/.

Diamond, Jared M. *Collapse: How Societies Choose to Fail or Succeed.* Harmondsworth: Penguin Books, 2006.

Dimock, Michael, and Richard Wike. "America Is Exceptional in the Nature of Its Political Divide." Pew Research Center, November 13, 2020. https://www.pewresearch.org/short-reads/2020/11/13/america-is-exceptional-in-the-nature-of-its-political-divide/.

Duggan, Maeve. "Online Harassment 2017." Pew Research Center, July 11, 2017. https://www.pewresearch.org/internet/2017/07/11/online-harassment-2017/.

Dunne, Nora. "Analyzing Brain Structure in Schizophrenia." Northwestern Medicine News Center, July 2, 2015. https://news.feinberg.northwestern.edu/2015/07/02/analyzing-brain-structure-in-schizophrenia/.

Elias, Norbert. *The Civilizing Process.* Oxford: Blackwell, 1994.

Elias, Norbert, Eric Dunning, Johan Goudsblom, and Stephen Mennell. *The Civilizing Process: Sociogenetic and Psychogenetic Investigations.* Revised ed. Oxford and Malden, MA: Blackwell Publishers, 2000.

Fricker, Miranda. *Epistemic Injustice: Power and the Ethics of Knowing.* Reprint. Oxford: Oxford University Press, 2011.

Fukuyama, Francis. *Identity: The Demand for Dignity and the Politics of Resentment.* 1st ed. New York: Farrar, 2018.

Funkhouser, Eric. "Beliefs as Signals: A New Function for Belief." *Philosophical Psychology* 30, no. 6 (August 18, 2017): 809–31. https://doi.org/10.1080/09515089.2017.1291929.

Furet, François. *Interpreting the French Revolution.* Cambridge, New York, and Paris: Cambridge University Press. Editions de la Maison des sciences de l'homme, 1981.

Hannon, Michael, and Jeroen de Ridder. "The Point of Political Belief." In *The Routledge Handbook of Political Epistemology.* 123–134. London and New York: Routledge Taylor & Francis Group, 2021.

Henrich, Joseph. *The Secret of Our Success: How Culture Is Driving Human Evolution, Domesticating Our Species, and Making Us Smarter*. Princeton, NJ: Princeton University Press, 2015.

Gibson, Ginger. "Trump Says Immigrants Are 'Poisoning the Blood of Our Country.' Biden Campaign Likens Comments to Hitler." *NBC News*, December 17, 2023. https://www.nbcnews.com/politics/2024-election/trump-says-immigrants-are-poisoning-blood-country-biden-campaign-liken-rcna130141.

Geiger, Abigail. "Section 1: Growing Ideological Consistency." Pew Research Center, June 12, 2014. https://www.pewresearch.org/politics/2014/06/12/section-1-growing-ideological-consistency/.

Goldstone, Jack A. *Revolution and Rebellion in the Early Modern World: Population Change and State Breakdown in England, France, Turkey, and China, 1600–1850*. 25th anniversary ed. New York: Routledge, Taylor & Francis Group, an Informa Business, 2016.

Haidt, Jonathan. *The Righteous Mind: Why Good People Are Divided by Politics and Religion*. New York: Vintage, 2012.

Haidt, Jonathan. *The Anxious Generation: How the Great Re-Wiring of Childhood Is Causing an Epidemic of Mental Illness*. New York: Penguin Press, 2024.

Hirschfeld, Lawrence A. *Race in the Making: Cognition, Culture, and the Child's Construction of Human Kinds*. Learning, Development, and Conceptual Change. London, England, and Cambridge, MA: MIT Press, 1996.

Hobbes, Thomas. *Leviathan: With Selected Variants from the Latin Edition of 1668*. Indianapolis, IN: Hackett Pub. Co, 1994.

"Internet Modern History Sourcebook Abbé Sieyes: What Is the Third Estate? Excerpts." Fordham University, n.d. https://sourcebooks.fordham.edu/mod/sieyes.asp.

Ionesco, Eugène. *Rhinoceros: A Play in Three Acts*. Translated by Derek Prouse. New York: Samuel French, 1960.

Iyengar, Shanto, Yphtach Lelkes, Matthew Levendusky, Neil Malhotra, and Sean Westwood. "The Origins and Consequences of Affective Polarization in the United States." *SSRN Scholarly Paper*. Rochester, NY, May 1, 2019. https://doi.org/10.1146/annurev-polisci-051117-073034.

Jervis, Robert. *Perception and Misperception in International Politics*. New ed. Princeton, NJ: Princeton University Press, 2017.

Joshi, Hrishikesh. "What Are the Chances You're Right About Everything? An Epistemic Challenge for Modern Partisanship." *Forthcoming in Politics, Philosophy & Economics*, n.d. https://philpapers.org/archive/JOSWAT.pdf.

Justia Law. "Buck vs. Bell, 274 u. S. 200 (1927)." Accessed May 7, 2024. https://supreme.justia.com/cases/federal/us/274/200/.

Kahan, Dan M. "The Supreme Court 2010 Term - Foreword: Neutral Principles, Motivated Cognition, and Some Problems for Constitutional Law." *SSRN Electronic Journal* 129, 2011: 1–30. https://doi.org/10.2139/ssrn.1910391.

Kant, Immanuel. *Groundwork of the Metaphysics of Morals*. Translated by Mary J. Gregor and Jens Timmermann. Revised ed. Cambridge Texts in the History of Philosophy, 1785. Reprint, Cambridge: Cambridge University Press, 2012.

Kaplan, Jonas T., Sarah I. Gimbel, and Sam Harris. "Neural Correlates of Maintaining One's Political Beliefs in the Face of Counterevidence." *Scientific Reports* 6, no. 1 (December 23, 2016): 39589. https://doi.org/10.1038/srep39589.

Karlsgodt, Katherine H., Daqiang Sun, and Tyrone D. Cannon. "Structural and Functional Brain Abnormalities in Schizophrenia." *Current Directions in Psychological Science* 19, no. 4 (August 2010): 226. https://doi.org/10.1177/0963721410377601.

Kevles, Daniel J. *In the Name of Eugenics: Genetics and the Uses of Human Heredity*. 1st Harvard University Press paperback ed. Cambridge, MA: Harvard University Press, 1995.

"King James Bible." In *Samuel 2:12*, n.d.

Koonz, Claudia. *The Nazi Conscience*. 1. Harvard University Press paperback ed. Cambridge, MA: Belknap Press of Harvard University Press, 2005.

Laland, Kevin N. *Darwin's Unfinished Symphony: How Culture Explains the Evolution of the Human Mind*. Princeton, NJ: Princeton University Press, 2017.

Layne, Nathan, Gram Slattery Tim Reid, and Gram Slattery. "Trump Calls Migrants 'animals,' Intensifying Focus on Illegal Immigration." *Reuters*, April 3, 2024, sec. United States. https://www.reuters.com/world/us/trump-expected-highlight-murder-michigan-woman-immigration-speech-2024-04-02/.

Levin, Yuval. *The Fractured Republic: Renewing America's Social Contract in the Age of Individualism*. New York: Basic Books, 2016.

Levy, Neil. *Bad Beliefs: Why They Happen to Good People*. 1st ed. Oxford: Oxford University Press, 2021. https://academic.oup.com/book/38980.

Mason, Lilliana. *Uncivil Agreement: How Politics Became Our Identity*. Chicago, IL and London: The University of Chicago Press, 2018.

Mercier, Hugo. *Not Born Yesterday: The Science of Who We Trust and What We Believe*. 1st paperback printing. Princeton, NJ and Oxford: Princeton University Press, 2022.

Mill, John Stuart. *On Liberty*. Kitchener: Batoche Books, 1859.

Minster, Christopher. "Cortex and His Tlaxcalan Allies." *ThoughtCo*, October 1, 2019.

Moalem, Sharon, and Jonathan Prince. *Survival of the Sickest: The Surprising Connections between Disease and Longevity*. Harper Perennial ed. New York: Harper Perennial, 2007.

Murphy, Jack. "Jack Murphy Live." JD Vance – JML #070, 2021.

Prosbiec, Jacob and Lisec, Joshua. *Unhuman: The Secret History of Communist Revolutions (and How to Crush Them)*. New York: Simon & Schuster, 2024.

Putnam, Robert D. *Bowling Alone: The Collapse and Revival of American Community*. A Touchstone Book. London: Simon & Schuster, 2001.

Roberts, James, Luc Yaya, and Chris Manolis. "The Invisible Addiction: Cell-Phone Activities and Addiction among Male and Female College Students." *Journal of Behavioral Addictions* 3, no. 4 (December 2014): 254–65. https://doi.org/10.1556/JBA.3.2014.015.

Roeber, Blake. *Political Humility: The Limits of Knowledge in Our Partisan Political Climate*. New York: Routledge, 2024.

Saad, Lydia. "U.S. Political Ideology Steady; Conservatives, Moderates Tie." *Gallup*, January 17, 2022. https://news.gallup.com/poll/388988/political-ideology-steady-conservatives-moderates-tie.aspx.

Senju, Atsushi. "Spontaneous Theory of Mind and Its Absence in Autism Spectrum Disorders." *The Neuroscientist* 18, no. 2 (April 2012): 108–13. https://doi.org/10.1177/1073858410397208.

Singer, Peter. *Animal Liberation: A New Ethics for Our Treatment of Animals.* London: Cape, 1976.

Singer, Peter. *The Expanding Circle: Ethics, Evolution, and Moral Progress.* 1st Princeton University Press paperback ed. Princeton, NJ: Princeton University Press, 2011.

Skocpol, Theda. *States and Social Revolutions: A Comparative Analysis of France, Russia and China.* Cambridge: Cambridge University Press, 1979.

"Speciesism." In *Wikipedia*, August 17, 2024. https://en.wikipedia.org/w/index.php?title=Speciesism&oldid=1240794399.

Steinberg, Mark D. *The Russian Revolution, 1905–1921.* 1st ed. Oxford Histories. Oxford and New York, NY: Oxford University Press, 2017.

Suler, John. "The Online Disinhibition Effect." *CyberPsychology & Behavior* 7, no. 3 (June 2004): 321–26. https://doi.org/10.1089/1094931041291295.

Tackett, Timothy. *The Coming of the Terror in the French Revolution.* 1st Harvard University Press paperback ed. London, England, and Cambridge, MA: The Belknap Press of Harvard University Press, 2017.

Tajfel, Henri, and John C. Turner. "The Social Identity Theory of Intergroup Behavior." In *Political Psychology*, edited by John T. Jost and Jim Sidanius. New York: Psychology Press, 2004.

The Civil War. Documentary Series, 1990.

"The Walking Dead." AMC, n.d.

Thomas, Elizabeth Marshall. *The Harmless People.* Revised ed., 2nd Vintage Books ed. New York: Vintage Books, 1989.

Tomasello, Michael. *A Natural History of Human Morality.* 1st Harvard University Press paperback ed. Cambridge, MA: Harvard University Press, 2018.

Viala-Gaudefroy, Jérôme. "Why Do Millions of Americans Believe the 2020 Presidential Election Was 'Stolen' from Donald Trump?" *The Conversation*, March 3, 2024. https://theconversation.com/why-do-millions-of-americans-believe-the-2020-presidential-election-was-stolen-from-donald-trump-224016.

Walzer, Michael. *Just and Unjust Wars: A Moral Argument with Historical Illustrations.* London: Allen Lane, 1978.

Washington Post. "Full Text: Donald Trump Announces a Presidential Bid," June 26, 2015. https://www.washingtonpost.com/news/post-politics/wp/2015/06/16/full-text-donald-trump-announces-a-presidential-bid/.

Weisel, Ori, and Ro'i Zultan. "Social Motives in Intergroup Conflict: Group Identity and Perceived Target of Threat." *European Economic Review* 90 (November 2016): 122–33. https://doi.org/10.1016/j.euroecorev.2016.01.004.

Wenar, Leif. *Blood Oil: Tyrants, Violence, and the Rules That Run the World.* Oxford and New York: Oxford University Press, 2017.

Yong, Ed. *An Immense World: How Animal Senses Reveal the Hidden Realms Around Us.* 2023 Random House trade paperback ed. New York: Random House, 2023.

INDEX

Note: Page numbers followed by "n" denote endnotes.

For Product Safety Concerns and Information please contact our EU
representative GPSR@taylorandfrancis.com
Taylor & Francis Verlag GmbH, Kaufingerstraße 24, 80331 München, Germany